UNDERSTANDING
WITTGENSTEIN

UNDERSTANDING WITTGENSTEIN

Edited and with a Foreword by

GODFREY VESEY

Cornell Paperbacks

CORNELL UNIVERSITY PRESS

Ithaca, New York

First published in the United States of America in 1974

First printing, Cornell paperbacks, 1976

International Standard Book Number 0–8014–9160–6
Library of Congress Catalog Card Number 76–12818
Printed in the United States of America
*Librarians: Library of Congress cataloging information
appears on the last page of the book.*

CONTENTS

LIST OF ABBREVIATIONS

The following abbreviations, listed alphabetically, are sometimes used to refer to Wittgenstein's works.

BB   *The Blue and Brown Books*, with preface by R. Rhees (Oxford: Basil Blackwell, 1958). Followed by page number.

LLW   *Letters from Ludwig Wittgenstein*, with a memoir by Paul Engelmann, ed. B. F. McGuinness, trans. by L. Furtmüller (Oxford: Basil Blackwell, 1967). Followed by page number.

NB   *Notebooks 1914–16*, ed. G. H. von Wright and G. E. M. Anscombe, trans. by G. E. M. Anscombe (Oxford: Basil Blackwell, 1961). Followed by date of entry and/or page number.

OC   *On Certainty*, ed. G. E. M. Anscombe and G. H. von Wright, trans. by D. Paul and G. E. M. Anscombe (Oxford: Basil Blackwell, 1969). Followed by paragraph number.

PB   *Philosophiscke Bemerkungen*, ed. R. Rhees (Oxford: Basil Blackwell, 1964). Followed by page number.

PE   'Wittgenstein's Notes for Lectures on "Private Experience" and "Sense Data" ', ed. R. Rhees, *Philosophical Review* lxxvii (1968). Followed by page number.

PG   *Philosophiscke Grammatik*, ed. R. Rhees (Oxford: Basil Blackwell, 1969). Followed by page number.

PI   *Philosophical Investigations*, ed. G. E. M. Anscombe and R. Rhees, trans. by G. E. M. Anscombe (Oxford: Basil Blackwell, 1953). Part I, followed by paragraph number; Part II, followed by section, and, if necessary, page number.

PTLP   *Proto Tractatus – An Early Version of Tractatus Logico-Philosophicus*, ed. B. F. McGuinness, T. Nyberg, G. H. von Wright, trans. by D. F. Pears and B. F. McGuinness (London: Routledge and Kegan Paul, 1971). Followed by sentence number.

RFM   *Remarks on the Foundations of Mathematics,* ed. G. H. von
       Wright, R. Rhees, G. E. M. Anscombe, trans. by G. E. M.
       Anscombe (Oxford: Basil Blackwell, 1956). Followed by
       part and section number.

TLP   *Tractatus Logico-Philosophicus,* trans. by C. K. Ogden
       assisted by F. P. Ramsey, with introduction by Bertrand
       Russell (London: Routledge and Kegan Paul, 1922); trans.
       by D. F. Pears and B. F. McGuinness (London: Routledge
       and Kegan Paul, 1961). Followed by sentence number.

WWK   *Ludwig Wittgenstein und der Wiener Kreis,* shorthand notes
       recorded by F. Waismann, ed. B. F. McGuinness (Oxford:
       Basil Blackwell, 1967). Followed by page number.

Z   *Zettel,* ed. G. E. M. Anscombe and G. H. von Wright, trans.
       by G. E. M. Anscombe (Oxford: Basil Blackwell, 1967).
       Followed by paragraph number.

FOREWORD

WITTGENSTEIN's abiding philosophical concern was with the conditions of an utterance having sense – and so with what it is to mean something, to think, to understand, and to infer. This concern was constant, unchanging. What changed was not his concern with the conditions of sense, but his view as to what they are. Understanding Wittgenstein means understanding his change of view about the conditions of sense. I shall say something about this to provide a point of reference for my remarks, in the remainder of the Foreword, about the individual lectures that this volume comprises.

In the *Tractatus* Wittgenstein writes:

2.0211   If the world had no substance, then whether a proposition had sense would depend on whether another proposition was true.

2.0212   It would then be impossible to form a picture of the world (true or false).

In the *Investigations* and *Zettel*, on the other hand, he argues that a proposition's having sense *does* depend on other propositions being true. They are propositions about a certain sort of 'human agreement'.[1] There must be human agreement of a certain sort for our language-games to work.[2] But it is not agreement in *opinions*, that is, in what enters into the language-game. The things that enter into the language-game are true or false statements like 'The dress she bought is red', 'The shopkeeper gave me five apples', and 'He had toothache'. If someone says, in reply to the last statement, 'Yes, I remember now, he had', that is not the sort of agreement Wittgenstein has in mind.

Probably the least misleading thing to say is that it is agreement in what we *do*. The trouble is that the agreement in what we do which makes the language-game possible cannot be identified

[1] *PI*, I, 241.   [2] *Z*, 430.

without using the language-game in question. Unless people agree
in their reactions to colours they will not have the concept of
colour they need to have to see certain behaviour as 'agreement in
reactions to colours'. Unless they agree in their expressions of, and
reactions to, pain, they will not have the concept of pain they need
to have to see behaviour as 'pain behaviour'. (Arguments from
analogy haven't a leg, even *one* leg, to stand on.) The result is that
either we have the concept – or we cannot even imagine what the
concept may be that we haven't got. Under these circumstances
the concepts we have seem to exist unconditionally, so to speak.
And so people who haven't got the concepts we have seem to us
not to realise things we realise;[1] and people who have got other
concepts strike us as irrational.

There is another reason for it not being obvious that the possibility of a language-game is conditioned by certain facts. This is the
attractiveness of competing accounts of the sense of an utterance –
in terms of (a) the words in the utterance being correlated with
objects for which the words stand, or (b) something in our minds
(a conscious act of 'meaning' or 'understanding') which is thought
to make the difference between the utterance being mere sounds
and having sense.

Wittgenstein holds these accounts to be wrong. To give the
first of them is to think of all language (or all 'fact-stating' language)
as having sense in the same way. That had been his idea when he
wrote the *Tractatus*. In the *Investigations* and *Zettel* he combats the
idea that all language has sense in the same way by insisting on
'the multiplicity of language-games'.[2] And he combats the idea
that *any* language has sense in the way described in the *Tractatus*
by saying that 'our language-game only works . . . when a certain
agreement prevails'.[3]

Wittgenstein sometimes calls the agreement an agreement in
'form of life'. I think it would have been better if he had reserved
this expression for the sort of agreement that might be held to
underlie the sense of, say, religious utterances.[4] But perhaps he
wanted to bring out how the fact that words like 'red' have sense
is no less dependent on agreement in human behaviour than is the
fact that words like 'altar' and 'oracle' have sense.

His discussion of the conditions of mathematical words having
sense is central in all this.

---

[1] *PI*, II, xii.   [2] *PI*, I, 24.   [3] *Z*, 430.
[4] Cf. Wittgenstein, *Lectures and Conversations on Aesthetics, Psychology and Religious
Belief*, ed. Cyril Barrett (Oxford: Basil Blackwell, 1966), p. 58: 'Why shouldn't
one form of life culminate in an utterance of belief in a Last Judgment?'

Kant saw a problem in accounting for the necessity of propositions like '7 + 5 = 12'. They did not seem to him to be merely analytic. However long he analysed his concept of a possible sum of 7 and 5 he would, he thought, never find the 12 in it. He wrote:

We have to go outside these concepts, and call in the aid of intuition which corresponds to one of them, our five fingers, for instance . . . adding to the concept of 7, unit by unit, the five given in intuition. For starting with the number 7, and for the concept of 5 calling in the aid of the fingers of my hand as intuition, I now add one by one to the number 7 the units which I previously took together to form the number 5, and with the aid of that figure [the hand] see the number 12 come into being.[1]

The trouble with this is that we can go wrong. We can miscount on our fingers, even though as a rule we don't. But it isn't correct to say *'As a rule*, 7 + 5 = 12'.

Nevertheless, there is something in what Kant says about having to go outside the concepts. You and I, when we are asked to add on our fingers, as a rule get the same result. Why? Because by 'adding on our fingers' we mean the same thing. We *do* the same thing. For each successive finger we say a numeral in the series '1', '2', '3', '4', and so on, this being a series we have learnt by heart. There is this human agreement in what constitutes counting. It doesn't decide what is true or false in mathematics; but it is what makes the language of mathematics, as something more than a sign game, possible.

The problem can be put like this. In some sense, in knowing the formula for a series, one *knows* what will come at any point in the series. Yet, as Kant saw, one doesn't have to have *thought* of the whole series – it may be infinite – to be in a position to say that one knows, that is, has understood, the formula. How is it that we can talk of 'knowing' here? How is it that we can say that someone has interpreted a rule, a formula, correctly or incorrectly? What underlies there being such a thing as correctness and incorrectness, truth and falsity, in the language of mathematics – or, for that matter, in any language at all?

This is the subject of Wittgenstein's long and subtle discussion in *Investigations*, I, 138–99. In 154 he connects up his discussion of knowing a formula with his rejection of the account of the sense of an utterance in terms of something in our minds which

---

[1] *Critique of Pure Reason*, trans. Norman Kemp Smith (London: Macmillan, 1934), B15–16.

makes the difference between the utterance being mere sounds and having sense – (*b*) above. He writes:

> But wait – if 'Now I understand the principle' does not mean the same as 'The formula . . . occurs to me' – does it follow from this that I employ the sentence 'Now I understand . . .' or 'Now I can go on' as a description of a process occurring behind or side by side with that of saying the formula?
>
> If there has to be anything 'behind the utterance of the formula' it is *particular circumstances*[1] which justify me in saying I can go on – when the formula occurs to me.
>
> Try not to think of understanding as a 'mental process' at all. – For *that* is the expression which confuses you.[2]

'Try not to think of understanding as a mental process' is grammatically like 'Try not to think of him as your boss (now that you've married him)'. But the grammatical similarity is misleading. One musn't read what Wittgenstein says here as a *denial* that understanding is a mental process – as though we had, independently, a clear idea of what it is for something to be a mental process and saw that understanding was not one. If anything is to be called a mental process then surely it is such things as understanding, imagining, and remembering.[3] No; the point is that talk of a mental *process* makes us think of understanding (meaning, imagining, remembering, etc.) in a way which blinds us to our actual use of the words 'understand' ('mean', etc.). Photosynthesis is the process of carbohydrate formation that occurs in leaves. Similarly, we think, understanding is a process that occurs in another, but more mysterious, medium, the mind. It is not false that understanding is a mental process (how could it be?). But the picture we have of a mental process is an ill-formed one.[4]

It is helpful here to consider the meaning of 'I meant' (*BB*, pp. 39, 142; *Z*, 1–53, 231–48).[5] What is the meaning of the word 'meaning' in our talk of meaning someone (for example, 'When I said "Come here" I meant you, not Jones') or of meaning something

---

[1] The particular circumstances are 'that he had learnt algebra, had used such formulae before' (*PI*, I, 179). Note that having learnt algebra involves having acquired abilities shared with others who have learnt algebra.

[2] *PI*, I, 154.

[3] In *PI*, I, 154 Wittgenstein says that by a 'mental process' he means such things as 'a pain's growing more and less', and 'the hearing of a tune or a sentence', but I think he was confused as to his own philosophical method at this point.

[4] *PI*, I, 305–9.

[5] I am drawing, here, on things I said in my review of *Zettel*, 'Wittgenstein on the Myth of Mental Processes', *Philosophical Review*, lxxvii (1968) pp. 350–5.

(for example, 'When I said "Go to the bank" I meant the river bank')? In saying 'I meant . . .', when one has been misunderstood, is one saying something about something one did at the time of saying 'Come here' or 'Go to the bank'? If the ambiguity, the misinterpretability, of 'Go to the bank' struck one as one said it, then one would be seeing the sentence 'from outside', so to speak (Z, 233–5, 287), in which case one's thought and the sentence would be distinguishable. But for one to mean anything at all (and so, to *think*), *some* sentence (picture or the like) must serve as it stands – that is, *not* need an accompanying interpretation.

But is it not remarkable that we should say 'I *meant* . . .' (i.e. in the past tense) if there was only the sentence 'Go to the bank' and no accompanying interpretation? (Z, 39–40). Yes, if you look at it in a certain light, as those philosophers are apt to who go on to say that there *must* (Z, 286) have been more than the sentence in my mind for it to be the case that I meant such-and-such. But, remarkable or not, this *is* what we say; there *is* this language-game in which what happens later (Z, 7–8, 14, etc., cf. 100) is the criterion (Z, 22) of my meaning someone or something: asked whether I wanted Jones to come, I answer almost as I answer a question about my present sensations (Z, 7) and yet I say 'I *meant* you, not Jones'. Moreover, even where there was an accompanying interpretation, the use I make of 'I meant' bypasses it (Z, 25, 41, 88).

I said that in the *Investigations* and *Zettel* Wittgenstein argues that a proposition's having sense depends on other propositions being true, these other propositions being about a certain sort of human agreement. But Wittgenstein elsewhere acknowledges other kinds of proposition on which the sense of a proposition may depend. They may again be described as propositions about a certain sort of agreement, but it is not the same sort as he is concerned with in the *Investigations* and *Zettel*. For example, in the *Blue Book* he discusses the conditions of the phrase 'the same person' having the sense it has, and writes:

> Our actual use of the phrase 'the same person' and of the name of a person is based on the fact that many characteristics which we use as the criteria for identity coincide in the vast majority of cases.[1]

Coincidence, I suppose, is a form of agreement, but it is not agreement in things we do in the way in which agreement in, say, counting is agreement in things we do.

[1] *BB*, p. 61.

Finally, in *On Certainty*, 617, Wittgenstein refers to what he calls the 'sureness' of a language-game, and writes:

> Certain events would put me into a position in which I could not go on with the old language-game any further. In which I was torn away from the *sureness* of the game.
>   Indeed, doesn't it seem obvious that the possibility of a language-game is conditioned by certain facts?

I take him to mean '. . . is conditioned by our *not calling in question* certain facts'.[1] In 613 he compares doubting that heat makes water boil (instead of freeze) with doubting that some familiar friend is who he is. He writes:

> If the water over the gas freezes, of course I shall be as astonished as can be, but I shall assume some factor I don't know of, and perhaps leave the matter to physicists to judge. But what could make me doubt whether this person here is N. N., whom I have known for years? Here a doubt would seem to drag everything with it and plunge it into chaos.

It isn't that I am certain that he is N. N., for the question 'Is he N. N.?' doesn't arise. It is the fact that the question 'Is he N. N.?' doesn't arise, not the fact that he is N. N. (or that I am certain that he is), that conditions the possibility of the language-game – the one in which I may sensibly ask, about a stranger, 'Is he P. P.?' Against the background of *not* raising questions in certain cases (those which supremely satisfy our criteria, those which are, in a sense, our 'paradigms') we *can* raise questions in others. Our employing the criteria we do employ (treating as paradigms the cases we do so treat) might be described, in language reminiscent of the *Tractatus*, as our having a certain picture of the world. But how different such talk of a picture of the world would be from the *Tractatus* talk, may be judged from what Wittgenstein says in *On Certainty*, 94–9. A picture of the world, in the *Tractatus*, is itself what is true or false. In *On Certainty* it is 'the inherited background against which I distinguish between true and false'.

The picture of the world Wittgenstein means in *On Certainty* may alter. The role of propositions describing it 'is like that of rules of a game', and the rules may change. Does it follow, then, that Wittgenstein has to revise his earlier view about logic not being an empirical science? No. That rules may change does not mean

---

[1] On this and related points I am grateful to Rush Rhees for his comments on an early draft of this foreword. Whether the use I have made of them is one of which he would approve is another matter.

that there are no rules. 'If someone were to say "So logic too is an empirical science" he would be wrong. Yet this is right: the same proposition may get treated at one time as something to test by experience, at another as a rule of testing.' Seeing this is seeing the mistake in thinking 'that certain concepts are absolutely the correct ones'.[1] The insight that this is a mistake is not possible for someone who holds the 'picture theory of meaning' of the *Tractatus*. This illustrates the change in Wittgenstein's view about the conditions of sense.

Anthony Kenny, Fellow of Balliol College, Oxford, claims that Wittgenstein's 'own later statements about the *Tractatus* sometimes misrepresent it and mask the considerable continuity between his later views and his earlier views'. An example of continuity he mentions relates to the picture theory of meaning. Kenny argues that elements crucial to the picture theory are retained in the *Investigations*. One such is the bipolarity of the proposition: any proposition which can be true can be false. Another is the iso-morphism between the world and language. This, Kenny says, survives 'though with its poles reversed'. On this Kenny quotes Peter Hacker approvingly. Instead of language mirroring the logical form of the universe, 'the apparent "structure of reality" is merely the shadow of grammar'. In either case the structure of reality can only be shown, not described; and the structure of language cannot be justified.

Kenny says that 'it is commonly said that Wittgenstein after the *Tractatus* abandoned the picture theory'. For my part I would agree with what he says is commonly said. In spite of the 'considerable continuity' to which Kenny draws attention, there is more to *X* being a picture of *Y* than that they are isomorphic. For Wittgenstein, reversing the poles of the isomorphism went with regarding a proposition's having sense as being dependent on the truth of other propositions (e.g. about a certain sort of human agreement). And Wittgenstein himself says that if a proposition's having sense depended on another proposition being true 'it would then be impossible to form a picture of the world (true or false)'.[2]

Why should Wittgenstein have held the picture theory of meaning in the first place? And how did holding it lead him to the so-called 'logical atomism' of the *Tractatus*? Roger White, Lecturer in Philosophy at the University of Leeds, suggests that Wittgenstein misconstrued an innocuous connection between a proposition's making sense and its having true/false polarity in terms of a nocuous

[1] *PI*, II, xii.   [2] *TLP*, 2.0212.

theory (the picture theory) of a link between a proposition's making sense and its dividing possible states of affairs into two groups – those that make it true and those that make it false. This theory is put in jeopardy if one proposition's making sense is dependent on another being true, as is the case if (a) the proposition is about the bearer of a proper name, (b) a proper name is a sign which contributes to the sense of a proposition by standing for that bearer, and (c) the bearer of the proper name is, for example, a person, that is, an entity that may, after a time, no longer exist. To safeguard the picture theory, names of persons must be shown not to be *real* proper names, but disguised descriptions, or something of the sort. The real proper names must be of objects of which it makes no sense to suppose that they don't exist. And if you can't have language without real proper names then there must be such objects – the 'simple objects' of Wittgenstein's logical atomism, the 'substance' of the world referred to in *TLP*, 2.0211.

The reply to the *Tractatus* implicit in the *Investigations*, White says, involves a total change of perspective on the phenomena of language. Central to it is the idea that 'we rely on certain contingent features of our world in order to give our signs a sense, and in imagining those features not to have obtained, we are imagining a world in which propositions containing such signs would be incapable of formulation, not one in which they would be false'. With this change in perspective we can still talk of a proposition and its negation exhausting the possibilities, but they will now be 'the possibilities allowed for by the language, not the possibilities taken in some abstract sense, and these possibilities are conditioned by the form of life of the speakers of that language and by the features of the world within which they live that life'.

In talking about the truth '$7 + 5 = 12$', above, I said that the trouble with Kant's account ('calling in the aid of the fingers of my hand as intuition') is that we can go wrong. I then said that human agreement in what constitutes counting doesn't decide what is true or false in mathematics, but is what makes the language of mathematics, as something more than a sign game, possible. Wittgenstein could be said to have been concerned with the question 'What is logical inference if it is not merely the transformation of one configuration of signs into another, and if logical propositions are not merely very general empirical propositions?' This is the question Rush Rhees takes up on page 35 of his paper (the paragraph beginning 'The transition from one proposition to another in a logical proof . . .'). I cannot hope to summarise his treatment of this question in the remainder of his paper. He himself says that no single or formal answer can be given to the question what makes a transition from one proposition to another a logical inference; we can answer only by giving examples. But it is evident that he attaches considerable importance to the notion of a 'practice'. He writes:

> Describing what language is, describing what saying something ('a proposition') is, describing what drawing a conclusion is – means describing a practice. . . . It does not mean 'describing a routine'. A practice refers to a way of living in which many people are engaged. We could observe a habit in an individual man but not a 'practice'. Much of what Wittgenstein says about 'rules' is connected with this.

(Elsewhere Rhees says that rules were not made by the devil, but the word 'rule' was.)

Brian McGuinness, Tutor and Praelector in Philosophy at Queen's College, Oxford, in a paper that relates interestingly to that by Rush Rhees, discusses the history behind *TLP*, 4.0321, 'My fundamental idea is that the "logical constants" are not representatives; that there can be no representatives of the logic of facts.' It was Russell who had held that to understand 'logical' words – like 'or', 'not', 'all', and 'some' – we must be acquainted with 'logical objects', for which they stand. In *The Problems of Philosophy* he had similarly held that to understand a statement containing the word 'I' a person must be acquainted with his self, a view he renounced in *The Analysis of Mind*.

Russell's view about the self, known if not by acquaintance then by description as a Humean series of mental events, recur in his theory of judgment, according to which the relation between a proposition and a fact is explained in terms of a judging relation involving a subject, on the one hand, and particular and universal entities on the other. Wittgenstein, as Guy Stock, Lecturer in Logic at the University of Aberdeen, points out, rejected this psychologistic explanation of the relation of language to the world, in favour of, in the *Tractatus*, the picture theory of meaning. Stock quotes Ramsey, who said Wittgenstein 'explicitly reduces the question as to the analysis of judgment . . . to the question "What is it for a proposition token to have a certain sense?" ', and comments that Wittgenstein's answer to this question left no room in the world represented in thought for a subject that thinks, and, in conjunction with the polarity thesis, 'required that there be the possibility of indefinable names standing for objects which are "Roughly speaking, colourless" '.

Wittgenstein denied the self in which Russell believed when he wrote *The Problems of Philosophy*. But did he not believe in another self? In the *Tractatus*, 5.641, he wrote:

There is therefore really a sense in which in philosophy we can talk of a non-psychological I.

The I occurs in philosophy through the fact that the 'world is my world'.

The philosophical I is not the man, not the human body or the human soul of which psychology treats, but the metaphysical subject, the limit – not a part of the world.

Bernard Williams, Knightbridge Professor of Philosophy at the University of Cambridge, finds in Wittgenstein's *Tractatus* discussion of the self and solipsism three ideas which, he says, Wittgenstein may seem to have abandoned in his later work. One of them is the idea that 'we cannot conceive of it as a matter of empirical investigation to determine why my world is this way rather than that, why my language has some features rather than others, etc.'.

Did Wittgenstein abandon this idea? In the *Investigations*, II, xii, he writes: 'If anyone believes that certain concepts are absolutely the correct ones . . . then let him imagine certain very general facts of nature to be different from what we are used to, and the formation of concepts different from the usual ones will become intelligible to him.' I can understand this if by 'facts of nature' Wittgenstein means, for example, the coincidence of the characteristics we use as the criteria for personal identity. I can imagine the facts being different from what we are used to. For instance, I can imagine brains being transplanted, and our concept of personal identity changing as a consequence. But if he means such facts of nature as I earlier called 'agreement in what we *do*', such as agreement in reactions to colours, or agreement in what constitutes counting, then I think there is a problem – unless I was mistaken in saying that the agreement in what we do which makes the language-game possible cannot be identified without using the language-game in question. Perhaps what Wittgenstein means is that we can come to realise that our 'picture of the world' is not the only possible one (though not what other ones are possible). If so, and *if* saying this means being a transcendental idealist, then Wittgenstein is a transcendental idealist.

For Wittgenstein, writes A. Phillips Griffiths, Professor of Philosophy at the University of Warwick, the willing subject is no more a part of the world than is the thinking subject. 'It is an illusion that I can bring anything about. The world is the totality of elementary facts, and there is nothing in any one fact to explain another (which could do for the will)'. What, then, of ethics? Most of us take it to be about how we should act. If it is not, what is it about? What does Wittgenstein mean when he says, for instance (*TLP*, 6.43), that 'good or bad willing . . . can only change the limits of the world, not the facts'? Griffiths asks 'But how on earth could I, by a particular act, alter the limits of the world?' He tries to understand Wittgenstein by making what he calls 'some very radical assumptions'.

I remarked, earlier, on the possible misleadingness of Wittgenstein's prescription 'Try not to think of understanding as a "mental process" at all' (*PI*, I, 154). Renford Bambrough, Fellow of St John's College, Cambridge, and University Lecturer in Philosophy, refers to 'the strains to which language is subjected if it is used in an attempt to express Wittgenstein's meaning in general and theoretical terms' and says that 'every remark made in the course of such an attempt is misleading and needs immediate qualification'. Such reservations as I have about this relate to 'immediate qualification'. The point of a philosophical utterance like 'Thoughts are not mental processes' will be lost if one *immediately* counters it with the thought 'But, of course, in the common usage of the phrase "mental process" thoughts *are* mental processes'. In the philosophical utterance it is the misleading picture that goes with the word 'process' that is important – it is like saying 'The picture we have of thoughts when we refer to them as "processes" doesn't accord with our use of expressions like "I thought, or meant, such-and-such" ' – and one mustn't be cut off in pursuing that thought by an immediate reminder that 'literally' thoughts *are* mental processes.

Jenny Teichman, College Fellow of New Hall, Cambridge, is struck by the fact that there are about a page and a half of remarks in the *Blue Book* about the concept of a person, and the criteria of personal identity; but in the *Investigations* practically nothing about persons, but quite a lot about human beings. She speculates as to why there should be this change, and thinks that it may be because of the dualistic backdrop to the philosophical notion of a person. For some reason the notion of a human being is less likely to lead us into problems such as the Other Minds problem, than that of a person. Why? Because we think of human beings as having a natural history as members of a community; and of thinking, language and consciousness as part of that history. The overall conclusion she is tempted to draw is that 'language, and therefore the higher forms of consciousness, depend, logically, for their existence on the possibility of common "forms of life" ' and that 'if this conclusion, which is about the essence of language and thought, is a true conclusion, then it means that solipsistic doubt, and the Other Minds problem, have disappeared'.

I suppose my own contribution to this volume, entitled 'Other Minds', could be described as an attempt to show that Mrs Teichman's conclusion is a true one, and means what she thinks it means.

In the first section of his paper, 'Wittgenstein on the Soul', İlham Dilman, Reader in Philosophy at the University College of Swansea, also is concerned with the conditions of the possibility of higher forms of consciousness. Wittgenstein, he says, opposes the picture of the soul as a substance and says that the reality of the soul – i.e., the possibility of joy and sorrow, love, etc. – depends on the life of those capable of these things. Part of this life is our natural reaction to someone who has hurt himself. So the idea that 'we tend someone else because by analogy with our own case we believe he is experiencing pain too' is 'putting the cart before the horse' (Z, 542). In the last section of his paper Dilman discusses what Wittgenstein says in the *Notebooks* about the will, and draws conclusions about Wittgenstein's views on ethics which may be compared with those of A. Phillips Griffiths.

Les Holborow, Senior Lecturer in Philosophy at the University of Dundee, is puzzled by some of Wittgenstein's remarks about remembering, in *Zettel*. Such insights as I have do not seem to extend to them. I mean, for instance, the insight that in the language-game of 'I meant . . .', what happens *now* (what I say) is the criterion of my having meant (*then*) so-and-so. This helps me to understand why Wittgenstein refers to 'primitive interpretations of our concepts'. Calling meaning someone (as in 'I meant you, not Jones') a 'mental process' makes one think that there *must* have been more than the sentence 'Come here' in my mind at the time I said it. It makes us want to talk of 'an experience of meaning someone'. If there was no such 'experience' then there was nothing to parallel any supposed physical process in my brain. Along these lines I can understand Wittgenstein calling psychophysical parallelism a prejudice. But it doesn't help me to see why, for instance, he questions the necessity for memory traces (Z, 610).

Renford Bambrough discusses Wittgenstein's philosophical remark:

> I can know what someone else is thinking, not what I am thinking.
> It is correct to say 'I know what you are thinking', and wrong to
> say 'I know what I am thinking'. (*PI*, II, xi, p. 222)

He says that Wittgenstein is making a mistake, but with a point. 'Wittgenstein is protesting at the imposition of a *requirement* for the application of the word "knowledge". He is insisting that there can be knowledge where there can also be doubt.' Roger Squires, Lecturer in Logic and Metaphysics at the University of St Andrews, understands Wittgenstein's point differently. It is an attack on the 'internal eavesdropper' notion, that someone engaged in silent soliloquy knows something which 'can only be known in the first instance' to himself (Lewis) 'in a way that is not available to anybody else' (Ayer). The significance of the attack is that if it does not make sense to say a person knows what he thinks there could be 'no need to postulate inner processes and states to which a person has privileged access. The stream of consciousness would be an illusion.'

Sir Alfred J. Ayer, Wykeham Professor of Logic at the University of Oxford, says that Wittgenstein, in *On Certainty*, holds that our belief in the physical world 'is not an ordinary factual belief, but rather part of the frame of reference within which the truth or falsehood of our factual beliefs is assessed', and also that Wittgenstein maintains that the physical object language-game 'has its roots in action'. Ayer asks:

> But our actions are conditioned by our beliefs, . . . and our beliefs . . . are evinced by sentences which are intended to express what is true. When they fulfil this intention, it is . . . because things are as they describe them. So is not our use of language dependent not only on the rules of the game, but also, and indeed primarily, on the nature of things?

But how can we talk of 'the nature of things' except in some language? I think that when Wittgenstein says 'it is our *acting*, which lies at the bottom of the language-game' (*OC*, 204) he cannot mean the sort of acting that is conditioned by beliefs. He would not say that the acting which lies at the bottom of the language-game we play with 'pain' is conditioned by beliefs. It is not, when the acting is our own natural expression of pain. And it is not, he would say (Z, 540–2), when the acting is our 'primitive reaction to tend, to treat, the part that hurts when someone else is in pain'. I think the acting which lies at the bottom of the physical object language-game must be at this 'pre-rational' level.

The paper by Christopher Coope, Lecturer in Philosophy at the University of Leeds, also, deals with Wittgenstein's views on knowledge. His discussion of two, related, points has a bearing on some of the things Ayer says. The first is that, *pace* Malcolm, Wittgenstein says (*OC*, 519):

> But since a language-game is something that consists in the recurrent procedures of the game in time, it seems impossible to say in any *individual* case that such-and-such must be beyond doubt if there is to be a language-game – though it is right enough to say that *as a rule* some empirical judgment or other must be beyond doubt.

The second relates to the distinction Wittgenstein makes between *being mistaken* and other cases of false belief. Even if my belief that I have never been to the moon was false, it would not necessarily count as a mistake (*OC*, 661–3). It is necessarily true, Coope suggests, that a mistake, to *be* a mistake, could have been *avoided*. And, with the advent of space travel, there are mistakes to be avoided in 1973 which there were not in 1952.

GODFREY VESEY

Honorary Director
The Royal Institute of Philosophy

1

THE GHOST OF THE
TRACTATUS

Anthony Kenny

WITTGENSTEIN was unreliable as an historian of philosophy. When he criticised other philosophers he rarely gave chapter and verse for his criticism, and on the rare occasions on which he quoted verbatim he did not always do justice to the authors quoted. I will illustrate this first in the comparatively unimportant case of Augustine and then in the more serious case of Frege.

The *Philosophical Investigations* begins with a quotation from St Augustine's Confessions. Ever since the early thirties Wittgenstein had taken Augustine as the spokesman for a certain view of language: the view that naming is the foundation of language and that the meaning of a word is the object for which it stands (*PG*, 56–7). The passage quoted in the *Investigations* lays great stress on the role of ostension in the learning of words, and makes no distinction between different parts of speech (*PI*, I, 1). Despite this, Augustine is a curious choice as a spokesman for the views which Wittgenstein attacks since in many respects what he says resembles Wittgenstein's own views rather than the views that are Wittgenstein's target.

In the early pages of the *Investigations* Wittgenstein is concerned to argue that ostensive definition cannot have the fundamental role sometimes assigned to it in the learning of language because (*a*) the understanding of an ostension presupposes a certain mastery of language and (*b*) ostension by itself cannot make clear the role which the word to be defined is to have in language. Both these are points with which Augustine agreed. As a presupposition of the parents' being able to show objects to the child, he mentions that they express their intentions 'by the bodily movements, as it were the natural language of all peoples'. In saying this he is not saying that the child 'already has a language, only not this one' (*PI*, I, 32);

he is drawing attention to a point often made by Wittgenstein, that the setting up of linguistic conventions presupposes a uniformity among human beings in their natural, pre-conventional, reactions to such things as pointing fingers (*PG*, 94; *PI*, I, 185). Again, Augustine does not think that the ostension by itself will teach the child the meaning of the word: the child must also 'hear the words repeatedly used in their proper places in various sentences' (*PI*, I, 1).

For Augustine the beginning of the whole learning process is the child's own efforts to express its sensations and needs pre-linguistically: just before the passage quoted by Wittgenstein he says: 'By cries and various sounds and movements of my limbs I tried to express my inner feelings and get my will obeyed'.[1] Thus he agrees with Wittgenstein that 'words are connected with the primitive, the natural, expressions of the sensation and used in their place' (*PI*, I, 244). Augustine clearly distinguishes between this natural expression (for which he uses the verbs *edere, aperire, indicare*) and the relation between a word and what it signifies (for which he uses expressions involving the root *sign-* and the verb *enuntiare*). Finally, it is worth remarking that this spokesman for the name-theory nowhere uses the word *nomen* in this passage, and calls words *signa voluntatum* as often as he calls them *signa rerum*.

The misrepresentation of Augustine was not due to any hostility on Wittgenstein's part. On the contrary, a number of Wittgenstein's friends have recorded that he regarded Augustine as a great man and a clear thinker. What this shows is that even great admiration for a thinker did not ensure that Wittgenstein would represent him accurately.

This is much more obvious and much more serious in Wittgenstein's treatment of 'the great works of Frege'. In the *Tractatus* Frege is referred to in fifteen passages: in at least five of these he is misrepresented. I will illustrate this briefly.

(1) At 3.143 Wittgenstein says that Frege was able to call a proposition a composite name because of the obscuring effect of the way we write things, which means that no difference appears in print between a sentence and a word. This had nothing to do with Frege's reasons for calling a proposition a name.[2] In an ordinary arithmetic textbook, an equation looks exactly the same whether it is used to make a statement or only as the expression of an assumption:

---

[1] *Confessions*, 1, 8: *cum gemitibus et vocibus variis et variis membrorum motibus, edere vellem sensa cordis mei, ut voluntati paretur.*

[2] *Translations from the Philosophical Writings of Gottlob Frege*, ed. Peter Geach and Max Black (Oxford: Basil Blackwell, 1960) (hereafter *GB*), p. 63.

according to Frege it is a name in the latter case but not in the former (*GB*, p. 34 n).

(2) At 4.063 Wittgenstein says that Frege thought that the verb of a proposition was '. . . is true' or '. . . is false'. In the *Begriffschrift* Frege thought that the verb of a proposition was '. . . is true', but he soon abandoned this view, which was inconsistent with other things he said in that work; and at no time of his life did he think that the verb of a proposition was '. . . is false'. (Cf. G. E. M. Anscombe, *An Introduction to Wittgenstein's Tractatus*, p. 106.)

(3) At 5.02 Wittgenstein accuses Frege of having confused argument and index. Max Black comments on this passage. 'Wittgenstein's allegation is incorrect. Had Frege really thought of the names composing a proposition as "indices" in Wittgenstein's sense, he must have conceded that the meaning of a proposition could just as well have been conveyed by a simple symbol – say T for a true proposition and F for a false one. Now Frege would have agreed that the reference (*Bedeutung*) of a proposition could be identified by a name; but he also held that the sense of a proposition was a function of the senses of its components (as Wittgenstein himself seems to recognise at 3.318 in his allusion to Frege)' (*A Companion to Wittgenstein's Tractatus*, p. 239).

(4) At 5.521 Wittgenstein says that Frege 'introduced generality in association with logical product or logical sum'. There is no warrant for this in the way Frege introduces generality e.g. in *Function and Concept* (*GB*, p. 35).

(5) At 6.1271 Wittgenstein makes the proposal that one might derive logic from the logical product of Frege's primitive proposition. He goes on: 'Frege would perhaps say that we should then no longer have an immediately self-evident primitive proposition. But it is remarkable that a thinker as rigorous as Frege appealed to the degree of self-evidence as the criterion of a logical proposition'. One cannot help noticing how within the space of a sentence a counterfactual has changed into a categorical, and how Frege is taken to task for something which has been put into his mouth by Wittgenstein. Black comments 'This seems unfair to Frege and especially to his sharp separation of logical from psychological considerations. Frege held "that arithmetic is a branch of logic and need not borrow any ground of proof whatever from experience or intuition" ' (*GB*, p. 148). Frege does sometimes talk of self-evidence, as when commenting on the difficulties created by Russell's paradox for Axiom V of the *Grundgesetze*: 'I have never disguised from myself its lack of the self-evidence that belongs to the other axioms and that must properly be demanded of a logical law' (*GB*, p. 234). So

Black's defence of Frege is perhaps too generous. Still, if Frege sometimes talks of self-evidence, so does Wittgenstein – when criticising Frege! (E.g. 5.42: 'It is self-evident that ∨, ⊃, etc. are not relations in the sense in which right and left etc. are relations.')

The unfairness of some of Wittgenstein's criticism of Frege is no doubt partially to be explained by the inaccuracy of the account of Frege in the appendix to Russell's *Principles of Mathematics* on which Wittgenstein seems sometimes to have relied.

I draw attention to Wittgenstein's treatment of Augustine and Frege because I want to suggest that his carelessness as a critic affected not only his discussion of his admired predecessors but also his later polemic against his own early work. I wish to claim that his own later statements about the *Tractatus* sometimes misrepresent it and mask the considerable continuity between his later views and his earlier ones. In particular, I shall try to show that he came to misrepresent the *Tractatus* on the nature of names, on the nature of objects, on the nature of facts, and on the nature of propositions. If I can make out my case, one upshot will be that Wittgenstein will be shown to have overestimated in later life the distance which separated the picture theory of meaning from the discussions of meaning in the *Philosophical Investigations*. This should not surprise us. As an epigraph to the *Investigations* Wittgenstein sapiently placed a quotation from Nestroy: 'It is in the nature of every advance, that it appears much greater than it actually is'.

NAMES AND DEFINITION

From the early thirties onwards Wittgenstein thought it important not to identify the meaning of a name with its bearer, the object for which it stood. He also thought that it was erroneous to suggest that acquaintance with the bearer of a name was sufficient for knowledge of the meaning of a name; and hence, as we saw earlier, he attacked the primacy of ostensive definition in language learning. How far do these later attacks bear on the doctrine of the *Tractatus*?

There seems no doubt that the *Tractatus* identifies the meaning of a word with its bearer: 3.203: 'A name means an object. The object is its meaning.' And in conversation with Waismann in July 1932, having said that ostensive definition remains within language and does not involve any confrontation between sign and reality, he went on to say 'When I wrote the *Tractatus* I was unclear about logical analysis and ostensive definition. I then thought that there is a "linking up of language with reality"' (*WWK*, 209–10).

At *Tractatus*, 2.1513–4 Wittgenstein says that the correlations between the elements of a picture and things in the world are 'as it were the feelers of the picture's elements, with which the picture touches reality'. However, it is not said that the correlation is made by ostensive definition. 'Ostensive definition' does not appear in the index to the *Tractatus*, but that is unsurprising since the expression was not yet in use as a technical term. (I owe this point to Dr P. Hacker.) But no other term appears which could be a non-technical equivalent. *Hindeuten* and *hinweisen* appear in 5.461, 2.02331, 5.02, 5.522, but not in the appropriate sense. The nearest to an allusion to ostensive definition is the passage at 3.263: 'The meanings of primitive signs (*die Bedeutungen von Urzeichen*) can be explained by means of elucidations. Elucidations are propositions that contain the primitive signs. So they can only be understood if the meanings of those signs are already known.'

Max Black finds this passage 'disturbing'. On Wittgenstein's view, he says, 'It is impossible to explain a name's meaning explicitly: the only way to convey the meaning is to use the name in a proposition, thus presupposing that the meaning is already understood. On this view, the achievement of common reference by speaker and bearer becomes mysterious' (*A Companion*, p. 115). No more mysterious, one might think, than artificial respiration; but our concern is not with the plausibility of the view, but with its relationship to the *Investigations* criticism of ostensive definition.

One thing which Wittgenstein is very clearly *not* saying in 3.263 is that first we learn the meanings of names by ostensive definition, and then when we have hooked the names on to the world, we can put them together into sentences. Nor is he saying that before understanding propositions you have to understand the names that occur in them, and before understanding names you have to understand the propositions in which they occur. That would indeed make the learning of meaning mysterious and inexplicable. What he is saying is that the understanding of names and the understanding of propositions stand or fall together. And of course this is what you would expect the *Tractatus* to say in view of its claim that it is only in the context of a proposition that a name *has* a meaning (*TLP*, 3.3).

What is clear in both the *Tractatus* and the *Investigations* is that you can't learn the meaning of a name in isolation from its use (which is, *inter alia*, the way it fits into propositions). The *Investigations*, so far from contradicting, takes a stage further the *Tractatus* point that one cannot think of the meaning of propositions and the meaning of names as two separate lessons to be mastered in the course of coming to understand language. It points out that in very primitive cases of linguistic understanding it may not even be possible to identify names and propositions as separable elements of language (*PI*, I, 9–20). The *Tractatus*, so far from saying that it is acquaintance with the bearers of names which hooks the propositions on to the world, insists that the only way in which the primitive signs themselves can be understood is by using them in full-blown propositions. Certainly, Wittgenstein thought at that time that *the way in which* the use of names in propositions communicated their reference to others was a matter for empirical psychology, whereas later he thought it was part of the subject-matter of philosophy; but this extension of the realm of philosophy did not itself involve any going back on the theses which were already recognised as philosophical at the time of the *Tractatus*.

A passage in the *Philosophische Bemerkungen* makes quite clear that the ostensive definitions which don't take us beyond language are different from the elucidating propositions of the *Tractatus*.

> If I explain the meaning of a word 'A' to someone by pointing to something and saying 'this is A', this expression may be meant in two different ways. Either it is itself a proposition, in which case it can only be understood if the meaning of A is already known, i.e. I must leave it to chance whether or not he understands the sentence as I mean it; or it is a definition. Suppose I have said to someone 'A is ill', but he doesn't know who I mean by 'A', and I now point at a man, saying 'this is A'. Here the expression is a definition, but this can only be understood if he has already gathered the kind of object it is through his understanding of the grammar of the proposition 'A is ill'. But this means that any kind of explanation of a language presupposes a language already. (*PB*, p. 54)

Here it is the 'this is A' meant as a proposition, or 'A is ill', which would be elucidations in the sense of the *Tractatus*. 'This is A' meant in the second way is the ostensive definition which might wrongly be thought to take one outside language and presuppose nothing linguistic. The criticism of the role assigned to ostensive definition quite passes by the account briefly given in the *Tractatus*.

THE NATURE OF OBJECTS

Students of the *Tractatus* disagree whether that work is to be taken in a nominalist or Platonist sense: whether, that is to say, the objects which form the fixed substance of the world are to be interpreted as individuals (such as the material particles of physics) or as universals (such as the colour red or the property of tiredness). The *Notebooks* that precede the *Tractatus* show that Wittgenstein himself veered between nominalist and Platonist positions, and provide to that extent support for the rival interpretations of the *Tractatus*. However, it seems to me no accident that it is difficult to decide the question from the study of the *Tractatus* alone; when writing the book Wittgenstein chose his words carefully so as not to adopt either of the positions about which the *Notebooks* express his doubts and hesitations.

The conversations with Waismann contain a very interesting passage dated 22 December 1929. Wittgenstein was discussing the nature of objects as conceived by Frege and Russell and the possibility of representing all colour statements by means of an apparatus like the colour octahedron.

If the four primary colours would be adequate for this purpose, he said, they could be called 'elements of representation', and it is these elements of representation that are the 'objects'. 'It makes no sense to ask whether the objects are something thing-like, whether they are something that stands in the subject place, or are something like a property, or are relations and so on' (*WWK*, 43). This thought is continuous with the one expressed in the *Philosophical Investigations* (*PI*, I, 50): 'What looks as if it had to exist [what has been discussed is the nature of objects in the *Tractatus* (*PI*, I, 46)] is part of our language. It is a paradigm in our language-game: something with which comparison is made. And this may be an important observation; but it is none the less an observation concerning our language-game – our method of representation.'

In the conversations with Waismann, as in the *Tractatus*, Wittgenstein refuses to adopt either the Platonist or the nominalist notion of objects; but commonly in the thirties he writes as if the objects of the *Tractatus* had been like Platonic Ideas. A striking case in an unexpected context occurs in the 1931 *Remarks on the Golden Bough*: 'To cast out death or slay death; but he is also represented as a skeleton, as in some sense dead himself. "As dead as death." "Nothing is so dead as death; nothing is so beautiful as beauty itself." Here the image which we use in thinking of reality is that beauty, death etc. are the pure (concentrated) substances, and they are found in the beautiful object as added ingredients of the mixture. – And do I not recognize here my own observations on "object" and "complex"?' (*The Human World*, 3, 36).

In an essay which now appears as an appendix to the *Philosophische Grammatik* there is a discussion of objects which begins with the quotation 'An object cannot, in a certain sense, be described'. That seems to be an allusion to *Tractatus*, 3.221: 'Objects can only be *named*. Signs are their representatives. I can only speak *about* them; I cannot put them into words. Propositions can only say how things are, not what they are.' There follows an allusion to Plato's *Theaetetus* (201E) and the remark 'By description is meant "definition"'. For it is naturally not denied that the object can "be described from the outside", that say properties can be ascribed to it'. That may well be true of the *Tractatus*, but it is not true of Plato: in Socrates' dream in the *Theatetus* it really is being denied that any true predications can be made of the elements. But no matter, our concern is not with Wittgenstein's exegesis of Plato, but Wittgenstein's exegesis of Wittgenstein. For this purpose the most interesting feature of the passage is that the examples it takes of objects are colours considered as universals, the colours blue and red, the references of the names 'blue' and 'red' considered as undefinable signs. The passage ends by saying 'If you call the colour green an object you must say that this object occurs in a symbolism. Otherwise the sense of the symbolism, and therefore its being a symbolism, would not be guaranteed' (*PG*, 209).

This passage too fits well with the discussion in the *Investigations* where Wittgenstein imagines samples of colour being preserved in Paris like the standard metre, so that one can define, e.g. 'sepia' as the colour of the standard sepia kept hermetically sealed there. Such a sample will be not something represented, but a means of representation (*PI*, I, 50). But again the *Tractatus* is being misrepresented, for in that work it is said explicitly that colours are not simple objects, since colours have a logical structure which explains the impossibility of the simultaneous presence of two colours at the same place in the visual field (*TLP*, 6.3751).

FACT AND COMPLEX

The most interesting of the later criticisms of the *Tractatus* is contained in an essay of 1931 entitled 'Komplex und Tatsache' which appears as an appendix both to the *Philosophische Bemerkungen* and to the *Philosophische Grammatik*. I will quote the crucial part, in Roger White's translation.

> Complex is not like fact. For I can e.g. say of a complex that it moves from one place to another, but not of a fact.
> But that this complex is now situated here is a fact.
> 'This complex of buildings is coming down' is tantamount to: 'The buildings thus grouped together are coming down'.

I call a flower, a house, a constellation complexes: moreover, complexes of petals, bricks, stars, etc.

That this constellation is located here, can of course be described by a proposition in which only its stars are mentioned and neither the word 'constellation' nor its name occurs.

But that is all there is to say about the relation between complex and fact. And a complex is a spatial object, composed of spatial objects. (The concept 'spatial' admitting of a certain extension.)

A complex is composed of its parts, the things of a kind which go to make it up. (This is of course a grammatical proposition concerning the words 'complex', 'part' and 'compose'.)

To say that a red circle is composed of redness and circularity, or is a complex with these component parts, is a misuse of these words and is misleading. (Frege was aware of this and told me it.)

It is just as misleading to say the fact that this circle is red (that I am tired) is a complex whose component parts are a circle and redness (myself and tiredness). (*PG*, 199–200)

This passage is surprising in various ways. It suggests that Wittgenstein once held the view that a fact was a complex of objects, and that he was cured of this erroneous view by reflection on a remark of Frege's. But in fact in the years before the *Tractatus* Wittgenstein constantly attacks the idea that a proposition like 'this circle is red' stands for a complex, and (rightly or wrongly) attaches part of the blame for that erroneous idea to Frege. For instance, in the 1913 *Notes on Logic*: 'Frege said "propositions are names": Russell said "propositions correspond to complexes". Both are false; and especially false is the statement "propositions are names of complexes". Facts cannot be names' (*NB*, 93; cf. *TLP*, 3.144). And the *Tractatus*, though it speaks of objects as constituents (*Bestandteile*) of states of affairs, and states of affairs as concatenations of objects (2.01) never says that a fact is a complex of objects, or commits itself to the existence of Platonic objects like redness and tiredness. Indeed it contains an attack on Frege for confusing (in the case of the proposition) a complex with a fact (3.143).

The contrast is so striking that one casts about for a different way of reading the passage. Is this really a criticism of the *Tractatus* at all? Does the sentence 'Frege was aware of this and told me it' perhaps mean, not that it was Frege who first brought the matter to Wittgenstein's attention, but that Frege, in spite of Wittgenstein's accusations, had been aware of this all along and told Wittgenstein

so (i.e. told Wittgenstein that he had), more by way of self-defence
than of imparting instruction?

I do not think we can take these ways out. Various parallel
passages make clear that this is an attack on the *Tractatus*. For
instance, on p. 58 of the *Grammatik* we read:

> It is possible to speak perfectly intelligibly of combinations of
> colours and shapes (e.g. of the colours red and blue and the
> shapes square and circle) just as we speak of combinations of
> different shapes or spatial objects. And this is the origin of the
> bad form of expression: the fact is a complex of objects. In this
> the fact that a man is sick is compared with a combination of two
> things, one of them the man and the other the sickness.

An earlier version of this passage is more explicit: instead of '*des
schlechten Ausdrucks*' it reads '*meines irreleitenden Ausdrucks*': my misleading expression: the fact is a complex of objects. In the *Blue
Book*, p. 31 we are told: 'We are misled by the substantives "object
of thought" and "fact" and by the different meanings of the word
"exist". Talking of the fact as a "complex of objects" springs from
this confusion (cf. *Tractatus Logico-Philosophicus*).' Peter Geach
records that Wittgenstein told him that after reading the *Tractatus*
Frege asked him whether a fact was larger than an object which was
a constituent of it. In the essay 'Complex and Fact' we read: 'The
part smaller than the whole. Applied to fact and constituent that
would give an absurdity' (*PG*, 201).

There seems no doubt then that Wittgenstein meant the strictures
of the essay to apply to the *Tractatus*. One of the strictures gets home.
TLP, 5.5423 says: 'To perceive a complex means to perceive that
its constituents are related to one another in such and such a way'.
PG, 200 says: 'We also say "to point out a fact", but that always
means: "to point out the fact that . . ."' Whereas "to point at (or
point out) a flower" doesn't mean to point out that this blossom is on
this stalk; for we needn't be talking about this blossom and this
stalk at all.' This is a fair point. It anticipates the well-known
passage about the broomstick and the broom in the *Investigations*
(*PI*, I, 60). But here and in the *Investigations* what is in question is
not facts considered as complexes, but complexes considered as
facts: Wittgenstein is saying (correctly) that spatial complexes are
not the same as the fact of the existence of the spatial complexes.
But it is quite a different thing to claim that a fact is itself a complex
of objects. This is the claim the essay principally attacks, and this is
the one that it is unfair to saddle the *Tractatus* with.

The unfairness consists principally in ignoring the distinction made in the *Tractatus* between *Tatsache* (fact) and *Sachverhalt* (state of affairs). In the *Tractatus* Wittgenstein wrote:

In a state of affairs objects fit into one another like the links of a chain. In a state of affairs objects stand in a determinate relation to one another. (*TLP*, 2.03, 031)

In the *Grammatik* he takes up this metaphor to criticise it:

A chain is composed of its links, not of these and their spatial relations. The fact that these links are so concatenated isn't *composed* of anything at all. (*PG*, 201)

But in the *Tractatus*, too, the fact that links were concatenated (whether literal links in a literal chain, or objects in a state of affairs) would be a fact, the *existence* of a *Sachverhalt*, and that too would not be composed of anything. The *Grammatik* insists that there is an important difference between the complex consisting of *a*-standing-in-the-relation-*R*-to-*b* and the fact that *a* stands in the relation *R* to *b*. In the *Tractatus* at 3.1432 that distinction is already drawn with complete sharpness and given an important place in the theory of the proposition.

THE PICTURE THEORY

It is commonly said that Wittgenstein after the *Tractatus* abandoned the picture theory of the proposition. He certainly came to regard it as incomplete, and he certainly came to think that he had misconceived the relation between thought and proposition. In the *Tractatus* he regarded the thought as a ghostly intermediary between sentence and fact, where, in the ghostly medium of the mind, the projection lines were drawn between the proposition and what it represented (3.11). He later came to think that it was language which linked thought to reality, not the other way round; and he came to think that no lines of projection could do what the *Tractatus* thought was supposed to do (*PG*, 214).

In my book *Wittgenstein* I have argued that it is a mistake to overestimate the philosopher's change of mind with regard to the picture theory. Many of the logical features of the theory, I have argued, survived with more or less modification the abandonment of the atomism of the *Tractatus*. I do not wish to repeat here what I have written elsewhere: instead I will single out one feature of the picture theory which remained influential throughout Wittgenstein's

B

life: the bipolarity of the proposition. Any proposition which *can* be true, Wittgenstein insisted from 1913 onwards, *can* be false. This thesis, which is a crucial element of the picture theory, is tantamount to the thesis that there are only contingent propositions. If every genuine proposition is capable of being false, then there are no necessary truths: synthetic *a priori* truths are impossible and analytic truths are 'propositions' only by courtesy. The thesis of bipolarity is constantly reaffirmed throughout Wittgenstein's life: in the conversations with Waismann (*WWK*, 67, 88, 97), in the *Philosophische Grammatik* (129), in the *Blue Book* (p. 54), in the *Philosophical Investigations* (I, 251). It is tantamount to the insistence that what gives a proposition its sense must be independent of what gives it its truth, which is also a notion which recurs from the early *Notebooks* (107) through *Bemerkungen* (*PB*, 78) into the argument against private languages in the *Investigations*.

Even the isomorphism between the world and language survives, though with its poles reversed, in the later philosophy. Dr Hacker has put it neatly in his book *Insight and Illusion*: 'In the *Investigations* the structure of language . . . is still isomorphic with the structure of reality, not because language must mirror the logical form of the universe, but because the apparent "structure of reality" is merely the shadow of grammar'. Whichever way it is facing, the isomorphism has the effect that the structure of reality can only be shown not described, and that the structure of language cannot be justified.

The first entry in the *Notebooks* is 'logic must take care of itself'. That is an abiding thought of Wittgenstein's philosophy. Throughout his life he continued to deny that philosophy could provide a justification for logic, or as he would later call it, grammar, or language games. One of the clearest passages about this is in the *Philosophische Grammatik*, which stands in the middle of his life firmly anchoring the earlier to the later philosophy.

> The rules of grammar cannot be justified by shewing that their application makes a representation agree with reality. For these justifications must themselves describe what is represented. And if something can be said in those justifications and is permitted by their grammar – why shouldn't it be also permitted by the grammar that I am trying to justify? Why shouldn't both forms of expression have the same freedom? And how could what the one says restrict what the other can say? (*PG*, 186)

He might have said at the end of the *Investigations*, about attempts to justify grammar, what he said at the end of the *Tractatus*: whereof one cannot speak thereof one must be silent. Instead, if one had to choose an epigram to end his later work, one might choose something which expresses the same thought, but in a more tolerant vein: a thought which he attributes to St Augustine but which, like the theory of language with which the *Investigations* began, is difficult to locate in the actual text of the Saint.

Was, du Mistviech, du willst keinen Unsinn reden? Rede nur einen Unsinn, es macht nichts! (*WWK*, 123)

2

CAN WHETHER ONE PROPOSITION MAKES SENSE DEPEND ON THE TRUTH OF ANOTHER? (*Tractatus* 2.0211–2)

R. M. White

WITTGENSTEIN'S *Tractatus* contains a wide range of profound insights into the nature of logic and language – insights which will survive the particular theories of the *Tractatus* and seem to me to mark definitive and unassailable landmarks in our understanding of some of the deepest questions of philosophy. And yet alongside these insights there is a theory of the nature of the relation between language and reality which appears both to be impossible to work out in detail in a way which is completely satisfactory, and to be bizarre and incredible. I am referring to the so-called logical atomism of the *Tractatus*. The main outlines of this theory at least are clear and familiar: there are elementary propositions which gain their sense from being models of possible states of affairs; such propositions are configurations of names of simple objects, signifying that those simples are analogously configured; every proposition has its sense through being analysable as a truth-functional compound of elementary propositions, thus deriving its sense from the sense of the elementary propositions when this view is taken in conjunction with the idea that the sense of a proposition is completely specified by specifying its truth-conditions. In this way the *Tractatus* incorporates in its working out a philosophical system analogous to the classical philosophical systems of Leibniz or Spinoza which are regarded by many people, in a sense rightly, as the prehistoric monsters of philosophy which are not to be studied as living organisms, but studied as the curiosities of human thought. And we may here agree that in the end we must simply reject a philosophy which incorporates such features as its postulation of simple eternal objects, or of a possibility of an analysis of a proposition which was presented as a pre-condition for the propositions that we ordinarily utter to make sense, and yet the specific form of which we are unaware of, and so on.

And yet paradoxically it is this last fact – the incredibility of the picture of the relation of language and reality which Wittgenstein offers – which makes the *Tractatus* a constant stimulus to further reflection on a wide range of the most fundamental questions of philosophical logic. (We could incidentally say that the same is true *mutatis mutandis* for those other philosophical systems such as Leibniz' monadology in as much as we do not approach them with a crude philistinism or mere dilettante aesthetic curiosity.) For what the *Tractatus* represents is in fact a systematic and rigorous thinking out with full consequence of a series of ideas on the inter-relations between a proposition's making sense, its being true or false, its having a negation, where we usually appeal to these ideas sporadically and unsystematically, without thinking them through to the end. These ideas are entirely natural and apparently self-evident, and yet taken at their face value are shown in the *Tractatus* to lead to the consequences which we find so bizarre and unaccept-able. In this way we are forced to rethink the interrelations, say, between the idea of a proposition's making sense and its being true or false, either abandoning ideas which seem self-evident or else being forced to realise that those ideas have to be understood far more subtly than we naively assume. That the *Tractatus* can be regarded as the rigorous thinking through of certain very natural ideas about what it is for a proposition to make sense, and that the theories of the *Tractatus* are therefore not merely to be regarded as oddities, is, I think, mainly overlooked for two very different reasons.

The first and most obvious reason is the mode of exposition which Wittgenstein adopts in the *Tractatus* – what he was to call later a 'dogmatic' method of exposition. The explanation of this method of exposition, apart from aesthetic considerations, appears to have been twofold: the first relates to the difficulties Wittgenstein refers to in conversation with Waismannin [1] communicating what he had to say at all, of organising his ideas into a coherent and intelligible form when he was constantly groping for what he wanted to say, and the second is that it was I think always true that Wittgenstein thought that in philosophy if you spared someone the difficulty of thinking something out for himself, you also deprived him of the opportunity of really understanding what it was that was to be said.

[1] *WWK*, pp. 182ff.

But be that as it may, in the case of the *Tractatus* this has led a large number of people to think of the book as a series of aphorisms without the deep underlying structure of argument ever coming into focus, with the result that they fail to recognise how doctrines of the *Tractatus* are in fact supported by an attempt to give substance to many of our most basic ideas in philosophical logic, and therefore that repudiating the *Tractatus* must lead to a subtle shift in our understanding of those basic ideas in as much as we do not simply reject them.

The second reason why discussions of the *Tractatus* do not do justice to the strength of the arguments of the book is a more curious one: this is the way that the doctrines of the *Tractatus* are presented for criticism in the *Investigations*. I am sure I am not alone in the feeling at times that the author of the *Investigations* appears in its early sections not to have understood the *Tractatus*, that what we are offered there are almost straw men, certainly crude caricatures of the positions of the *Tractatus*, and that the actual ideas of the *Tractatus* were far subtler than anything that is put under critical review in those parts of the *Investigations* which deal explicitly with the *Tractatus*. If I am right in this impression, it is certainly an odd one, which is, I think, susceptible of two explanations: the first and obvious one is that Wittgenstein was so out of sympathy with certain of the ideas of the *Tractatus* that he had lost the ability to give them even a sympathetic exposition before criticising them, but the second and, I think, real reason is that the criticism of some of the crucial ideas of the *Tractatus* was in fact so radical that it involved a total shift of perspective on the nature of the relation between language and reality, and was thus not capable of the succinct exposition in which the views of the *Tractatus* would be refuted by brief arguments. The real criticism of those ideas of the *Tractatus* which he found to be misguided is, rather, diffused throughout the book, and is to be found in a change of perspective which permeates the later book; the early remarks about the *Tractatus* are to be regarded as shots across the bows, and the real criticisms are to be found less directly but, once found, represent a real engagement with the *Tractatus* at the deepest level. But those early remarks may have distracted readers from the nature of the critique of the *Tractatus* offered in the *Investigations* and consequently caused them to read a grossly oversimplified position back into the *Tractatus*. It is at least to indicate the nature of what I take to be the real engagement between the two books with which I am concerned in this talk.

Near the centre of Wittgenstein's concerns in the *Tractatus* is the intimate relation between a proposition's making sense and its having truth/falsity polarity: that to understand the sense of a proposition is to know what is the case if it is true and what if it is false. Where of course there is not merely an accidental relation between what must be the case for a proposition to be true and what for it to be false. In making it clear what is to be the case for a proposition to be true, we *ipso facto* determine what it is for it to be false. What I have said thus far is innocent and perhaps even platitudinous: it is in its interpretation and working out that we get involved in the more suspect features of the *Tractatus*. This stress on the relation between making sense and having truth/falsity polarity is clearly right; we would not understand what was meant by someone's understanding a proposition and yet being unclear what it would be for the proposition to be true. Equally it is clear that we define the sense of a proposition by making it clear what it is for it to be true and what it is for it to be false simultaneously: as Wittgenstein stresses, we have missed the point of the notions of truth and falsity if we think that we give distinct accounts of a proposition's being true and of its being false. When we make an assertion, we put forward an utterance as the appropriate thing to say, as true, and if we fail, if it is clear that the utterance is inappropriate, we have made a false assertion.

Now the stress on these points, which if taken correctly can be seen as innocuous, can suggest a certain picture which if worked through is far from innocuous. This picture can be given as follows: we imagine there to be a spectrum of possible situations and we demarcate a region within that spectrum as comprising the possible situations which make a particular proposition true. A proposition gains its sense by thus demarcating a part of a spectrum of possible states of affairs. If the actual situation falls within that part of the spectrum then the proposition is true, otherwise it is false. So that the proposition divides a spectrum of possible situations in two, and thereby simultaneously defines what it is for it to be true and what for it to be false, and any adequate account of the sense of a proposition should make it clear what its truth value is in the face of any possibility. One may see part of what is at stake here in Wittgenstein's emphatic endorsement of Russell's theory of definite descriptions. Whereas Frege said of a proposition of the form 'The F is G' that such a proposition presupposed but did not imply that there was one and only one F, Russell construed the sense of such a proposition in such a way that it did directly imply there to be one and only one F. The immediate consequence of this was that for Frege we could envisage a situation in which we were clear that a proposition was not true, and yet did not thereby deem it false, whereas Russell had given an account of the sense of the propositions involved which made it clear that in determining the proposition not to be true, we were *ipso facto* determining it to be false.

For Frege, for the proposition 'the *F* is *G*' to be true or false, which is in *Tractatus* terms what it is for it to make sense, another proposition – namely that there is one and only one *F* – had to be true, thereby rendering unclear for Wittgenstein the role of the notions of truth and falsity, by making room for the possibility of our being clear that a proposition was not true, that it was incorrect to assert it, while not thereby deeming it false, so that the relation between being true and false becomes obscured, since it now appears that a proposition may have to satisfy a condition over and above not being true in order to be false. The fact that in a concrete situation it may be well known to all concerned that a certain possibility does not obtain, does not prevent us from saying of a proposition which if that possibility had obtained would have been false, that it implies or asserts that that possibility does not obtain. And for us not to say this is to obscure the relation between a proposition's making sense and its division of the possibilities into those which make the proposition true and those which make it false: it may seem that those who have talked like Frege and, more recently, Professor Strawson, of possibilities which are presupposed but not implied by a proposition's being true are simply confusing our purpose in asserting a proposition with the content of what we assert. If it is known to us and our audience that a certain possibility does not obtain it may well be that when we assert a proposition which implies that that possibility does not obtain, it is not part of our purpose to deny that possibility, but that does not prevent what we assert from implying that that possibility does not obtain. If I am told that Richard Nixon has been re-elected president of the United States, then the use of the word 're-elected' makes it clear that it is being claimed that he was elected previously, even though that may be common knowledge and not the purpose of the announcement: to try in the concrete to draw a distinction between those implications of a proposition which are common knowledge and so to be designated presuppositions of the proposition rather than true implications seems not only a virtually impossible exercise, but also a pointless one, lumbering us with an irrelevant distinction which does not seem, without further explanation, to clarify the sense of what is being claimed, what would make the claim true or false. It is clear that I cannot within the scope of this talk do more than sketch a position and not go into the intricacies of the debate over the tenability, say, of Strawson's account of the theory of descriptions, and if I were to make that the subject of a talk I would wish to elaborate what I have only indicated here, where the theory of descriptions has only the function of giving a preliminary indication of Wittgenstein's position which is to lead him to a form of logical atomism.

Up to this point, I have been expressing ideas with which I have broad agreement and with which I think Wittgenstein retained broad agreement throughout his life. What we now have to see is the way of taking those ideas which led him to the positions which I described at the outset as bizarre and incredible. Within the *Tractatus* Wittgenstein envisages our putting forward a proposition as constructing a model of a situation in the world, and how the world is will make that model right or wrong, the proposition true or false, but, and this is in line with what we have been saying up to now, how the world is cannot prevent the model from presenting us with a possible situation, and so how the world is can make our model wrong, not prevent it from showing how the world would be if it were right. In line with this, if we specify a possibility and say 'In this case the model would not be right' then we are not specifying a possibility which prevents the model from being a model, the proposition from making sense. And an account of the sense of the model, the proposition, must be construed so as to allow no possible situation to be such that we would deny that the proposition was right, was true, without *ipso facto* making it false.

Now let us in the light of this consider a very everyday proposition, and the natural account that we would give of its sense. We may take the proposition 'Martin Luther wrote a commentary on Genesis'. Our everyday understanding of such a proposition would involve us in saying that 'Martin Luther' here functioned as a proper name, that is to say a sign which has a bearer and contributes to the sense of the proposition by standing for that bearer, and that the proposition is true or false according as Martin Luther did or did not write such a commentary, and this is surely right, it is in such a way that we do understand the proposition. And yet we may note straight off that such an account at least *prima facie* falls foul of what we have been saying up to this point. There is at least one possibility which is catered for neither by our account of what it is for the proposition to be true or to be false, or in other words neither by the proposition 'Martin Luther wrote a commentary on Genesis', nor by what we would regard as its negation 'Martin Luther did not write a commentary on Genesis', namely the possibility of the non-existence of Luther. We must at this point be clear what we are referring to when we talk of this possibility: for it is in different ways of understanding this possibility that we may notice a bifurcation in the programme of analysis in which Wittgenstein and Russell were collaborating, a bifurcation which explains the different natures of the logical atomism advocated at this period by Russell and of the doctrine of the *Tractatus*. For we may take the phrase 'the possibility of the non-existence of Luther' either to refer to that envisaged by the proposition 'It is possible that there was no such person as Luther', or to that envisaged by the proposition 'It is conceivable that Martin Luther should never have existed'. Where the first of these propositions alludes to the possibility of doubting that in fact there was such a person as Luther, while the second says that even though we know there to be such a person, we can well imagine what it would have been like for the history of the world to be different – say for Luther's mother to have died before reaching the age of childbirth – in such a way that it would not have come about that Luther existed. It is important to notice that these two different ways of taking the phrase 'the possibility of the non-existence of Luther' point in completely different directions, very different possibilities are being envisaged, and that it is essential to the first that we should not prejudge whether it is a counterfactual possibility, whereas the second is quite definitely envisaging a possibility that we know does not obtain. The former, the epistemo-logical possibility of doubt of Martin Luther's existence, partly because of curious features of the theory of judgment he held during this period, was the one of crucial importance to Russell, and was what led his logical atomism to assume the simple objects to be sense-data, and the logically proper names to be the words 'this' and 'that' used to refer to them: here we had escaped the sphere of what could be doubted. This theory, a hybrid combination of logical and epistemological features, although starting out along the same lines as the *Tractatus* has in its final form little in common with the final position of the *Tractatus*. Epistemological considerations play no part at all in Wittgenstein's thought, in fact it is crucial to under-standing Wittgenstein's position to see him as treating as completely irrelevant that we know a certain possibility not to obtain when we determine the sense of a proposition which can only be true if that possibility does not obtain: our knowing that it does not obtain does not alter one jot the fact that the proposition implies that it does not.

What we have in Wittgenstein's case is something like the follow-ing situation: if we take a proposition containing a term that we would ordinarily regard as a proper name, then if we are to be able to regard it as having truth/falsity polarity, as dividing the logically possible situations into two groups, those which make the proposition true and those which make it false, we run up against the conceivability of the non-existence of the object named, and our account of the sense of the proposition must cater for this possibility, must show, say, the proposition to be false in case that possibility had occurred. Thus the proposition is taken to imply that that possibility did not obtain, and the supposed proper name is analysed in such a way that it no longer contributes to the sense of the proposition by standing for its bearer, for that sense must cater for the possibility that such a bearer might never have existed, otherwise whether the proposition makes sense, divides the possibilities into two groups, depends on another proposition being true: i.e. the proposition to the effect that the history of the world did not go in the way envisaged by the claim 'Luther might never have existed'.

Now if it is essential to language that there should be proper names, as it is in the theory of the proposition as a truth-functional compound of models of reality, then those proper names can only be of objects of which it makes no sense to suppose that they might never have existed. In the detailed working out of the *Tractatus*, Wittgenstein here contrasts complexes and simples. Given an object which is complex, which is made of parts, it is easy enough to conceive of its non-existence, i.e. we simply imagine those parts not to have been put together in this way. This concrete working out of the theory is in many respects slightly fishy, but does not affect the substance of what Wittgenstein is arguing for in the *Tractatus*: that if we take a proper name as a sign which has a bearer and contributes to the sense of a proposition by standing for that bearer, then our ordinary proper names can only be regarded as such if we make the question whether one proposition makes sense depend on the truth of another, and thus put in jeopardy our idea of the link between a proposition's making sense and its dividing possible situations into two groups – those that make the proposition true and those that make it false: we must therefore reconstrue such propositions, give them an analysis which shows these everyday names to be, from a logical point of view, only apparent names, and that the real names must be names of objects for which it makes no sense to suppose that they might not have existed; the existence of such objects is then the precondition for our being able to produce a model of the world. We may summarise the path we have followed in the language of the *Tractatus* itself, where the sense of certain key theses which have been found obscure should by now be intelligible:

(1) A proposition which talks of a complex will not be nonsense if this complex does not exist but simply be false.

(2) If the world had no substance then whether one proposition made sense would depend on whether another proposition was true. In that case, we couldn't sketch out a picture of the world (true or false).

Now what are we to say to this whole line of thought and its result? It is clear that the queerness of the outcome does not of itself show what is wrong with Wittgenstein's pattern of argument, and if we find the argument fishy, then we should reflect on the fact that at those points where we are most suspicious all Wittgenstein does is to take at their face value certain of our most fundamental ideas about logic and think them through to the end. If, for instance, we object to the insistence that the possibility countenanced by the proposition 'Luther might never have existed' is one that is to be taken into account when explaining the truth-conditions of 'Luther wrote a commentary on Genesis', then we cannot object glibly, for at a number of points we appeal to a notion of possibility which stands in deep need of explanation if we do reject certain possibilities as relevant. For instance, we construe the negation of a proposition as a proposition whose sense is explained by the fact that it, together with the original proposition, exhausts the possibilities. If we now cite logical possibilities which yet are not counted as relevant within that formula, then the notion of possibility involved, and with it the notion of the negation of a proposition, becomes a notion that we realise we have a much less clear grasp on than we had previously thought.

Within the scope of this talk, all I want to do is to indicate the way in which the range of questions prompted by the unsatisfactory character of some features of the *Tractatus* led Wittgenstein to subject the question of the relation of language to reality to a profound re-examination culminating in many of the most characteristic ideas of the *Philosophical Investigations*. The pattern of argument in the *Tractatus* is no superficial sophism, but a train of thought which calls forth as a reply as deep an investigation as that which runs through the *Investigations*: I cannot hope to do more here than to make tentative suggestions of how to regard the *Investigations* as at least in part a reply to the kind of argument I have here ascribed to the *Tractatus*.

There is one preliminary remark that needs making: the argument that I have sketched out I have developed with reference to proper names, but the points at issue are by no means restricted to names: proper names have figured so largely in the account so far for two reasons: Firstly and most simply that the *Tractatus* account of language, the so-called picture theory highlights the role of proper names in language and it is therefore in the context of a discussion of names that the argument will naturally be developed. Secondly, there is a pragmatic justification in that the argument can be expounded most simply for the case of proper names of contingent entities – the complexes of the *Tractatus* – for here the possibilities which are not catered for either by a proposition's being true or false, and therefore the propositions whose truth seems presupposed to the sense of that proposition, are capable of being specified with most simplicity. But the reply to the *Tractatus* implicit in the *Investigations* only deals incidentally with proper names, involving as it does a total change of perspective on the phenomena of language, which is being expounded at a time when proper names no longer had the all-important role assigned to them by the *Tractatus*. This means two things: firstly, that in seeing the material in the *Investigations* as a reply to the *Tractatus* we may recognise that there is far more at stake than a doctrine of proper names – indeed, at one of the crucial points we shall discuss, Wittgenstein sees the nature of logic at stake: 'this appears to abolish logic but does not do so'; and secondly that it is easy to overlook the way in which the *Investigations* does attempt to criticise the *Tractatus*, since the interrelations are not as close to the surface as they would have been if he had presented his new position in more explicit connection with the ideas of the *Tractatus*. I certainly find it easier to recognise the deep continuities within Wittgenstein's thought, than the real nature of the contrasts: one only comes to recognise these for what they are after prolonged engagement with the two works.

We may begin this part of my discussion by returning to the argument with which we began and note that the parallel which I put forward between Wittgenstein's endorsement of the theory of descriptions and his treatment of ordinary proper names masks a fundamental contrast between the two cases which may serve as a preliminary stage in the criticism I am to develop here. It is certainly the case that with both the propositions 'The present queen of England is married' and 'Luther wrote a commentary on Genesis', we may countenance the counter-factual possibility 'The present queen of England might never have existed' and 'Luther might never have existed'. But there is an ambiguity in the first of these which isn't present in the second. For the first could mean 'There might not have been one and only one queen of England', or that 'Whether or not there were a queen of England, the present one (i.e. Elizabeth Windsor) might never have existed'. It is the first of these two interpretations that is catered for by the theory of descriptions, and yet it is the second alone which is analogous to the claim 'Luther might never have existed'. The reason for this is clear and instructive: if we say that the theory of descriptions shows 'the present queen of England is married' as false in case there is no present queen of England, then we can say this because even if this possibility had obtained we could still have formulated the proposition in question. Whereas when we imagine the history of the world to have developed differently, so that Luther did not exist, we are not imagining a world in which the proposition 'Luther wrote a commentary on Genesis', using the name Luther as a proper name as we do, would have been false, we are imagining a world in which there would have been no such proposition, in which it would not have come about that people would have been in a position to formulate a proposition tantamount to our 'Luther wrote a commentary on Genesis': there would be no Luther for them to refer to and make this claim about. (As an aside, I may remark that in the proposition 'Luther might never have existed', 'Luther' is being used *there* as a proper name, and had this possibility obtained, people would not have been able to state its having obtained.) We then see the beginnings of a reason for denying that the phrase 'a proposition's being true and being false exhaust the possibilities' is to be interpreted in the radical and simplistic way we have taken it in our preceding discussion: that is, that given certain propositions then there are logically possible histories of the world in which it would be inappropriate for us to say that the propositions are either true or false for the simple reason that in envisaging those histories to have obtained, we are envisaging a situation in which it would have been impossible to formulate the propositions in question. Quite simply, we rely on certain contingent features of our world in order to give our signs a sense, and in imagining those features not to have obtained, we are imagining a world in which propositions containing such signs would be incapable of formulation, not one in which they would be false. And in the light of this, we may say that we must interpret our phrase 'exhaust the possibilities', to refer to the possibilities allowed for by the existence of our language, and not to an abstract notion of logical possibility independent of the features which make our language capable of saying what it does. We could say: by possibilities here, we mean the possibilities envisaged by the language. In the light of this, Wittgenstein's first move away from the kind of doctrine sketched out in the *Tractatus* is to say 'I will count anything which looks as if it has to exist in order for a proposition to make sense as an instrument of the language'. This position, to be found for example in the *Bemerkungen*, is slightly unhappy, at least in its expression, for it is surely odd to say of the man Martin Luther, that he is an instrument of the English language. But what we see here is the first hint of something worked out with immense subtlety and on a very broad scale within the *Investigations*: that language evolved as a system of communication within the world, and relies, in giving a sense to its propositions, on certain contingent features of the world; and also that one cannot simply disregard the fact that language has evolved as a system of communication between men within this world, and that in imagining certain features of the world not to have obtained, one may be imagining the world to be such that it would be impossible to formulate the propositions which men do in fact utter. To that extent, we cannot say that those propositions assert the existence of those features and their negations must cater for the possibility of their not having existed, for in imagining those features not to have existed, we are equally imagining here the impossibility of formulation both of a proposition and of its negation. Here we are then in a position to see a good sense in the much over-used notion of presupposition; if in envisaging a certain possibility to obtain we are *ipso facto* envisaging a situation in which a proposition can no longer be formulated, we may say that the proposition presupposes that feature of the world, since in thinking that feature away, we are not envisaging the falsehood of that proposition but a situation in which there is no longer such a proposition to be true or false. To the extent that this is not so in the case of a definite description, the notion of presupposition is being made to do unnecessary work when contrasted with the clear simplicity of Russell's account of definite descriptions, but in as much as this is so in the case of most of the proper names we employ, then the notion becomes unavoidable. We may now reformulate: 'A proposition's being true and false exhaust the possibilities envisaged by the language, i.e. not presupposed to the existence of the language' and this gives us the kind of connection we require between a proposition's making sense and being true and false – in the phrase of the *Investigations*, does not 'abolish logic' – without leading us like a will o' the wisp into the quagmires of logical atomism.

We now move from the abstract consideration of language conceived as a device for the construction of a model of the world, to looking at it as a system of communication used by men within the world, relying on certain features of their world and their mode of existence – what Wittgenstein calls their form of life – to establish that system of communication, and by extension of this line of thought to seeing language as part of a broader activity including other forms of social intercourse and life: it is at this point that the frequently overworked metaphor of a language-game is introduced to convey his point: that we cannot divorce the use of language from its wider human context and that we must understand an utterance as 'a move in the game' of human beings engaged in a common social and therefore rule-governed way of life.

From this broadened and deeply enriched perspective we may see a wide variety of phenomena which are presupposed to the propositions of our language being formed, making sense, being true or false. I can, of course, do no more than indicate the range of Wittgenstein's thought; but I hope that the provision of the context for that thought which this talk is aimed at should show how misleading it is to talk, as for instance most recently Pears has done, of Wittgenstein engaging in an empirical investigation of the actual phenomena of language in his later work. His concern is still with the nature of logic and what it would be for any language to relate to reality, not merely the particular characteristics of our language: he in fact talks about his anthropological method, where this does not mean anthropological field work or anything of that sort, but rather the reverse – imagining hypothetical tribes whose lives run along very different lines from ours, in order that we may see in that context what it is for there to be a language about reality.

I will end by sketching a few of the kind of phenomena which Wittgenstein draws attention to in this connection, over and above the simple case with which I have developed this talk, the use of everyday proper names being dependent on the existence of bearers of those names.

(1) In order that there should be a common language – or, indeed, a language at all – there must exist the possibility of human beings following rules, since this notion is involved in our using a word again in the same sense, with the same use. But if there are to be rules common to human beings, there must be agreement in human reactions to phenomena: for instance, if we think crudely of teaching someone how to use the word 'red' by the use of samples of objects which are and are not red, then sooner or later we come to the point where we say 'Now, go on' and he must be able to respond to this training in a way which is the same as other members of his community, if he is to have a common language with them, so that confronted by a new shade of red, an object not actually used in the teaching, he must react in common with other human beings to this colour as though prefigured in the training. The fact that human beings do in general react in the same way in such situations is a contingent anthropological fact, but one without which language could never get off the ground, for there would be no such thing as human beings all following the same rule. I have used here the phrase 'agreement in reactions' in preference to Wittgenstein's

'agreement in judgments' for although I think the idea is the same, Wittgenstein's phrasing has in fact frequently misled people as to what he is saying, although most of those misunderstandings should have been averted by Wittgenstein's prefacing his introduction of the phrase by the remark: ' "So you are saying that agreement among men decides what is true and what is false?" – It is what human beings *say* that is true and false; and they agree in the *language* they use. That is not agreement in opinions but in form of life.'[1] Here, more than anywhere, I feel the inadequacy of my gesture towards an account of Wittgenstein, but all that was possible here was to indicate how the long and profound discussion of what it is to follow a rule relates to my topic.

(2) There is yet another sense of 'agreement in reactions' without which the formation of certain concepts would be unintelligible. For instance, to take an example that Wittgenstein discusses at great length, if human beings did not agree in finding pain unpleasant, if there were not characteristic patterns of behaviour evoked by pain, the formation of a concept of pain would become unintelligible: for certainly the word 'pain' does not designate such behaviour, and yet but for such behaviour we could not imagine the formation of a language in which pains were referred to.

(3) Wittgenstein frequently imagines tribes – particularly in the *Brown Book* period – which differ significantly from normal human beings, to show the ways in which they would form concepts which would be unintelligible to us, and for whom our concepts would not be applicable. For instance, to use an example which isn't Wittgenstein's but which is like many of his, it is a contingent matter of fact that when someone is hurt, the part of the body where the injury is inflicted, the part where the damage results, and the part where treatment should be applied, in general, coincide: we could easily imagine that when someone was hit in the stomach, this had major repercussions in the lungs which should be treated by attending to the nose and throat, and so on. If there were not such general coincidence, our concepts of pain location might very well run along very different lines, and feeling a pain in the arm might relate to very different phenomena of being injured from those which lie behind our ability to form our concepts of pain location. In all three kinds of case I have indicated, we should not say it would then be false to say what we now say – it would not, for instance, in the last case, be false to say of a man that he felt a stomach ache, we would be imagining a form of life which ran along such different lines that we could no longer apply our concepts of pain location to

[1] *PI*, I, 241.

him: we could not attach any sense to saying of such a man that
in our sense he felt a pain in the stomach, although a tribe of such
people might well develop a system of pain locations different from
ours which would have a point, given their physiology. To summarise by Wittgenstein's epigram, given a very different form of
life, certain propositions which make sense for us, would cease to
make sense, to be true or false, and *vice versa* and 'If a lion could
speak we would not understand him'.

So we may return by saying in reply to the *Tractatus* that a
proposition and its negation exhaust the possibilities allowed for by
the language, not the possibilities taken in some abstract sense,
and these possibilities are conditioned by the form of life of the
speakers of that language and by the features of the world within
which they live that life.

After this discussion, Wittgenstein's criticism of the notions of
the *Tractatus* should, I hope, have become clearer, and also perhaps
the nature of the repercussions for philosophical logic, even if not
their detailed working out. And we are now in a position to leave
the final word with Wittgenstein, where he summarises the nature
of his *Investigations*, and, I hope, to see how this represents the
deepest engagement with the train of thought developed in his
earlier book: certainly this passage is not to be seen as a curt dismissal of the *Tractatus* as utterly misguided, indeed, certain reported
remarks of Wittgenstein suggest that he saw the *Tractatus* as the
only possible alternative account of language to that which he later
developed. This should not be seen as an arrogant estimate of the
value of his own work, but rather as a reflection of the fact that
the *Tractatus* posed certain deep problems which either led to a
variant on the theory of the *Tractatus* period, or could only be overcome by the very different approach represented by his later work.
That it required the *Investigations* to answer the *Tractatus* is a
tribute to the importance of the earlier work. At II, xii of the
Investigations, then, Wittgenstein writes:

> If the formation of concepts can be explained by facts of nature,
> should we not be interested, not in grammar, so much as in nature
> which forms the basis of grammar? – Our interest certainly
> includes the way concepts answer to very general facts of nature.
> (Such facts as usually do not strike us because of their generality.)
> But our interest does not revert to these possible causes of concept-
> formation; we're not doing natural science; nor even natural
> history – since we can indeed construct fictitious natural history
> for our purposes.

I do not say: Were such and such natural facts different, men would have had different concepts (where this is taken as an hypothesis). What I am saying is: If someone believes certain concepts to be the unavoidably right ones, and that someone who possessed different ones would simply not have seen what we see, then let him imagine certain very general facts of nature to be different from what we are accustomed to, and different concept-formations from the ones we are accustomed to will become intelligible to him.

3

QUESTIONS ON LOGICAL INFERENCE

Rush Rhees

A FUNDAMENTAL notion of the *Tractatus* is that of the repetition of an operation. The operation specially mentioned is the simultaneous negation represented by the Sheffer stroke. 'If an operation is applied repeatedly to its own results, I speak of successive applications of it. . . . In a similar sense I speak of successive applications of *more than one* operation to a number of propositions' (5.2521).

Every possible propositional form can be derived in this way – by the successive application of the operation $N(\bar{\xi})$ to elementary propositions. And the general form of operation is the most general form of transition from one proposition to another.

By reference to the repetition of the operation and the resulting series of forms, the *Tractatus* can give a recursive definition of the natural numbers.

So there is an internal connection between the conception of a number and the conception of the transition from one proposition to another – or the transformation of one propositional form into another. And an internal connection with the idea of a *series* of forms; so that the general form of number is the general term of a series of forms, and might be taken as a symbol for mathematical induction: $(0, \xi, \xi+1)$.

This is an enormous simplification compared with the introduction of 'number' in the works of Frege and of Russell; and also, compared with Frege's demonstration of the logical character of mathematical induction.

It is not a reduction of mathematics to logic. But it helps to explain what Wittgenstein wrote in the margin of Ramsey's copy of the *Tractatus*: 'Number is *the* fundamental idea of calculus and must be introduced as such'[1] – where 'calculus' means 'formal series or system of transitions from one propositional form, or one formula, to another'.

If we speak of 'generality' in logic or in mathematics – we do not mean any reference or application to 'all the members of a class'. The *Tractatus* says in 6.031:

> that the generality we have to do with in mathematics is not the *chance* generality.

A 'chance generality' would be the general application of a predicate to all the members of a class – 'All men die before they are 200 years old'.

In the *Philosophische Bemerkungen* he would say: 'The generality of arithmetic is (mathematical) induction'.

The *Tractatus*, in 5.11ff, speaks of logical inference in the sense: I can infer q from p if the truth of q follows from the truth of p.

Russell had given the rule of inference in words: 'Anything implied by a true elementary proposition is true. Pp.' ('Elementary proposition' in *Principia Mathematica* (*PM*) does not mean just what it does in the *Tractatus*.) He added: 'We cannot express the principle symbolically, partly because any symbolism in which p is variable only gives the *hypothesis* that p is true, not the *fact* that it is true'. The Introduction to the Second Edition of *PM*, which was largely influenced by Wittgenstein's work, does not raise the difficulty, and '*the rule of inference*' is written symbolically, although in the stroke notation rather than that of Peano.

The *Tractatus* refers to the symbolic expression of it: $p \supset q . p : \supset : q$. (E.g. in 6.1221.) But this becomes a *rule* only when it is written as a *tautology*. And then we see that we can write the rule of inference simply as

$$p \supset q = \text{Taut.;}$$

i.e. 'If I can give p and q such values that $p \supset q$ is a tautology, then this is a rule of inference and q follows from p'.

As it is given in the Introduction to the First Edition of *PM*, Russell's rule has sometimes been called 'the principle of detachment'; inference has been described as 'the dissolution of an implication'; and the deductions of *Principia Mathematica* seem to depend on taking it this way. Wittgenstein believed he had shown that Russell's proofs have the form of tautologies. And he thought the role assigned to Russell's principle came from a confusion: giving it the character both of a rule of material inference and a rule of logical inference. In any case, for Wittgenstein in the

[1] See the article by Dr C. Lewy, *Mind* (July 1967) p. 422.

Tractatus, there is no distinction among logical propositions between primitive propositions or axioms and the system of propositions derived from these, directly and indirectly, through substitution and detachment. Starting with elementary propositions as bases, it is possible through the successive application of an operation to construct all possible forms of proposition and to show the relation of logical propositions to any others.

Every logical proposition is itself a rule of inference from one material proposition to another.

He speaks, in *TLP*, 5.1362, of the 'internal necessity' of a logical inference (he is contrasting it with causal inference). This lies in the internal relation between the structures of the proposition p and the proposition q which follows from it: what would be 'truth-grounds' of q would also be truth-grounds of p. But the structures of any propositions constructed through a logical operation stand also in internal relations to one another. And the transition from one structure to another in this way would have the inner necessity that logical inference has.

The *Tractatus* finds nothing problematic in the notion of 'the repetition, or successive application, of an operation'. It does not ask, 'How do I know it is the *same* operation at every step?' 'How can I be sure that this transition is by the *same* operation as that which I applied to the elementary propositions in the beginning?' Any such question would be ruled out by an unambiguous notation.

The Sheffer stroke notation does seem to make it plain that we've always to do with the same operation. But in the *Tractatus* it is taken as a symbol for simultaneous negation. The successive application of it brings, often, a multiple combination of negations. Suppose you apply simultaneous negation twice simultaneously in the same operation. No doubt there is a rule to tell you what happens here. But is this rule itself derived from 'the nature of negation'?

When Wittgenstein returned to philosophy (11 or 12 years after the *Tractatus*), he would return in his manuscripts again and again to negation, and often to 'the law of double negation'. This is not the '*simultaneous* negation' of the stroke notation, of course; but 'the successive application' of the stroke could raise similar questions. 'When you have two "not's" – when it is not not p – then if you use the second "not" in the same way as you use a single "not", you must get an affirmative.' But what *is* using 'not' *in the same way* as you'd use it by itself in this situation? In logic we may naturally say two negatives make an affirmative. In other sorts of discourse and in other languages, including earlier English, two negatives make a stronger negative – or anyway, not an affirmative. We cannot ask which is right. 'The nature of negation' cannot tell us the right way to apply it. Rather the other way round. 'Not' or any other sign of negation has its meaning in the use that is given it, the consequences and reactions and so on.

'Continue the same operation' need not be indefinite at all. I want to extend the development of this decimal fraction, for instance. And there is a right and a wrong way and a 'necessity': if he calculates correctly he can't possibly get any other result. But the necessity comes from elsewhere: from the use of division and decimals in all sorts of other situations. We wouldn't call it 'division' in this operation if it happened only here.

When *Tractatus*, 5.11 explains what is meant by saying that the truth of one proposition, *q*, follows from the truth of another proposition, *q*, this is the logical inference of one *material* proposition from another material proposition. The logical proof of a *logical* proposition would be something entirely different. It is the *sense* of *p* and the sense of *q* that show the inner necessity of the logical inference discussed in 5.11. But a logical proposition is a tautology and has no sense. When we 'prove' a logical proposition we do not bother about any sense or meaning; we construct the logical proposition solely by rules for the combination of signs (6.126). This may help us to recognise a very complicated tautology. But it would always be *possible* to recognise the tautology in the symbol itself.

In later years there was a time when Wittgenstein would speak of arithmetic as 'a sort of geometry of signs'; perhaps without clearly adopting this way of speaking as his own. He did call attention to 'visual demonstration' – certain geometrical proofs which do not depend on propositions but simply on juxtaposing or altering figures drawn on a blackboard or on paper. A simple example: If you draw lines joining the angles of a regular pentagon with one another you get a pentagram. Or this:

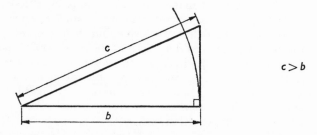

$c > b$

Under which he wrote: 'It convinces my *eyes*'. (There are more complicated examples, but there is a limit to them.) Here there is a logical conclusion without any general form of operation, and without reference to a general rule of transformation.

In the *Remarks on the Foundations of Mathematics* (Part II of the 1956 edition) Wittgenstein is examining the question whether there is something 'primary' about the view of mathematical proof as: proving that the proposition or theorem in question can be constructed. 'Can I say: "Any proof proves *first and foremost* that this formation of signs must result when I apply these rules to these formations of signs"?...
That would seem like saying: 'the very least that we must accept, if we accept the proof, is that these signs etc., etc. – and accepting this underlies our accepting further'. But Wittgenstein comments: 'To this I'd want to say: the sequence of signs in the proof doesn't necessarily bring any kind of acceptance. But when the acceptance does enter it need not begin as "geometrical" acceptance' (*RFM*, II, 38).

In the pages that follow Wittgenstein seems first to reject the geometrical view of proof and then to advocate it – although I imagine both expressions are tentative and belong to his method of turning the question first on one side and then on the other. He discusses whether there is some 'primary' or 'original' form of calculation, one in which, say, all integers would be written as successive additions of 1, and whether the 'shortened' calculation we ordinarily use presupposes this. And the idea that the sign-geometrical proof is what is fundamental in all mathematical proof would be a form of the same way of thinking. Both of these would differ from Russell's view that what a mathematical proof 'rests on', or what makes it a *proof*, is a *logical* proof in the symbolism of *Principia Mathematica*. But Wittgenstein was no more drawn to a view like Hilbert's than he was to Russell's. For each of them neglects the relation of a mathematical proof to *application*.

The geometrical view of proof may have attracted him because it does not suggest that what makes the proof effective is any rule of deduction or any general form of reasoning or general schema. 'It is not something behind the proof, but the proof, that proves.' And if I am not convinced that this sequence *is* a proof of the proposition with which it ends, it is not enough to call my attention to the *form* which it has in common with those proofs and those. I want to know: 'Why is this "proof" a proof of *this* proposition?' I must be able to see *in this particular case* the necessity of the transition from this configuration to that one.

In Part I of the *Remarks on Foundations of Mathematics* Wittgenstein is discussing what point it would have to speak of a 'rule of inference' in connection with *Principia Mathematica*. There is the transition from one proposition to another in the development of the proofs. And at best the rule of inference tells you something about the way the propositions are arranged in the *book*. 'The rule merely informs us that in this book only *this* transition from one proposition to another is employed. . . . The correctness of the transition must make itself apparent each time in the particular place where it occurs. And the expression of the "logical principle" is then the *sequence of the propositions* itself' (*RFM*, I, 20).

As the expression of a general form of transition, the logical principle will not help you anywhere.

Two or three years later he wrote that the transformations effected in a mathematical proof do not prove only propositions of sign-geometry, but also propositions of a great variety of different *contents* (*RFM*, III, 14).

For instance, a proof in *Principia Mathematica* shows how a *logical* proposition can be constructed from the axioms by the use of these rules. But then it is taken as a proof that the conclusion is a tautology (this is what proving that the conclusion is a *true* proposition would mean here). This can be shown only through the relation of the formula (say $p \vee \sim p$) to propositions outside logic and to the way they are used there.

' "The tautology (e.g., $p \vee \sim p$) says nothing" is a proposition from the language-game in which the proposition p is used' (*RFM*, III, 14).

' "It's raining or it's not raining" tells us nothing about the weather.' When Wittgenstein says this we understand him, because the positive and the negative sentences here come up constantly in the language we speak, and because we know what it is for a sentence to tell us something about the weather.

We can understand the proof because we know how its expressions are used outside logic, or outside mathematics.

The transition from one proposition to another in a logical proof is not *merely* the transformation of one configuration of signs into another. We wanted to say it was this and nothing else, because we thought we'd lose the *formal* character of logic otherwise: treating logical propositions with propositions about material things and happenings, distinguished only by their greater generality. Then logical necessity and logical impossibility are lost. And we've lost the relation that logical principles and logical inferences do have to empirical statements and empirical investigations. Wittgenstein had insisted against Ramsey that logic could not be an empirical science – for Ramsey's thought about it was moving that way. This seemed a reason for placing the emphasis Wittgenstein did upon symbolism. He might almost have said at this time: We cannot look to the way words are used in everyday language to guide us to an understanding of the rules and connections of the symbols in logic. Rather the other way round: it is the logical syntax embodied (and often obscured) in everyday language that makes this *language*.

He later called this a misunderstanding of logic – although Ramsey's was a misunderstanding the other way. The idea of 'primary' signs and of connections as immediately given as they are – like connections of figures in visual space – well even if we had them, and rules for their transformation, there would be nothing of logical inference in this, nor of proof. Wittgenstein came repeatedly to the discussion of 'the logical "must" ', or the notions of 'paradigm' and of 'logical exactitude'.

We are given a proof in logic or in mathematics, and we go through it to see if it is correct. This is possible only where there is an established technique or procedure for such proofs. This makes it possible to *ask* whether it is correct; the question would not mean anything otherwise: and expressions like 'formally correct' or 'formal proof' would have no meaning. Obviously it is not like asking whether my account of what happened is correct.

If I have learned elementary arithmetic, I have learned how to add and divide and so on, and this is something I don't lose. But I have also acquired a way of looking at certain things that people do. Perhaps I go on and learn new forms of calculation. I have a different conception of arithmetic now: of the operations and signs that come into it. Very often I can follow a calculation or a proof as you write it out, and I tell you that 'I can see that'. This may not mean you have convinced me of anything; it might mean just that I can see that that would be the next step. But suppose you were teaching me about decimal fractions. Suppose you showed me the decimal development of $\frac{1}{7}$ and wrote out the quotient and remainders like this:

$$\underline{1} \div 7 = 0.142857$$
$$30$$
$$20$$
$$60$$
$$40$$
$$50$$
$$\underline{1}$$

You underscored the 1 of the dividend and the 1 which is remainder and left it at that. If I see that this means that going on with the division will always give the same six numbers over again, I have drawn a logical conclusion; or I may say you have *convinced* me of that. This means that I have a new concept of what a periodic decimal is, and a new concept of division and quotient. For the quotient when it is written like this is complete. There is nothing further we could add to show what completing the division would be. And if we say the division *yields* this quotient, this is a different sense of 'yields' and a different sense of 'quotient' from what we should have if we said that $1 \div 4$ yields 0.25.

This illustrates what Wittgenstein meant when he used to say that 'a proof *convinces* you of something'; that you express this when you say 'I can see that it *must* be'; and that being convinced of this means that you have a new conception of the proof – in our case, that you have a different conception of the division. The proof has led you to adopt a new way of calculating. And in other cases this is even more obvious.

On the other hand, I might have followed you as you went through the division to the first six places of the decimal, and I might have nodded when you pointed out that now the remainder was the same as the dividend – and I might *not* then see that this showed it was periodic. If I've done hardly any arithmetic, you might even say this was likely. If I have mastered elementary arithmetic, you may wonder what's wrong. ('If he could see the other things, why can't he see this?') In practically every case a pupil who has shown he can do arithmetic will see this. But . . . is it something you taught him when you taught him to express fractions as decimals? What is clear is that he wouldn't say 'It *must* be' if he had *not* been taught that arithmetic.

Suppose you show me how, by using coordinates, I can express the properties of geometrical figures in algebraic equations. I must have learned already to work with equations, just as I must know elementary geometry. But then when you explain the method and I follow you, I say 'Of *course*'. I know one can prove geometrical theorems by analytic geometry. My concept of geometrical proof is not just what it was before. But even within elementary geometry: if the proof of the theorem of Pythagoras convinces me, I have a new concept of commensurability of the sides of a triangle.

Wittgenstein sometimes said I 'adopt' a new concept, or I switch to the new form of operation, because in a sense it is my move. Of course when I recognise the periodicity, I don't imagine any alternative – that wouldn't mean anything. But I take a step which the man who doesn't see it, doesn't take. But if I acquire or adopt a new concept, I can do this only within a *system* of concepts, only where I recognise the continuity or 'identity' between the concepts

I had learned already and the concept I have now. (When I say 'I can do this only within . . .' the 'can' is grammatical.) Even if we say it's my move, nothing is arbitrary or 'personal' in what I have acquired or adopted.

That I have a new concept will appear in what I am prepared to say and do, what questions I now ask, and in the fact that there are certain questions I no longer ask, certain things I no longer try to do; and so on. Suppose, for instance, we say that when the proof convinces me that there is no general method of trisecting an angle with ruler and compass, this changes my concept of trisection – then certain things are no longer puzzling, I no longer try to do them, etc. If I adopt new forms of calculating or new forms of inference, this will appear in the ways in which I discuss these things with other people. The new concept or new method is just as much and just as little 'mine' as is the language which I speak with them.

A concept has been thought of as 'a possible predicate' (Frege) or as a propositional function; something which appears in a sentence. This is connected with the notion of a concept as a universal, as something which has instances. Wittgenstein thought this account was wrong. Partly because there can be language-games employing generic terms – concept terms – which do not appear in subject-predicate propositions at all; like the terms 'tile' and 'beam' in the language-game of the builders. And because of the difficulties when we try to say what it is a possible predicate *of*. We meet them in Russell's account of generality. In the language of Russell's notation it must make sense to say *everything* is a tree, for instance. If it makes sense to say $(x) . \phi x \supset \psi x$ – 'For all x, x is a metal implies x is heavy' – then it must make sense to say $(x) . \phi x$: 'For all x, x is a metal', or 'everything is a metal'. But in many cases we should not know what to do with such a statement: 'Everything is a tree', 'Everything is a song', etc. It was important when Frege pointed out that numbers are always used of generic names or of concepts. But to know that something is a generic name tells you little or nothing of how it is used.

In 1941 Wittgenstein said tentatively that mathematical propositions are concept-forming propositions. He was wondering how the relation of grammatical propositions and material propositions should be expressed, for his earlier discussions suggested a sharp cleavage and were misleading. (Some rules of grammar had been empirical propositions at one time; and there may be cases where we'd waver if we had to say which it was. People may look for '*evidence*' in discussing 'There can't be a reddish green'. And it is interesting that they should discuss it at all.) As a rough formulation

he suggested: 'Self-evident propositions are concept-forming propositions' – cf. 'The limit of empiricism – is *concept-formation*' (*RFM*,
III, 29). He soon saw that for mathematical propositions this
must be qualified. Concept formation in mathematics is different
from concept formation in chemistry. And it is only when they
appear as the results of proofs, or else as postulates, that mathematical propositions are concept-forming.

Someone shows me a calculation by which he has arrived at

$$S = \frac{n(n+1)}{2}$$

as the formula for the sum of the first *n* positive integers. I check
through his calculation and say 'Yes, that's what it *must* be'.

This is not what the proof says. It is what I say when I have checked
that the proof is correct. And anyone knowing elementary algebra
would say the same. 'It would not be *addition* if the result were
anything else here.'

From the formula reached we can derive the sum for the first 25
integers, for the first 30 integers and so on. In this sense what has
been proved is a rule. But Wittgenstein said also that when I
multiply 25 by 25 and see that it is 625, I recognise the equation as
a rule; where the word must mean something else. – It 'plays a role
in our lives' – but this could mean all sorts of things.

> In the course of building A has measured the length and breadth
> of an area and he gives B the order: 'bring 15 × 18 slabs'. B is
> trained to multiply and to count out a number of slabs according
> to the result he reaches.
> The sentence '15 × 18 = 270' need never be uttered . . . (*RFM*,
> V, 23).

If you ask B whether it was 'the *correct* result', he might not know
what you were asking.

Wittgenstein goes on to imagine that

> we condition a man in such and such ways; then exert an
> influence on him with a question; and get a numeral. We go on
> to use the numeral for our purposes and it proves practical. That
> is calculating. – Not yet! . . . Just as we might imagine that for
> purposes which our language now serves sounds were produced,
> without thereby forming a language. It belongs to what we mean
> by calculating that all the people who calculate correctly produce
> the same pattern of calculation. And 'calculating correctly'
> doesn't mean calculating when one's mind is clear and without
> being disturbed; it means calculating like *this*. (*RFM*, V, 24)

But this still does not give the sense of 'rule' which Wittgenstein had in mind when he spoke, for instance, of a multiplication like 25 × 25. One point is this: If I said I know or accept that multiplication, this acceptance would show in the way I scrutinised other calculations, and also in the way I scrutinised shipments of goods delivered to me, the circumstances in which I would say 'there are still so and so many to come', and so on. The ways in which it shapes the attention I give to other things. 'Our recognition of it consists in turning our back on it' (*RFM*, III, 35).

In this there is a close analogy between mathematical propositions and the laws of logic. Wittgenstein used to ask what it would mean if you said that this man recognised the law of contradiction; or, what would it mean if you asked whether he does? Perhaps he tries to keep from contradicting himself in what he is saying. This may be because he finds that people misunderstand him unless he is careful about this. But the logical law *rules out* a contradiction. And if someone asked what this means, we'd point to a calculation. To recognise the law of contradiction is to *calculate*.

In another place (Part VI of the 1974 edition of *RFM*) Wittgenstein says:

Is $25^2 = 625$ a fact of experience? You'd like to say, 'No'. – Why not? – 'Because according to the rules it can't be anything else.' – And why is that? – Because *that* is the meaning of rules. Because that is the procedure on which we erect all our judgements (*RFM*, VI, 28).

And a little later:

When I say 'If you follow the rule, that *must* be the result', this does not mean 'it must because it always has been the result'; but rather: that it is the result belongs to the ground on which I stand. ((. . . ist einer meiner *Grundlagen*.))
What *must* result is something judgment stands on, which I don't touch (*RFM*, VI, 46).

This says much more than that the notion of calculating includes that of calculating correctly.

We can think of incorrect moves in a dance or a game, or of doing it correctly, and this is decided by the rules. But we don't have *proofs* here; whereas in mathematics we can't think of rules without proofs; unless they are postulates – and the sense of this lies in their relation to proofs. There are proofs in the *theory* of chess, but these don't give character to the rules. And when we are carrying on the *game*, as opposed to the theory of it, we do not make inferences.

Insofar as a mathematician really is 'playing a game' obviously he is not drawing inferences. For 'playing' must mean here: *acting* in accordance with certain rules. He would already have moved outside the mere game if he were to infer that at this juncture the general rule would allow him to act in this way. . . .

Nor is it a logical inference if I transform one configuration into another (one arrangement of chairs into another, say) unless these arrangements have a function in language outside this transformation. (*RFM*, IV, 1-2)

I think the point of this is partly: To understand the mathematical character of the transformation, we have to see how the mathematical proposition enters as a norm in describing physical things. We need to see how the formation of concepts in mathematics shapes our thinking about things – determines the ways in which we think of them, what it is we try to find out about them, gives meaning to 'a more satisfactory description, a more accurate description' and so on. In *RFM*, V, 37, he asks whether

mathematics . . . teaches us to formulate empirical questions. Can't we say it teaches me for example to ask whether a certain body is moving in accordance with a parabolic equation? – But what is it that mathematics does in this case? Without mathematics, or without the mathematicians, we should certainly not have arrived at the definition of this curve. But was defining this curve itself a piece of mathematics? Would it be something stipulated by mathematics, for instance, if people studied the movement of bodies to find if its path could be represented by an ellipse constructed using a string and two nails? Would whoever invented this sort of inquiry have been doing mathematics? He did create a new *concept*. But was it in the way mathematics does this? Was it like the way in which the multiplication $18 \times 15 = 270$ gives us a new concept?

Asking whether its movement conforms to a parabolic *equation* and asking whether its path can be represented by an ellipse we construct with a string and two nails. When the equation comes into our question, this determines what we mean by 'conforms to' (the meaning is not obvious in the other case); we take measurements and use coordinates; we draw the curve, perhaps, and measure divergence; and so on.

In learning to count we learn to ask 'How many?'.

Teaching us the equation of an ellipse is like teaching us to count. But it is also like teaching us the question: 'Are there a hundred times as many marbles there as here?' (*RFM*, V, 38)

What is mathematical about the equation? (When we had drawn
an ellipse with a string and two nails, we might have drawn the
main axis through it and measured the perpendiculars from this
axis to the circumference where it cuts each of the foci. We find these
are equal in the figure we have just drawn. And we write this down
using the sign of equality.) The equation means nothing apart from
the methods of analytic geometry. It has its meaning in a system of
calculations. But it has its meaning also in the way it is applied – for
instance, in the form it gives to questions about the path of a
moving body.

We might say it is used as a rule within mathematics, as we say
it of other equations. This sense of 'rule' has not vanished when we
look to the equation in our study of moving bodies, but it is not
what we mean when we say the equation determines what our
problem is.

'We treat it as a rule here' – if we say this, none would add: 'treat
it as a general rule'; or if he does, something has come between him
and the case we were mentioning. (Rules were not made by the
devil, but the word 'rule' was.)

'Generality' is one source of confusion. We look to the general
formula if we want to know the value when $n =$ (whatever we read
on the dial). But what interests us here is the fact that we do look
to the general formula: we take it for granted; it is part of the
question we started asking. If you asked why we ask the questions
that we do – well, certainly not because of any general rule or
general principle. 'It would be crazy *not* to; that's all' – which does
not mean 'You will get into trouble if you don't'. That people I live
among (and whose books and speeches I read) just take it for granted
that it is intelligent to ask questions in this way – is part of what
makes it possible to understand and speak with one another. And
if overnight I found that people weren't like this any longer, I'd
wonder where I was. 'What do you call "*thinking*", then?'

> . . . What compels us to proceed according to a rule, to take
> something as a rule? What compels us to talk to ourselves in the
> forms of the language we have learned? (*RFM*, III, 30)

When we follow this practice we are not following a rule of very
general application.

If I say the proof teaches me something and that as a result of
the proof I think about, say, decimal fractions differently, this does
not mean that there is some general characteristic of what I learn
from mathematical proofs, or some general account of how mathe-

matics develops my thinking. – I say that when I am convinced by a proof (say the proof of the Pythagoras theorem) this gives me a new concept of . . . well, of the relation of this theorem to this proof, for instance: which I express by 'it must . . .'. This is vague; and the expression 'concept' is vague. We can make clear what we mean here by giving particular *examples*. We shall be in trouble if we look for clarity of a different sort. For instance, it will not help if we say that the concepts developed in mathematics are dependent on the structure (or formal character) of the system, and then go on to give rules determining *which* concepts can be formed. The concept formed in a mathematical proof is not itself part of the proof. It shows in how I go on from the proof (what I do with it) both inside mathematics and – as with the ellipse and the equation – in studying physical things. If we take the word 'proof' to mean what is sometimes called the 'figure' of the proof: 'these constructions transformed by these rules *thus*' – it may not change my concept of anything nor add to my understanding of anything. For me it is just routine calculation, like continuing the division in the development of the decimal, and I would not say it proves anything. Whether it – the 'figure' – proves anything, depends on whether it's interesting.

Wittgenstein gives an example in 'visual demonstration'. (The meaning of 'figure' is obvious here, but it can be clearly applied to a proof in analysis that is written out.) There was the visual proof in *RFM*, I, 50, that a rectangle can be made of two parallelograms and two triangles. And then in *RFM*, I, 70 he asks

Why do I say the figure (50) makes me realize something any more than this one:

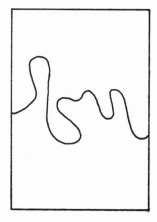

Rush Rhees

After all it too shows that two bits like these yield a rectangle. 'But that is uninteresting', we want to say. And why is it uninteresting?

Partly because the two halves are not shapes we immediately recognise and constantly use in our descriptions of other shapes and of physical bodies. And partly for this reason we do not think of this figure (70) as a demonstration within a system of demonstrations showing other figures 'internally' related to it.

A proof figure is interesting if it shows me a way of *doing* things, or changes my view of what can be done; when it makes me realise that 'this is really just that and that' – and this means: shows me a new way of calculating, a new form of transformation; or if it solves a problem.

'Whether it is interesting.' We see the transformation as a feature of a language-game. Often this means we see its place in a series or system of calculations: we see how it bears on other calculations, or we see what has to be given up if this proof is accepted.

Wittgenstein said of Aristotelian logic that it gives a general schema of forms of reasoning – a schema into which a great number of examples of logical inferences could be fitted – but that this schema does not help us to understand in any way the particular inferences which may be expressed in this form. He said the same of Russell's logical symbolism (and when he says 'the Aristotelian logic' he often means Russell).

Suppose someone spoke of 'the general idea of a *function* in mathematics' and wrote down

$$x = f(y)$$

What does this expression show or explain? We cannot know what a substitution for x or y would be until we know *what* function it is. The mathematician may go on to give a number of *illustrations* of what he means by 'a function', and these may all be such that you could, if it were convenient, use '$x = f(y)$' for any one of them. But then the formula is simply a way of writing. It is not the symbol of a 'very general' function – as though the illustrations had been given as special cases of this function. If we say

'the function f assigns (or correlates) the value x to the argument y' this is helpful in explaining the kind of schema it is. But it has not made it into something we could use in calculating anywhere.

An S-P schema of the syllogistic figures does not help to show in a particular case that from these premisses this conclusion follows. The 'subject-predicate form' covers a great variety of forms, and the Aristotelian schema does not help us to see what there is about any of them that makes these premisses yield just this conclusion. If we have seen independently that the conclusion follows, then we may be able to fit the argument into the general schema.

As we may also do when we express an argument in Russell's notation.

If we give a definition of inference in terms of the logical or mathematical notion of models, as Tarski did, this does not help us to understand that this conclusion follows from this proof. We understand this from the particular proof itself, or not at all. Tarski was emphasising that a formal proof belongs to a system; and obviously this is important. The various proofs of a system are logically related to one another, in the sense that they are developed from the same set of axioms. But Tarski seemed to speak as though every proof of a particular theorem in the system was equivalent to every other. A statement in this sense might be natural in discussing, say, the roles of axioms and theorems in a calculus. But we have to understand the phrase 'the proof of a particular theorem'. Already in his definition of logical consequence Tarski was moving *away* from this (away from the recognition in the particular case that this follows from that). He never says nor considers the sense of saying that the *premisses* yield this conclusion ('given them, this *must* be'). He says only that if the proposition X stands to the class of propositions K in a relation of the same form as another proposition of the same form as X stands to another class of propositions of the same form as those of the Class K, then X is a logical conclusion from K. This reminds me of one of Wittgenstein's objections to Russell's definition of 'number'; for instance in the remark which Waismann reports:

> If I ask 'How many chairs are there in this room?' and you tell me: 'As many as in that room', I should answer: 'That isn't an answer to my question. I asked how many chairs are standing here, not where I could find just as many.' (*WWK*, p. 221)

Or his remark in *Philosophische Grammatik*, p. 417:

> This proof is constructed according to a particular plan (one on which other proofs are constructed as well). But this plan cannot make the proof a proof. . . . The proof must speak for itself and the plan is merely embodied in it – not itself a constituent part of the proof. . . . So it doesn't help me if someone calls my attention to the similarity between proofs in order to convince me that they are proofs.

Philosophical difficulties about inference – for instance: 'What is the difference between reaching a conclusion by calculation and reaching a conclusion by an experiment?'; 'What is the difference between drawing an incorrect inference and not drawing an inference at all?' – in these it is generally something in the use of 'inference' outside logic that perplexes us: in mathematics or in science or in numbers of discussions of other forms.

If someone asked 'Why do we draw logical inferences at all?' (perhaps he has found that they are 'trivial'), we should reply, I think, by asking: 'Why do we say what's happening or ask questions?'

Misunderstandings may come especially with the notion of generality. Generality is important somehow ('it wouldn't be an inference if only one inference had ever been drawn'). We might say it would not be inference – we would not call this transformation an inference – it it did not play some role in our lives. This is like Wittgenstein's remark about mathematics: that although we have to admit a wide variety under the term 'mathematics', and there is no single line to demarcate what is mathematics from what is not, we do not for this reason think it is of no consequence whether this or that is included under it. A role or an application in our lives. And now we are speaking about 'a practice'.

Describing what language is, describing what saying something ('a proposition') is, describing what drawing a conclusion is – means describing a practice. And Wittgenstein adds: 'Das ist eine sehr schwierige Erkenntnis' ('That is something it is very hard to recognise' or 'hard to keep clear'). For of course it does not mean 'describing what regularly happens' or 'describing a routine'.

A practice refers to a way of living in which many people are engaged. We could observe a habit in an individual man, but not a 'practice'. Much of what Wittgenstein says about 'rules' is connected with this. So we may feel like saying that a practice is 'general', even if this adds nothing to what the word means anyway. It's not the generality of 'all' or 'always'. It is often what gives force to a conclusion or an argument.

> If you look in the mouth of this mouse you will see two long incisor teeth. – How do you know? – I know that all mice have them, so this one will too. (And one does not say: 'And this thing is a mouse, so it too has . . .') Why is this such an important move? Well, for example, we examine animals, plants etc., etc.; we form general judgments and apply these in the particular case. – But it is a truth, surely, that this mouse has the attribute, *if all* mice have it! That is a stipulation regarding the application of the word 'all'. The real generality lies elsewhere. For example, in the general practice of that method of investigation and of its application. (*RFM*, IV, 50)

(Or perhaps: 'The actual generality lies elsewhere: namely in the generality with which that method of investigating comes into play and is applied.')

At first sight, what he is calling 'the actual generality' here might seem to be an *empirical* generality. – But it is not.

He is describing a practice. And the emphasis is not on the fact that it happens often, but rather that this is the way we do things.

It is like describing a feature of the ways in which people speak with one another.

If someone asked, 'But *why* bring into this case the general judgment you've formed through examining others?', we might answer: 'Well, it's *obvious* that one would'. We have no *reason*. It is what we'd expect from any intelligent person; and we could not educate anyone nor work with him unless that move were a feature of his thinking.

Wittgenstein gives two more examples in the same section (*RFM* IV, 50):

> Or: 'This man is a student of mathematics.' How do you know? – 'All the people in this room are mathematicians; only mathematicians have been admitted.' –

> The interesting generality is: that we often have a means of ascertaining the general proposition before we consider particular cases; and that we then use the general method.

The interesting generality is not the general proposition, but that we are often in a position to proceed from a general proposition in this way. – 'Drawing a conclusion is part of a language-game'.

The third example is:

> We have given the porter instructions to admit only people with invitations and we take it for granted now that this man, who has been admitted, has an invitation.

> The interesting generality in the logical proposition is not the fact which it appears to express, but rather the constantly recurring situation in which this transition is made.

The 'logical proposition' is the whole sentence giving the example. The 'transition' is a logical inference. What is interesting is that we constantly do find ourselves in situations in which we make transitions of this form.

What is it that makes a transition from one proposition (or a set of propositions) to another a logical inference? We cannot give a single or formal answer. In any case no such answer would help a man who had asked that question. We can answer by giving examples; like these which Wittgenstein has given (these were chosen for a question about generality, but that will be central anyway). And the discussion can go on from there.

4

THE *GRUNDGEDANKE* OF THE *TRACTATUS*

Brian McGuinness

I TAKE as my text propostion 4.0312 of the *Tractatus*:

The possibility of propositions is based on the principle that objects have signs as their representatives.

My fundamental idea is that the 'logical constants' are not representatives; that there can be no representatives of the logic of facts.

Practically the same words occur (with two additional sentences) in Wittgenstein's *Notebook* for 25 December 1914, where Miss Anscombe translates them:

The possibility of the proposition is, of course, founded on the principle of signs as *going proxy* for objects.

Thus in the proposition something has *something else* as its proxy. But there is also the *common* cement.

My fundamental thought is that the logical constants are not proxies. That the *logic* of the fact cannot have anything as its proxy.

If this is the fundamental idea or fundamental thought of Wittgenstein's early philosophy or even just of the *Tractatus*, it would be presumptuous to attempt to bring out all its implications in a single lecture. I will set myself two more modest tasks: first, the historical one, of showing that this was the first or one of the first philosophical insights that Wittgenstein had and of sketching the historical background against which, and the set of problems from which, it arose; as a second task I shall set myself the exegetical one of indicating roughly how fundamental it is to the *Tractatus* and how wide its implications were, or seemed to Wittgenstein to be.

The idea that I am primarily considering is the one that the so-called logical constants do not represent, in the sense of stand for or go proxy for, objects of any kind. The details of the way in which other words do go proxy for objects came later in his thought. Taking the narrower thesis, then, we find it foreshadowed in the very first philosophical remark of Wittgenstein's that has been preserved. In a letter to Russell of 22 June 1912 he wrote:

> Logic is still in the melting-pot but one thing gets more and more obvious to me: The propositions of logic contain ONLY APPARENT variables and whatever may turn out to be the proper explanation of apparent variables, its consequence *must* be that there are NO *logical* constants.

> Logic must turn out to be of a *totally* different kind than any other science.

It is clear from many other passages in the pre-war letters and Notes that Wittgenstein regarded the occurrence of real variables among the primitive propositions of *Principia Mathematica* – 'the old logic' as he rather condescendingly called it – as a blemish: to take one example, he says that the true form of the Law of the Excluded Middle is not $p \vee \sim p$ but $(p)p \vee \sim p$ giving as his reason that the former contains the nonsensical function $p \vee \sim p$ while the latter only contains the perfectly sensible function $p \vee \sim q$. He would want then to re-write all logical laws as completely general propositions; and to explain generality (the quantifiers, if you prefer) in a way that did not involve the existence of logical objects. But was there any more direct connection between the idea that real variables might be necessary and the idea that there were logical constants?

I think there was one: any statement involving real variables would be a statement about the form of a proposition, treated as an object. In 'Notes on Logic'[1] Wittgenstein takes the trouble to assert that there are no such things as the forms of propositions.

The supposed logical constants, then, whose existence Wittgenstein was concerned to deny were not only the supposed references of words like 'and', 'or', 'not', etc.; nor these together with the supposed referents of the words 'some', 'all' and 'is identical with' – though these (truth functions, generality, and identity) did in time become the three ranges of so-called logical constants that he thought he had to deal with. Originally the notion covered much more: all the forms of propositions – the general notion of predicate, the

---

[1] *NB*, p. 99.

general notion of dual relation, triple relation, and any other forms
there might be of whatever complexity and level had been supposed
to be logical objects, and Wittgenstein was denying them that status.

Supposed by whom and why? Clearly, in Wittgenstein's view,
by Frege and Russell: he says as much at *Tractatus*, 5.4. Now as to
Frege it is clear that he did think there were mathematical objects,
for example the natural numbers. It is also clear that Wittgenstein
was fascinated by this belief of Frege's (from the account reported by
Geach of Wittgenstein's last conversation with Frege). But it is
doubtful whether, in criticising Frege in the *Tractatus*, he can have
had only those in mind. For one thing, it is not in the context of
numbers but in that of truth-functions that he expresses his dissent
from Frege. It must be remembered that when Wittgenstein says
'There are no logical constants or logical objects' he does not mean
– but there may perfectly well be logical functions or logical concepts.
Indeed this is just what he goes on to deny. In Wittgenstein's view,
truth-functions must not be assimilated to ordinary or material
functions. Yet this is just what Frege does and on Frege's own
principles, these functions must have a reference just as much as any
other function. Similarly for the function of identity and for the
higher-level functions which correspond to our quantifiers. Now, I
will not say anything here regarding Frege's doctrine as to the
reference of functions in general. I believe that Wittgenstein in
fact learned from it (as may appear shortly). In any case he is not
criticising that in general, but its application to logical notions. It
was partly this application that led Frege to his view that besides
the real or actual physical world and the subjective world of our
ideas, there existed a third world, inhabited by thoughts (in Frege's
sense) and numbers and countless other things (in the widest
sense) to which the attribute 'objective but not actual' could be
applied. It is clearly of this world that Frege is speaking when he
scoffs at those who take the laws of logic to be mere laws of thought
and when he insists instead that they are laws of truth – *Grenzsteine
in einem ewigen Grunde befestigt*, boundary stones fixed in an eternal
soil.

In this deeply felt passage Frege does not go far enough to show
how totally different logic is from any other science; but he does go
some way. Moreover he does not sin against the other commandment that Wittgenstein has in mind. Precisely because of his view
about the meaning of functions and their unsaturatedness, he does
not think that they can have meaning in a proposition unless their
gaps are filled. He too would not allow real variables to occur in the
propositions of logic.

It is Russell, much more than Frege, that Wittgenstein is criticising in his denial of logical constants, and to see why, we need to look briefly at the position both in the foundations of mathematics and in the philosophy of logic as it presented itself in 1912 and 1913 when Russell and Wittgenstein had their discussions. Despite the great technical achievements of *Principia Mathematica*, it was clear that the reduction of mathematics to logic still rested on axioms (such as that of reducibility) which were not at all obviously logical. Indeed Russell himself offered the justification that they at any rate led to the desired results and to none that were not desired. Again, as to the general status of logic, there was considerable confusion. The *a priori* was explained in *The Problems of Philosophy* essentially as that which was more self-evident, i.e. which recommended itself more strongly to the human mind, than other apparently self-evident propositions.

It was not a situation to be tolerated, and Russell set himself to write a book on *Epistemology*, originally intended to deal with Acquaintance, Atomic Propositional Thought, and Molecular Propositional Thought. The third part never got written and the second part and one-third of the first part never got published. What did appear (although the publication was delayed) was the first six chapters, in the *Monist* for 1914 and 1915 (the first three are reprinted in *Logic and Knowledge*). With these six chapters we shall not concern ourselves here, but the last three chapters, and particularly the last chapter of Part I and the whole of Part II are directly relevant to our theme. Russell discusses the acquaintance involved in our knowledge of relations. He uses all the terminology familiar to readers of the early Wittgenstein: atomic and molecular complexes, the atomic ones consisting of two kinds of constituents, the objects related and the relation relating them. He assumes that we have acquaintance with the relation relating two terms (as it were with another object alongside them) and has his old difficulty with what then it is to know or think that the relation actually does relate the two objects in the desired sense of direction. The next chapter is concerned with our acquaintance (if any) with predicates and raises what he calls the logical problem whether there are complexes with only two constituents: on the whole he thinks that experience is in favour of this, although formally speaking colour predicates could be replaced by the relation of 'colour-similarity' to a certain given example of the shade in question. (Perhaps this is Russell's theory of manufactured relations referred to in 'Notes on Logic', *NB*, p. 103.)

This is only to show that we are in the general realm of Wittgensteins' discussions and to set the scene for the next chapter, which deals with 'Logical Data' or 'the basis of acquaintance that must underlie our knowledge of logic'. Russell is not certain in what sense this acquaintance is a dual relation, but is clear that there must be some logical experience which enables us to understand terms like 'particulars', 'universals', 'relations', 'dual complexes', and 'predicates'. The 'logical constants' involved in such experience are really concerned with pure *form*, Russell says, and are attained by carrying abstraction to the utmost. For example, to understand the proposition 'Socrates precedes Plato' we must have acquaintance not only with Socrates and Plato and 'precedes' but also with the *form* of the complex *xRy*, in which none of *x*, *R*, or *y* is itself a constant. Similarly, where non-atomic complexes are concerned, we must be' acquainted with the logical objects associated with words such as *or*, *not*, *all*, and *some*. Russell admits that it is very difficult to detect in introspection these objects, or our acquaintance with them, but he regards the logical argument from our understanding of these notions to the existence of such objects and of our acquaintance with them as outweighing this difficulty.

The general idea of this passage is not new. It is a fuller statement of what is contained in the Preface to the first edition of *Principles of Mathematics*, where Russell said:

> The discussion of indefinables – which forms the chief part of philosophical logic – is the endeavour to see clearly, and to make others see clearly, the entities concerned, in order that the mind may have that kind of acquaintance with them which it has with redness or the taste of a pineapple. Where, as in the present case, the indefinables are obtained primarily as the necessary residue in a process of analysis, it is often easier to know that there must be such entities than actually to perceive them; there is a process analogous to that which resulted in the discovery of Neptune, with the difference that the final stage – the search with a mental telescope for the entity that has been inferred – is often the most difficult part of the undertaking. In the case of classes, I must confess, I have failed to perceive any concept fulfilling the conditions requisite for the notion of *class*. And the contradiction discussed in Chapter *X* proves that something is amiss, but what this is I have hitherto failed to discover.

Nonetheless, though the *Principles* presuppose such a view of the nature of logic, it is fair to say that the book does not develop it or argue for it, whereas such was evidently part of the aim of the un-published *Epistemology*, and would clearly have had to be pursued yet further in the projected but unwritten third part on Molecular Propositional Thought.

Moreover, for our present purposes, it is fairly clear that it is with the problems and in the terminology of *Epistemology* that Wittgenstein and Russell were wrestling at this time. Part II, for example, clearly contains the analysis of judgment that Wittgenstein criticised in summer 1913, a criticism that left Russell, on his own admission, paralysed. To mention some themes more relevant to our main subject, Part II discusses propositions and says that the fundamental characteristic that distinguishes them from other objects of acquaintance is their being true or false. Conversely, truth and falsity are described as being *properties* of beliefs, propositions, etc., such that a proposition is true when there is a complex consisting of its objects, otherwise false. (Russell recognises that this requires modification to allow for the difference between the truth of *aRb* and that of *bRa*.) Finally, when he proceeds beyond belief to knowledge, Russell says that all knowledge must rest on self-evidence, and the self-evidence of a judgment consists in the fact that at the time of making it the person who makes it *perceives* its *correspondence* with some *complex*, whether this be a complex given in sensation or one given in our acquaintance with the meanings of words.

Before turning to the consequences of these views and to Wittgenstein's reactions to them, I shall mention one further historical fact: we know from Russell's correspondence with Lady Ottoline Morrell that it was Wittgenstein's criticisms of this book that led Russell to put it (for the most part) aside and only return to this sort of philosophical writing in *Our Knowledge of the External World*, where, on page 208 of the first edition (Chicago and London, 1914), he withdraws some of the characteristic position described above, saying:

If the theory that classes are merely symbolic is accepted, it follows that numbers are not actual entities, but that propositions in which numbers verbally occur have not really any constituents corresponding to numbers, but only a certain logical form which is not a part of propositions having this form. This is in fact the case with all the apparent objects of logic and mathematics. Such words as *or*, *not*, *if there is*, *identity*, *greater*, *plus*, *nothing*, *everything*, *function*, and so on, are not names of definite objects, like 'John' or 'Jones,' but are words which require a context in order to have meaning. All of them are *formal*, that is to say, their occurrence indicates a certain form of proposition, not a certain constituent. 'Logical constants,' in short, are not entities; the words expressing them are not names, and cannot significantly be made into logical subjects except when it is the words themselves, as opposed to their meanings, that are being discussed.[1] This fact has a very important bearing on all logic and philosophy, since it shows how they differ from the special sciences. But the questions raised are so large and so difficult that it is impossible to pursue them further on this occasion.

[1] In the above remarks I am making use of unpublished work by my friend Ludwig Wittgenstein.

Where then did Russell's 1913 account leave logic, given that it was already in difficulties with axioms such as that of reducibility and infinity? On Wittgenstein's view, it left logic no better off than any other science. It seemed to be an account of what was true of a particular set of objects. Moreover it was an account of what was *accidentally* true of them; all the *necessity*, what he was later to call the hardness of the logical 'must', had gone out of logic. We have seen that, as regarded *Principia Mathematica*, there was much truth, which Russell could acknowledge, in this criticism.

In the early letters to Russell, Wittgenstein attempts to eliminate all talk about forms of propositions and about logical constants. First he formulates them all as *copulae* – predicational, relational, or finally truth-functional (though that term was not yet used). Logical forms and logical objects generally arose (or were thought to come into being) when all material components had been thought away by abstraction and only the cement that formerly held them together was left: and this, of course, is, in the typical case, the copula. It then occurred to him that if you could understand the way in which the copula functioned in an atomic proposition (Russell's term – Wittgenstein later used 'elementary proposition', which meant something else for Russell) – if you could understand this, then all the problems would be solved. We have an echo of this, for it remained his view, in the *Tractatus* remark (I syncopate it slightly) that in an elementary proposition all the logical constants are present (5.47). The next move in 1912–13 occurred, significantly, after a visit to Frege:

> I now think that qualities, relations (like love), etc. are all copulae! That means I for instance analyse a subject-predicate proposition, say, 'Socrates is human' into 'Socrates' and 'something is human', (which I think is not complex). The reason for this is a very fundamental one: I think that there cannot be different types of things! etc. etc. (Letter to Russell, January, 1913)

The thought here is one clearly derived from Frege. In a properly constructed language the names of objects and the signs for concepts are such that you cannot construct the nonsensical statement 'mortality is Socrates'. 'Socrates' fits into 'something is human', but 'something is human' does not fit into 'Socrates', And in this respect the properly constructed signs (and our own signs when properly understood) exactly match that for which they stand.

From this time on Wittgenstein's efforts were mainly devoted to his theory of the bipolarity – the necessary truth-or-falsity of atomic propositions, from which feature he hoped to derive the truth-functions, generality, and identity. But before turning to that aspect, I want to emphasise the importance which this Fregean doctrine retained for Wittgenstein, which can be seen precisely in the quotations with which I opened.

Signs go proxy for objects precisely because when properly constructed – or, what comes to the same thing, properly understood – they cannot be combined in ways which are impossible for the objects. This guarantees that every possible proposition is well-constructed; that no nonsensical proposition can be formulated; and consequently that no theory of types is necessary. In the passage we have quoted from *Notebooks*, 25 December 1914, Wittgenstein says that this is what makes propositions possible. Socrates is the sort of thing that can be human, and being human is the sort of thing that Socrates can be. For our part we can *say* that Socrates is human because the expression 'Socrates' has been given a meaning for the context '. . . is human' and the expression '. . . is human' has been given a meaning for the context 'Socrates is human'. These two trivialities are the same triviality: they are an attempt to say what is shown by the sense of 'Socrates is a man', namely – to attempt the impossible again – that *the same* relation of possible argument for a function (and conversely possible function for an argument) holds between Socrates and what it is to be a man and between the linguistic units 'Socrates' and '. . . is human'. This common relation – in the general case that of function and argument – is, I suppose, the common cement that Wittgenstein talks about in the *Notebooks* passage. It surely is the pictorial form that picture and fact have in common in the *Tractatus* (2.17). But, to stay within the *Notebooks* terminology, if we try to put in some proxy for the *logic* of the fact in question, assuming for simplicity's sake that Socrates *is* human, we find it impossible. We try it, for example, by saying 'Socrates has the *property* of humanity', but this still has the same common cement as before – 'Socrates' is a possible argument of the function '. . . has the property of humanity'.

Notice the historical fact which this exposition of the *Notebooks* passage brings out: in his denial that logical constants can have proxies, Wittgenstein is still thinking in the first place of attempts to grasp or isolate or describe the form of a proposition – precisely, in fact, of those logical notions with which Russell in *Epistemology* said that we had acquaintance.

It is clear enough – or at any rate as clear as I can make it – that Wittgenstein thought that the forms of elementary propositions were given to us by mere acquaintance with the objects composing them, by mere understanding of the names composing them. (I may say in passing that I take it that the names and the objects, by the time of the *Tractatus* at any rate, were alike simple in the sense of containing no parts that were names or objects. In this sense something like '. . . is human' might be a name, and stand for an object.) But how did he extend this doctrine that logical words did not stand for anything to words such as 'and', 'or', 'some', 'all', and 'is identical with'? We have seen already *why* he wanted to do so: logic must not be the science of a particular set of objects. Its difference from all other sciences must consist in anything logical's being non-contingently and obviously true of any objects whatsoever. We find the conclusion he wants to reach enunciated most clearly at *Tractatus*, 5.47:

> Wherever there is compositeness, argument and function are present, and where these are present, we already have all the logical constants.

But *how* did he get to this conclusion? What was the route by which he reached it? It seems to me very interesting as a fact in his philosophical biography that he already felt this in the summer of 1912, when he wrote to Russell saying:

> I believe that our problems can be traced down to the *atomic* propositions. This you will see if you try to explain precisely in what way the Copula in such a proposition has meaning.

> I cannot explain it and I think that as soon as an exact answer to this question is given the problem of ' ∨ ' and the apparent variable will be brought very near to their solution if not solved. I now think about 'Socrates is human'. (Good old Socrates!)

Not that he didn't try out blind alleys of many kinds in the course, for example, of writing his *Notebooks*, but the general direction of his thought remains the same throughout. Events like the picture theory's occurring to him were not, I suspect, as crucial as they have been thought. That theory was principally a way of putting more clearly something he had already grasped.

Clearly, even if I saw the whole development of this theme in Wittgenstein's early writings, I should not have time to expound it here; but in any case there is in this respect a tantalising gap. We have very little to show us what Wittgenstein thought was the connection between his Fregean way of explaining, or explaining away, the copula and what he called (in 1913–14) 'the bipolarity business'. For it was in this latter that the seeds of those views that flowered in the picture theory lay hidden. The bipolarity business was Wittgenstein's theory of how propositions had sense and how they differed from names. The view is perhaps most fully expressed in the 4th MS of the original version of *Notes on Logic*, now alas scattered among the various sections devised by Russell.[1]

The idea, roughly, is this: whereas a name has meaning by referring to an object, there is no object or complex for which the proposition 'p' is a name. What there is, is either the fact that p or the fact that $\sim p$. Whichever of these is a fact is the meaning both of 'p' and of '$\sim p$'. So to understand 'p', we must know both what is the case if it is true and what is the case if it is false. We understand 'p' as soon as we understand its constituents and forms (this was Wittgenstein's terminology at the time).

This understanding via constituents and forms comes about in the following way: suppose we have the proposition aRb: we must know what object 'a' stands for, and what object 'b' stands for. We must also know how the form of the proposition – in this case 'xRy' – symbolises (Russell's text here erroneously and indeed meaninglessly says 'how it is symbolised'): here I will insert Wittgenstein's crucial paragraph:

> But the form of a proposition symbolises in the following way: Let us consider symbols of the form 'xRy'; to these correspond primarily pairs of objects, of which one has the name 'x', the other the name 'y'. The x's and y's stand in various relations to each other, among others the relation R holds between some, but not between others. I now determine the sense of 'xRy' by laying down: when the facts behave in regard to 'xRy' so that the meaning of 'x' stands in the relation R to the meaning of 'y', then I say they they [the facts] are 'of like sense' [*gleichsinnig*] with the proposition 'xRy'; otherwise, 'of opposite sense' [*entgegengesetzt*]; I correlate the facts to the symbol 'xRy' *by* thus dividing them into those of like sense and those of opposite sense. To this

[1] See my article in *Revue Internationale de Philosophie*, 1972, pp. 444-60.

correlation corresponds the correlation of name and meaning. Both are psychological. Thus I understand the form '*xRy*' when I know that it discriminates the behaviour of *x* and *y* according as these stand in the relation *R* or not. In this way I extract from all possible relations the relation *R*, as, by a name, I extract its meaning from among all possible things. (*NB*, pp. 98-9)

Wittgenstein, of course, later abolished this distinction between 'forms' and 'constituents' in propositions, but we shall not deal with the point for a moment. The essential thing is that in the process of giving meaning to the components (forms and constituents) of the propositions, we have given the proposition a sense. We have made it *say* that things are so and not not-so: we have discriminated possible facts into two classes and indicated which class we prefer. Wittgenstein expresses this by saying that the proposition has two poles '*a*' and '*b*' and that one of these is, somehow or other (I shall not discuss that question) designated as the preferred pole. If we, then, write the proposition in the form '*a-p-b*', it is obviously, once it has been stated, possible to use this proposition to express the opposite sense to that originally intended. This is the operation of negation and is symbolised by attaching a further '*a*' and '*b*' in the opposite direction, yielding '*b-a-p-b-a*'. By a further extension – once again luminously simple once it has been explained – it is possible to take a pair or any number of propositions and to produce any desired *ab*-function, or in effect truth-function, of the original proposition. An important case, of course, is that of Sheffer's stroke, which (in the VEL-form, as opposed to that used in the *Tractatus*) is represented as

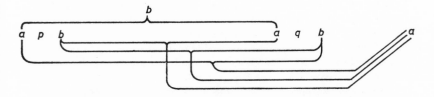

Now, about these *ab*-functions, Wittgenstein says, on the next page of the 4th MS (in the Russell version this occurs on *NB*, p. 101):

The *ab*-functions use the discrimination of facts, which their arguments bring forth, in order to generate new discriminations.

In other words: the truth-functions do not *introduce* new discriminations of facts, new material functions, but merely operate with the discriminations already introduced when the components of propositions were given a meaning. I will not here discuss how Wittgenstein thought he could eliminate identity as a possible independent logical constant – that came after the *Notes on Logic* – or how he thought he could show that generality also did not introduce some new element not already given with the components of propositions. Those are important questions, but the chief thing Wittgenstein is saying is already clear: that nothing is introduced by the logical constants, which is not present in the atomic proposition.

The general consequences of this for the propositions of logic is familiar to all readers of the *Tractatus*. It may be put in something nearer the terminology of *Notes on Logic* by saying that supposing logical propositions to be ones in which only the logical constants occur essentially, then nothing is being said about anything in them: no components – constituents or forms – occur in them essentially. They are used merely to show (for example) that two apparently different discriminations of facts into two classes (with a preference for one class) are really only one discrimination of facts into two classes (with preference for that same class).

Before considering how this is not only one of the original ideas from which the *Tractatus* arose, but also an idea that underlies its most important conclusions, I will mention briefly the change which took place between *Notes on Logic* and the *Tractatus*: namely the abandonment of the notion that the components of propositions could be divided into constituents (names of individuals, apparently) and forms. Wittgenstein, anticipating much in his later philosophy, came to see – or to think – that naming also was not such a self-explanatory process as he had originally supposed. A name in his former sense also carried with it a conception of the form of proposition into which it would fit. Thus these names did not differ in principle from any other components of the proposition, all of which carry with them *some* principle for the discrimination of facts. All therefore come to be called names. I do not myself think that this was an error, but I see that it can be argued that proper names (as we use the term) do not dictate the form of the proposition – or the place at which they must occur in the proposition – in quite the way that other terms do; and I further see that this would raise the question whether, in that case, Wittgenstein envisaged the occurrence of anything at all like our proper names in a fully analysed proposition. The answer to this depends on how like is like. It is at any rate too large an issue for me to enter on here.

I will end with a few words on the importance of this idea that the logical constants do not represent. This idea hangs together

with the notion that our terms are given meaning and our propositions sense only by a process of discriminating facts into two
classes. From this conception it follows that anything else we may
do with language can only serve to bring out features of the discrimination of facts already effected. Whatever we do will not belong
to the realm of sense and reference and truth but only to that of
showing. As is well-known, it is not only logic that is transcendental
according to Wittgenstein: ethics, and hence aesthetics, also is so.
We know, that, according to him, a poem – for example the one by
Uhland quoted in Engelmann's book, can show something by its way
of saying something perfectly simple. We know also, from his letters
to Ficker, that the main point of the *Tractatus* (at any rate as he
viewed it in 1920) was to demonstrate what could *not* be said. Not
only the limits of philosophy, but also the nature of ethics and the
mystical, were reached by considering how and whether the logical
constants had meaning. It is not clear *when* the depth of the implications of this question became apparent to Wittgenstein. Perhaps
the connection between logic and life first became apparent to him
(it certainly became *more* apparent to him) during the war. Towards
the end of the *Notebooks* he says, in a passage, I think, mistranslated
by Miss Anscombe:

> My work has broadened out from the foundations of mathematics
> to the essence of the world. (My translation.)

On the other hand we have Russell's anecdote, which is perhaps
more than just a good joke, about a pre-war evening when Wittgenstein was pacing about his room and Russell asked him: 'Wittgenstein, are you thinking about logic, or about your sins?' – to which
Wittgenstein replied 'Both!'

5

WITTGENSTEIN ON RUSSELL'S THEORY OF JUDGMENT

Guy Stock

In the early years of this century the debate as to the nature of judgment was a central issue dividing British philosophers. What a philosopher said about judgment was not independent of what he said about perception, the distinction between the *a priori* and empirical, the distinction between external and internal relations, the nature of inference, truth, universals, language, the reality of the self and so on.[1]

I want to consider the *Tractatus* in the context of this debate about the nature of judgment, and in particular to consider Wittgenstein's criticisms of Russell's theory of judgment. I think that in this way both the extent of Wittgenstein's originality and the degree of difference between his and Russell's version of Logical Atomism can best be appreciated. However, from this viewpoint the accepted view that the *Tractatus* is not committed to any particular theory of epistemology at least requires re-interpretation. No doubt it is a mistake to assimilate simple objects to sense-data when the latter are conceived as objects of some subject's sensations. Moreover, in the *Tractatus* there is no theory of perception in the traditional empiricist sense of a theory to explain how a subject can obtain knowledge of what exists in the world around him. Nor is there any theory of the sort which attempts to show how the complex knowledge that a subject has of things more or less remote from him in space and time can be 'constructed' from immediately experienced

---

[1] Cf. B. Russell, *Principles of Mathematics*, chap. IV, p. 43; F. H. Bradley, *Essays on Truth and Reality*, 'Coherence and Contradiction', chap. VIII, p. 230; G. E. Moore, 'The Nature of Judgment', *Mind*, N.S. VIII (1899) 182-3. Cf. also G. Stock, 'Russell's Theory of Judgment in Logical Atomism', *Revista Portuguesa de Filosofia*, XXCIII (1972).

objects. However it would be a mistake to conclude from this that Wittgenstein just *happened* not to be interested in epistemological problems and was concerned to develop an account of logic and language which would be, as it were, epistemologically neutral. On the contrary, his account of the nature of thought and language, like any theory of judgment, is at the same time an account of knowledge. However, it is a consequence of the account of the relation between thought and reality developed in the *Tractatus* that 'epistemological questions' as traditionally put are unaskable and hence the so-called philosophical theories of knowledge and perception formulated to answer them are nonsense.

2. To illustrate this I want to consider Wittgenstein's dissatisfaction with Russell's theory of judgment and will therefore attempt to give an outline of the essential features of Russell's theory. This account will of necessity be selective and I do not wish to raise any questions as to its correctness as a description of a view held by Russell at any one time.

Wittgenstein says at *Tractatus*, 5.541 that

> . . . in certain propositional forms of psychology, like 'A thinks, that *p* is the case', or 'A thinks *p*', etc. . . . it appears superficially as if the proposition *p* stood to the object A in a kind of relation. (And in modern epistemology (Russell, Moore, etc.) those propositions have been conceived in this way.)

I will take this remark to be directed at Russell's multi-object theory of judgment which received its final statement in the *Lectures on Logical Atomism*.[1] This theory was essentially dualistic in a Berkelian kind of way.[2] At this time Russell argued against the *Neutral Monists* for the existence in time of a subject of experience. He argued that the identification of things more or less remote in time is only possible relative to some object of *present* experience (i.e. some object of sensation or perception) and the idea of *an experience* requires that there be a subject of experience.[3] The subject itself, however, need not be a possible object of acquaintance. We can, as it were, have knowledge of the subject by description. As Russell puts it: '. . . the datum when we are aware of experiencing an object O is the fact "something is acquainted with O" '.[4] Hence

---

[1] Although by that time Russell himself had already begun to doubt its adequacy: cf. *Logic and Knowledge*, ed. R. C. Marsh, 'The Philosophy of Logical Atomism', e.g. p. 226.

[2] *Logic and Knowledge*, 'On the Nature of Acquaintance' p. 127.

[3] Ibid., pp. 163–8.   [4] Ibid., p. 164.

even if the subject itself is not a possible object of acquaintance nevertheless its existence can be admitted, and thus what Russell calls 'the selectiveness of experience'[1] can be explained in a way which is not open to the *Neutral Monist*, or, for that matter, to any philosophy that denies the existence in time of the unique subject of experience.

Thus Russell's theory of judgment, and his account of empirical knowledge in general, is egocentric. A subject can be acquainted with *particulars*, i.e. sense-data, in sensation and with *facts* in perception.[2] Perception is distinguished from sensation in that it requires not only acquaintance with particulars but also acquaintance with universals. Consequently an object of perception can never be a particular but is always what could be expressed by a true proposition. Perception is incorrigible[3] but in a different way from that in which sensation is incorrigible: perception yields knowledge of *truths* whereas acquaintance with particulars in sensation does not. The verbal expression of a perception involves the use of *logically proper names* and at least one word standing for a universal and therefore the object of knowledge in perception always has propositional form[4] and can never be simply named.[5]

But if perception is incorrigible, we can ask Socrates' question: how is false judgment possible? On Russell's account, as I interpret it, falsity only becomes possible with a judgment that is not merely analytic of what is given in present experience but goes beyond to things more or less remote in space and time. In the case of such judgments the particulars which they are 'about' cannot themselves be the *logical subjects* of the proposition judged since they are not objects of acquaintance. *Propositional functions* are their logical subjects[6] and hence the verbal expression of such judgments involves the use of *incomplete symbols* in the way explained in the *Theory of Descriptions*. It follows that the more or less permanent physical objects which we locate in our immediate spatio-temporal environments are not, in the strict sense of 'object', *objects* of perception. A judgment about such an object involves a claim about the *existence* of particulars beyond the subject's present experience; hence such a judgment can be discovered to be false or, what is

---

[1] Ibid., p. 174, i.e. the apparent fact that 'one part of the world is closer to me than another'.

[2] Ibid., p. 165.

[3] B. Russell, *Philosophical Essays*, 'On the Nature of Truth', pp. 182–3.

[4] B. Russell, *Mysticism and Logic*, 'Sense-data and Physics', p. 147.

[5] 'Philosophy of Logical Atomism', p. 188.

[6] *Mysticism and Logic*, 'Knowledge by Acquaintance', p. 232.

equivalent, such an object can be discovered not to exist. Thus the verbal expression of a judgment about a physical object located relative to one's body will have an incomplete symbol as grammatical subject and such objects will be *logical constructions*.[1]

On this account acquaintance with particulars in sensation provides the subject with an immediate cognitive contact with the particular constituents of the physical world and hence perception of facts is not only the ultimate source of verification for the subject's empirical knowledge[2] but also is the foundation of his capacity to denote unambiguously, e.g. by means of ordinary proper names and definite descriptions, things in space and time beyond what he can presently perceive.[3]

This egocentric version of Atomism left Russell with what he called 'irreducibly mental facts'. When, for example, A makes the perceptual judgment that *aRb*, in addition to the physical fact *aRb*, there will be the fact expressed by the proposition 'A judges that *aRb*'. This will be a *mental* fact in that the proposition expressing it involves reference to a mental constituent, namely the perceiving subject A.[4] This mental fact will not only involve a series of dyadic relations of acquaintance between subject, A, and the particular and universal constituents of the physical fact. It will be a *complex unity* consisting of the constituents A,*a*,*R* and *b* related in an order which is determined by the *sense* of the judging relation, *J*. The judgment will be true if and only if the constituents *a*,*R* and *b*[5] are related in the context of the mental fact by the judging relation *J* in the same order as they are in a corresponding physical fact. Given that the judgment is true the order of the particulars in the corresponding physical fact will be determined not, of course, by the *sense* of the judging relation, *J*, but by the *sense* of the 'object' relation, *R*.[6] Perception, in that it is always true, will constitute the limiting case of judgment.

3. It is these irreducibly mental facts like 'A judges that *aRb*' and 'A perceives *aRb*', the assertion of which involves reference to a subject, that provide Russell with a 'new species' for his zoo and he

[1] *Mysticism and Logic*, 'Sense Data and Physics', pp. 155ff; and 'Constituents of Matter', pp. 129ff.

[2] 'Philosophy of Logical Atomism' p. 288.

[3] B. Russell, *The Problems of Philosophy*, chap. v, p. 56; 'On the Nature of Acquaintance', p. 168.

[4] 'On the Nature of Acquaintance', p. 127.

[5] i.e. the *objects* of the judgment or belief, in contrast to the subject.

[6] *The Problems of Philosophy*, chap. xii, pp. 127–8; and also 'On the Nature of Truth', pp. 178ff.

credits Wittgenstein with their discovery.[1] Russell is not happy with them but so long as he wants to retain the existence in time – albeit momentary – of a subject of experience whose ability to think about things more or less remote in space and time is explained in terms of the *unique* cognitive relation he has in perception to things in his immediate sensible environment then he *must* admit the existence of such hybrid facts.

Wittgenstein, however, denies their existence at 5.542 when he says: 'But it is clear that "A believes that p", "A thinks p", "A says p", are of the form " 'p' says p"; and here we have no co-ordination of a fact and an object, but a co-ordination of facts by means of a co-ordination of their objects'.

Thus Wittgenstein is maintaining that to say 'A thinks p' or 'A perceives p' is *not* to mention a thinking or perceiving subject[2] existing in the world; nor therefore is it to describe any kind of relation between such a subject and other objects in the world. The relation between a thought and the world, or a perception and the world, is the same as that obtaining between a picture and its object which it represents truly or falsely.[3] In other words the thought or perception stands to the world in that 'pictorial internal relation, which holds between language and the world'.[4]

Hence when Russell asked Wittgenstein what the constituents of a thought are Wittgenstein could reply, 'I don't know *what* the constituents of a thought are but I know *that* it must have constituents which correspond to the words of language. Again the kind of relation of the constituents of the thought and the pictured fact is irrelevant. It would be a matter of psychology to find out.'[5]

For Wittgenstein the question as to the nature of the constituents of a thought *qua* fact was of no more philosophical interest than would have been a question about the chemical constituents of the ink used in 'a propositional sign in its projective relation to the world',[6] i.e. than would have been a question about the constituents of the ink used in writing a proposition.

The thought or perception and its perceptible expression 'like the two youths, their two horses and their lilies in the story . . . are all in a certain sense one'.[7]

[1] 'Philosophy of Logical Atomism', p. 226.

[2] Even, as Russell puts it, as an 'apparent variable', cf. 'On the Nature of Acquaintance', p. 164.

[3] *TLP*, 2.173.   [4] *TLP*, 4.014.

[5] Quoted by G. E. M. Anscombe, *An Introduction to Wittgenstein's Tractatus*, chap. I, p. 28.

[6] *TLP*, 3.12.   [7] *TLP*, 4.014.

The thought that *aRb*, the perception that *aRb* and the applied propositional sign '*aRb*' are all one in the sense that their identity depends on what they represent as being the case in the world and they all represent the very same thing as being so. From the point of view of logic what is important is what they have in common in virtue of which they can represent reality, truly or falsely, as being so.

Thus for Wittgenstein, as much as for Russell, what is thought or perceived is always what could be expressed by a proposition, but Wittgenstein is involved in rejecting:

(*a*) the possibility of *an account* of perception in terms of an immediate cognitive relation between a unique subject at a point in the spatio-temporal series and particular objects existing contemporaneously with the subject; and, *a fortiori*, an *account* of conception as a relation in time between a subject and a subsistent universal.[1]

And consequently in rejecting:

(*b*) any attempt to explain the nature of the relation between a name and an object in terms of the existence of an immediate experiential relation between some unique subject and an object of his experience; and, likewise, any attempt to explain the relation between a proposition and a fact in terms of a judging relation involving a subject, on the one hand, and particular and universal entities on the other.[2]

So, although for Wittgenstein, a proposition is the perceptible expression of a thought[3] and hence is nothing independent of thought, a proposition's relating to the world is not explained in terms of some subject's capacity to think about things in the world or to perceive things in the world.[4] For Wittgenstein, in so far as a thought or a perception is a *fact* and yet can be *true*, its relation to the object ('reality') it represents truly or falsely must be the same as the relation of the *perceptible expression* of the thought or perception to the object ('reality') which it represents truly or falsely. The one is not to be explained in terms of the other. They all bear the same internal pictorial relation to the world and that relation cannot itself be represented. If the thought *qua* fact could be observed empirically then the 'language' of thoughts would have to be understood in

---

[1] *The Problems of Philosophy*, chap. v, p. 52.

[2] This I take to be the kind of psychologistic 'explanation' of the relation of language to the world that, as Paul Engelmann points out, Wittgenstein took philosophy to be infected with. Cf. *LLW*, chap. v, p. 100.

[3] *TLP*, 3.1.

[4] Cf. the criticism that the Augustinian account of language treats the child as if it 'could already *think*, only not yet speak . . .' (*PI*, I, 32).

precisely the same way that the propositional sign expressing *what* is thought has to be understood. As Wittgenstein put it in the *Investigations*:

'If God had looked into our minds, he would not have been able to see there whom we were speaking of.'[1]

What God would see there would have to be applied or taken in its *projective relation* to reality of which it could be either true or false. In other words God would have to *think* its sense.[2]

4. If the above interpretation is correct then Wittgenstein's *motive* for rejecting any account of propositions of the form 'A thinks *p*' which construes them as involving reference to a subject of cognitive experience is not to be found simply in a desire to preserve a truth-functional account of all complex propositions. Rather, his motive must be seen as lying in his account of what Engelmann calls the 'comprehensive logical category of *depiction*'.[3] The truth-functional account of complex propositions is subservient to the idea of a proposition, or a thought, or *anything capable of representing its object truly or falsely*, as a kind of 'living picture'.[4] The fundamental requirement for the possibility of representation of this kind is that it should be possible to express 'a new sense with old words'.[5] There must be types of element in a proposition which are capable of retaining their meaning, i.e. of standing for the same objects, when rearranged with other such elements in different ways analogously to the way in which in a *tableau vivant* the same elements can be rearranged to present a 'new' fact regarding the object pictured. The identity of the object of the picture ('reality') depends on the objects the pictorial elements stand for: the coordinations of these elements with objects are 'the feelers' by means of which the picture is connected with what is pictured – 'reality'.[6] In virtue of alterations in the configurations of elements in the picture different configurations of objects, i.e. different facts regarding the object of the picture ('reality') can be *presented*.

The traditional criticism of such an account of meaning and sense was that it could not account for, e.g. negative and disjunctive propositions.[7] However, the idea that such propositions could have sense by being truth-functions of other propositions allowed for the

---

[1] *PI*, II, xi, p. 217.
[2] *TLP*, 3.11; and *PTLP*, 3.12–3.13 and cf. *PI*, I, 73.
[3] *LLW*, p. 99.   [4] *TLP*, 4.0311.
[5] *TLP*, 4.03.   [6] *TLP*, 2.1515.
[7] Cf., for example, F. H. Bradley, *Essays on Truth and Reality*, 'Truth and Copying', p. 109.

'fundamental thought that . . . the "logical constants" do not represent'.[1] Thus the truth-functional account of complex propositions made it possible to maintain an account according to which, in general, language stands to the world in a pictorial internal relation. But it is *this* account, as a completely general account of the form of *any* possible mode of representation which can represent reality truly or falsely, which leaves no room for a subject of thought.

It leaves no room for the subject *in* the world since the world can only be represented in thought and whatever is represented in thought 'is world'.[2] The subject cannot stand outside 'its' thought[3] and represent the relation between 'its' thought – as it were, a state of its 'conscious self' – and the reality which the thought represents truly or falsely. In so far as a thought can be represented in thought then what is represented is a fact and a fact *as such* is neither true nor false: it simply is so. A fact can only be true or false if it has a sense, i.e. if it is thought as representing a configuration of objects *outside* itself which might or might not obtain.[4] Only such configurations of objects can be represented in thought, never the subject that thinks them.

The subject that thinks, therefore, can never represent itself in the context of a state of affairs. For example, I can think of spatio-temporal relations holding between objects (the table as presently in front of G.S.'s eyes), but the subject that represents such relations between things cannot represent itself as related, spatio-temporally or otherwise, to any of the things it represents as related.[5] As Wittgenstein put it when talking about the Will in the *Notebooks*: '. . . the consideration of willing makes it look as if one part of the world were closer to me than another (which would be intolerable)'.[6]

Given the account of a thought as standing in an internal pictorial relation to the world, the subject cannot be an object in the world representable in thought. The subject's relation to the world must be analogous to that of the physical eye to its visual field.[7] Therefore if the *Tractatus* account of the form of 'A thinks p' is correct then Russell's account of judgment is wrong since Russell presents the judging subject as related in a *describable* way to the things the judgment is about.

[1] *TLP*, 4.0312
[2] *NB*, p. 89 entry dated 9 November 1916.
[3] *TLP*, 4.12.   [4] *TLP*, 2.173.
[5] Cf. F. H. Bradley, *Essays on Truth and Reality*, p. 410: what Bradley says about the 'finite centre' has similarities to what can be 'said' about the subject in the *Tractatus*.
[6] *NB*, p. 88.   [7] *TLP*, 5.632–5.6331.

But why *should* Russell's account of judgment be rejected in favour of the account of thinking given in the *Tractatus*? Wittgenstein states his reason at 5.5422. He says: 'The correct explanation of the form of the proposition "A judges *p*" must show that it is impossible to judge a nonsense. (Russell's theory does not satisfy this condition.)'

But how does Russell's theory fail to make it impossible to judge a nonsense? And how does Wittgenstein's account succeed where Russell's fails?

5. I think it is important to see that both Russell and Wittgenstein wanted to resist an account according to which (*a*) knowing the *meaning* of a name involved a subject's possessing a concept, and (*b*) knowing of the existence of an object in the world e.g. perceiving O, consisted in the subject having some kind of immediate experience of O and his subsuming O under the concept of an O – the concept being *true* of the object.

As Russell put it: 'I do not think that, when an object is known to me, there is in my mind something which may be called an "idea" of the object, the possession of which constitutes my knowledge of the object'.[1]

In saying this Russell expressed allegiance to his multi-object theory of judgment and to the idea of a cognitive contact with particulars in sensation which is *logically independent*[2] of the knowledge had of them in perceiving them *as* related in such-and-such a way in fact. According to this theory perceiving a particular in the context of a fact *as* so-and-so requires acquaintance with a universal, i.e. requires the possession of a concept, but the particular *itself* is not known via an idea or concept.

We can, for example, assume that a subject perceives that *aRb*. The fact *aRb* is supposedly a *contingent* fact: the relation *R* holding between *a* and *b* is a merely *external* one. The doctrine of acquaintance as cognition of *a* and *b* which is *logically independent* of perceiving them *as* related in the context of the fact *aRb* is required to allow for the mere externality of the relation *R*. The particulars are known as related by *R* in *fact*. But the doctrine of acquaintance, according to which the subject has knowledge of them which is logically independent of knowing them *as* related by *R*, is required to make it possible to think that *a* and *b* *might* have been related otherwise in another conceivable world.

---

[1] 'On the Nature of Acquaintance', p. 147.
[2] *The Problems of Philosophy*, chap. v, pp. 46–7.

But can the Russellian doctrine of acquaintance do what is required of it? Given the account of acquaintance the constituents of the perceived fact, particulars and universal, are known *completely* separately from one another in a way which is *logically independent* of knowing the true proposition '*aRb*'. But if this is so, surely there are no logical limits placed on the constituents which can be combined with one another in a judgment?

Either (and this I take to be Wittgenstein's point) it seems that anything goes, and there is nothing that could count as judging nonsense and therefore nothing that could count as *sense* either. *Or*, looking as it were at the obverse, no sense could really be given to the supposal that *a* might not have been related by *R* to *b* since nothing could account for the identity of *a* and *b* in such a supposal. In other words, nothing could account for the counterfactual supposal being a supposal about the *very same* particulars *a* and *b*.

At least on an account of judgment in which the subject's knowledge of objects is always via concepts *true* of them the limits of what can be sensibly judged about 'the world' are set by immutable internal relations between concepts.[1] However, it is clear that the *Tractatus* did not revert to an account involving the notion of a proposition or thought as a 'third realm' entity capable of coming into different kinds of relation with different minds.[2] The account of thinking which is given in the *Tractatus* represents a complete break with accounts of judgment, and *consequent* accounts of how language relates to the world, involving the more or less traditional philosophical distinctions between particular and universal, concept and object, and so on.[3] The notion of an object in the *Tractatus* is relative to the account of thinking as picturing, and this is why it is futile to raise the question as to the nature of simple objects and expect some answer in terms of notions internal to the accounts of thinking and judgment that Wittgenstein is rejecting *in toto*.

Fundamentally the concept of an object in the *Tractatus* is that of an entity which an element in a picture stands for. The *same* object can be represented as combined in different ways with other objects by means of alterations in the ways in which the pictorial element is combined with other such elements. For any given pictorial element there will be limits on the possibilities of its combination with other elements. Some combinations of pictorial

---

[1] Even if this kind of account does leave truth and existential propositions in a peculiar position. Cf. G. E. Moore, 'The Nature of Judgment', *Mind*, VIII (1899).

[2] Cf., e.g. G. Frege, 'The Thought', *Mind*, LXV (1956).

[3] F. P. Ramsey, *The Foundations of Mathematics*, 'Universals', pp. 132–4.

elements will be 'ruled out' as not representing possible states of affairs. In such cases the *natures* (the 'internal properties') of the objects the pictorial elements stand for will be such as to make it impossible for them to be combined in the way the combination of pictorial elements presents them as being.

So far this would appear to be nothing more than a description of 'how a *tableau vivant* actually functions'. However, there are two crucial identifications involved when it is seen as giving the form of *any* representation which can be true or false of its object. In other words, when it is seen as giving the form not only of the relation between a proposition and what it is true or false of but equally of the relation between a thought and what it is true or false of.

Then:

(*a*) knowing the meaning of a name (a pictorial element) must be identical with knowing the object the name stands for.[1] There cannot be two distinct 'epistemological acts'. The object cannot be identified by means of a *true* thought first and *then* named since in order to think truly or falsely of *it*, it must already be represented in thought, i.e. named.

And:

(*b*) knowing the meaning of a name in turn comes to be identical with knowing the *possibilities* of its combination with other names in the context of propositions and consequently with knowing the *possibilities* of combination of an object with other objects in states of affairs. Knowing an object cannot require knowing any *actualities* since knowing an object is already required both in the capacity to know *how* an object is in fact combined with other objects and also in the capacity to think how the *same* object *might have been* combined but in fact is not.

So Wittgenstein says at *Tractatus*, 2.0123: 'In order to know an object, I must know not its external but all its internal qualities'.

To understand this it is important to see the role that the so-called *argument* from determinateness of sense plays at this point. In fact it is not so much an argument as a *thesis* about the sense of propositions and consequently about truth and falsity also.[2] It is not argued that *if* the sense of a proposition is to be determinate *as opposed to* indeterminate then there must be the possibility of indefinable names and simple objects. Rather, it is maintained that the sense of any proposition that can be discovered by experience

---

[1] *TLP*, 3.203.

[2] *TLP*, 3.23: 'The postulate of the possibility of the simple signs is the postulate of the determinateness of sense'.

to be true or false of reality must be 'determined in advance of experience' otherwise there could be no such thing as truth at all.[1] And this is equivalent to the demand that anything that can be known to be true of reality *a posteriori* can sensibly be thought to have been false.[2] But if it is required that it be possible to think that any thought known to be true *a posteriori* might have been false, given the account of thinking implicit in the picture theory, it follows that there must be objects of thought such that their only *thinkable* properties are external properties: there must be objects which are 'roughly speaking, colourless'.[3] In other words there must be objects such that for *any given object* any property it can be represented in thought as having it can equally well be represented as *not* having. The identity (the *what*) of such an object therefore must be independent of *any* properties it can be represented in thought, truly or falsely, as having.

What is known in knowing such an object – apart from its external properties – are its internal properties. Such properties, since thinking consists in representing possible combinations of objects, cannot themselves be represented in thoughts that are true of an object. They must simply *show* in the 'syntactical employment' of the name standing for the object, i.e. in the ways in which the name can and cannot be combined with other names in the context of propositions which are true or false of reality. Thus knowing the meanings of names – knowing objects – is required in the capacity to think truly or falsely about reality and at the same time is what makes nonsensical judgment impossible. However, any attempt to *state* the syntactical employment of a name, i.e. the internal properties of the object the name stands for, by attempting to

---

[1] *PTLP*, 3.20103: 'The requirement of determinateness . . . can be formulated in the following way: if a proposition can have a sense, the syntactical employment of each of its parts must have been established in advance . . . Before a proposition can have a sense, it must be completely settled what propositions follow from it.'

[2] Cf., *TLP*, 5.634: '. . . everything we see could be otherwise . . .': Bradley's theory of judgment in so far as it doesn't allow any judgment to be completely false involves a rejection of the thesis of the determinateness of sense; an account involving the concept-object distinction retains it – at a cost – by making out *sense* to be determined *a priori* by internal relations between concepts whilst the truth or falsity of *a posteriori* judgments depends on the existence or non-existence of something 'falling under' the concept or concepts involved.

[3] *TLP*, 2.0232: this is also the source of the doctrine of the logical independence of atomic propositions. And one might add that the notion of such a colourless object stands at the opposite end of a continuum from the Idealist notion of a *concrete universal*, any thinkable property of which is an internal property, cf. B. Bosanquet, *Essays and Addresses*, 'A True Theory of Identity', pp. 165–8. Reprinted from *Mind*, XIII (1888).

state *truths* about the meaning of the name would necessarily
fail.[1]

Thus, so far as the *Tractatus* is concerned, knowing objects, unlike
Russell's acquaintance with particulars, is not a kind of *experience*
which could explain the possibility of naming things in the world.
It is what is required in the capacity to think the *sense* of any
proposition which is true or false of reality and hence in the possibility of any *experience* of something being the case. As Wittgenstein
puts it at *Tractatus*, 5.552:

> The 'experience' which we need to understand logic is not
> that such and such is the case, but that something *is*; but that is
> *no* experience.
> Logic *precedes* every experience – that something is *so*.
> It is before the How, not before the What.

Russell's theory of judgment had made knowledge by acquaintance of an object a precondition of formulating a proposition about
it but at the same time inconsistently maintained that *what* was
experienced in acquaintance with the object was identical with
what could be *known to be the case* about it. This had the consequence
of making it unintelligible how an atomic proposition which was
supposedly *contingently* true could be thought to be false.

6. To sum up: Russell rejected an account of thinking or judgment
according to which a subject's knowledge of an object is always
mediated via a concept of that object. Consequently he introduced
the notion of acquaintance in sensation as an immediate cognitive
relation between a subject in time and contemporaneously existing
particulars which was *logically independent of*, and yet a *precondition of*,
knowing truths about such particulars in perception. The particulars were conceived as being externally related to one another and
knowing facts about them consisted in knowing them *as* related in
such-and-such ways. But Russell's account left it unintelligible
how a particular known in fact to have certain 'external' properties
could be thought not to have had them.

The *Tractatus*, likewise, rejected an account of thinking as
involving concepts and of knowing an object as 'subsuming' it
under a concept true of it. But it also rejected Russell's account of
acquaintance as an experiential relation between a subject in the
world and objects in the world. Thinking is picturing. The relation
between a thought and reality is the same as the relation between

---

[1] *TLP*, 3.331.

a proposition and reality: they stand in an 'internal pictorial relation' to that of which they are true or false. Hence, as Ramsey put it, Wittgenstein 'explicitly reduces the question as to the analysis of judgment . . . to the question "What is it for a proposition token to have a certain sense?" '[1]

The answer he gave to this question (i) left no room in the world represented in thought for a subject that thinks, (ii) left no possibility of giving an 'account' of the relation between words and the world in terms of the subject's cognitive experience of the world, and (iii) given the thesis that any proposition that can be discovered to be true *a posteriori* can sensibly be thought false, it required that there be the possibility of indefinable names standing for objects which are 'Roughly speaking, colourless'.

---

[1] *Foundations of Mathematics*, 'Critical Notice on the Tractatus', pp. 274–5.

6

WITTGENSTEIN AND IDEALISM

Bernard Williams

I. SOLIPSISM AND THE TRACTATUS

Tractatus, 5.62 famously says: '. . . what the solipsist *means* is quite correct; only it cannot be *said* but makes itself manifest. The world is *my* world: this is manifest in the fact that the limits of *language* (of that language which alone I understand) mean the limits of my world.' The later part of this repeats what was said in summary at 5.6: 'the limits of my language mean the limits of my world'. And the key to the problem 'how much truth there is in solipsism' has been provided by the reflections of *TLP*, 5.61.

> Logic pervades the world; the limits of the world are also its limits.
>
> So we cannot say in logic 'the world has this in it, and this, but not that'.
>
> For that would appear to presuppose that we were excluding certain possibilities, and this cannot be the case, since it would require that logic should go beyond the limits of the world; for only in that way could it view those limits from the other side as well.
>
> We cannot think what we cannot think; so we cannot think what we cannot *say* either.

Now Wittgenstein says that 'there is no such thing as the self that thinks and entertains ideas' (5.631), and this item is presumably the same as what at 5.641 he perhaps loosely, but comprehensibly, calls '. . . the human soul with which psychology deals' – that is to say, the item that does not really exist, the thinking and knowing soul *in* the world, is an item which people look for there as the subject of the phenomena with which psychology deals. In this interpretation I think I am substantially in agreement with Mr P. M. S. Hacker in his book *Insight and Illusion: Wittgenstein on Philosophy and the Metaphysics of Experience* (OUP, 1972), which I have found helpful on these questions. There are, however, respects in which I would put the position rather differently from him. Hacker, as against Black and others, says that what Wittgenstein does is to deny the existence of a knowing self *in* the world, and denies it, moreover, on Humean grounds[1] to the effect that it cannot be encountered in experience. At the same time, Wittgenstein, under Schopenhauerian influence, does believe in the existence of another, metaphysical or philosophical self, which is 'the limit of the world, not a part of it' (5.632, 5.641), and in some such sense he really is a solipsist; only that of course cannot be said, but only manifests itself. Since Wittgenstein denies the first of these selves and in some way or other accepts the second, he cannot mean them to be the same thing.

Granted the intensely paradoxical and ironical character of Wittgenstein's thought here, one is in any case in expounding it going to be choosing between different kinds of emphasis. But I would enter two qualifications to Hacker's account. First, as regards the negative movement against the knowing self, it is not just an unsuccessful Humean search that we are dealing with. Wittgenstein says:

> There is no such thing as the subject that thinks or entertains ideas.
> If I wrote a book called *The World as I Found It*, I should have to include a report on my body, and should have to say which parts were subordinate to my will, and which were not, etc., this being a method of isolating the subject, or rather of showing that in an important sense there is no subject; for it alone could not be mentioned in that book. (*TLP*, 5.631)

He adds, just before the analogy of the visual field, which I shall not consider (5.633): 'where *in* the world is a metaphysical subject to be found . . . ?' This seems to me to say, not just that there was something we were looking for and which turned out not in fact to be in the world – which is Hume's tone of voice, though the full content of Hume's negative discovery is not to be found in his failing to find something which he might have found, either. Rather Wittgenstein says: that which I confusedly had in mind when I set out to look is something which could not possibly be in the world. Hacker's

[1] Hacker, p. 59.

emphasis is: there is one specification, which is the specification of a possible empirical thing, and to that nothing as a matter of fact corresponds; but there is a quasi-specification of a non-empirical thing to which something does, in a way, correspond. But rather, what we first looked for was never a possible empirical thing. For it had to satisfy the condition of being something *in* the world as I experience it and yet at the same time necessarily there whenever anything was there, and there could not be anything which did that; which is why Wittgenstein can explain his thought in this connection by saying (5.634) that no part of our experience is at the same time *a priori* (the phrase translated 'at the same time' is important here). Thus Wittgenstein's thought is, as Hacker indeed says, very like Kant's criticism of the Cartesian *res cogitans*.

The other qualification affects the other half of the argument. We cannot in any straightforward sense say that there is, or that we can believe in, or accept, a metaphysical, transcendental, self instead; for neither *what* it is, nor *that* it is, can be said, and attempts to talk about it or state its existence must certainly be nonsense. That is why, as we have already seen, the non-occurrence of a subject in the book of *The World as I Found It* means that 'in an important sense there is no subject'. The sense in which it *is* a limit, also means that *at* the limit, it isn't anything at all (5.64):

> Here it can be seen that solipsism, when its implications are followed out strictly, coincides with pure realism. The self of solipsism shrinks to a point without extension and there remains the reality co-ordinated with it.

Indeed, granted this, I find puzzling why Wittgenstein can say (5.641) that there really is a sense in which philosophy can talk about the self in a non-psychological way. But I take this to mean that philosophy can talk about it in the only way in which by the end of the *Tractatus*, we find that *philosophy* can talk about anything: that is to say, not with sense.

Whatever exactly we make of that, we can recover from the *Tractatus* discussion of the self and solipsism three ideas which will be particularly important as points of reference in what follows: that the limits of my language are the limits of my world; that there could be no way in which those limits could be staked out from both sides – rather, the limits of language and thought reveal themselves in the *fact that* certain things are nonsensical; and (what follows from the first two, but is an important point to emphasise) that the 'me' and 'my' which occur in those remarks do not relate to an 'I' *in* the world, and hence we cannot conceive of it as a matter of empirical investigation (as the *Tractatus* is fond of putting it, a matter of 'natural science') to determine why my world is this way rather than that way, why my language has some features rather than others, etc. Any sense in which such investigations were possible would not be a sense of 'my', or indeed, perhaps, of 'language', in which the limits of my language were the limits of my world.

It may seem that these three ideas are foremost among those that Wittgenstein abandoned in his later work, and that they, and the forms of puzzlement which gave rise to them, were particular objects of the criticisms of the *Investigations*. In a sense that is true, and Hacker devotes a good deal of his book to explaining how the later interest in such things as the impossibility of a private language, the necessity for public criteria, etc., is related to a long-term project of exorcising solipsism – exorcising it even from some vanishing and unsayable transcendental redoubt. The later arguments about oneself and others are designed (among other things) to remove the need even to try to point, hopelessly, in a solipsistic direction. That need certainly exists in the *Tractatus*. The well-charted moves in the later work from 'I' to 'we' mark one and the most evident attempt to banish that need; equally the emphasis in the later work on language's being an embodied, this-worldly, concrete social activity, expressive of human needs, as opposed to the largely timeless, unlocated and impersonal designatings of the *Tractatus* – that emphasis also can naturally be thought of as a rejection of the transcendental and Schopenhauerian aspects of the earlier work: the *transcendentales Geschwätz*, the 'transcendental twaddle' as Wittgenstein wrote to Engelmann in a different context in 1918 (quoted by Hacker, p. 81).

But the question is not as simple as this, and my chief aim will be to suggest that the move from 'I' to 'we' was not unequivocally accompanied by an abandonment of the concerns of transcendental idealism. To some extent, the three ideas I mentioned are not so much left behind, as themselves take part in the shift from 'I' to 'we': *the shift from 'I' to 'we' takes place within the transcendental ideas themselves*. From the *Tractatus* combination (as Hacker justly puts it) of empirical realism and transcendental solipsism, the move does not consist just in the loss of the second element. Rather, the move is to something which itself contains an important element of idealism. That element is concealed, qualified, overlaid with other things, but I shall suggest that it is there. I shall suggest also that this element may help to explain a particular feature of the later work, namely a pervasive vagueness and indefiniteness evident in the use Wittgenstein makes of 'we'.

2. SOLIPSISM AND IDEALISM

Hacker says (p. 59) that an aim of his book is 'to show that the detailed refutation of solipsism and hence of idealism, which Wittgenstein produced in the 1930s and incorporated, in low key, in the *Investigations*, is directed against views which he himself held as a young man'. A refutation 'of solipsism and *hence* of idealism': this is a connexion of ideas, not immediately self-evident, which Hacker makes throughout. Thus at p. 214:

> The solipsist claimed that the present moment is unique, that he is privileged, that it is always he who sees, that what he has when he sees is unique, that his seeing is exceptional, that 'this' is incomparable. Each move is illegitimate. The illegitimacy of each move damns not just solipsism, but phenomenalism and indeed any form of idealism.

Yet it is not at all obvious that everything which could pointfully be called a form of idealism, or indeed which has been so called by the history of philosophy, would necessarily be refuted by arguments which, by undermining a private language, removed the supposed privileged first-person immediacies which are the basis of solipsism, whether expressed or presupposed.

To phenomenalism, which Hacker mentions, such criticism can indeed be extended; and it may help towards the business of sketching a kind of idealism to which that criticism does not extend, if we first consider one or two points about phenomenalism. Phenomenalists used stoutly to hold that it was a crass misunderstanding to regard their theory as any form of idealism. If they were right at all in holding that, clearly their denial applies at best only to non-transcendental idealism – what we may call, following Kant, *empirical* or *problematical* idealism, and which we can define for our present purposes as a form of idealism which regards the existence of the material world as dependent on minds which are themselves things *in* the world, empirical beings whose existence or non-existence is a matter of contingent fact[1].

In fact, it is not clear that phenomenalism even manages to avoid being that. The question of whether it does or not, turns on the issue of the status of the hypothetical observers whose equally hypothetical sense-data constitute the content, under phenomenalist translation, of statements about unobserved portions of the material

[1] This definition excludes Berkeley's completed theory from being an example of empirical idealism. Yet clearly Kant was right in distinguishing Berkeley's views from transcendental idealism. We need not, for the present purpose, pursue the important distinctions which are needed here.

world. If *they* are regarded as empirical items, then there may be a difficulty about phenomenalism's steering clear of empirical idealism. For if it is to do that, and so maintain its professed stance as a realist theory at the empirical level, then it must be able to translate into its language any comprehensible *empirical* proposition which denies the mind-dependence of material objects: thus phenomenalists are happy to translate into their language, as they hope, propositions saying that there were rocks, etc. in certain spaces before there were any observers of them. But what about the following proposition, which at least seems to be a comprehensible and indeed true empirical proposition in the material object language: 'Even if there were not any observers, certain material objects would exist'? If phenomenalist observers are empirical items, the question of their existence is an empirical question – the same empirical question, indeed, as is raised by the antecedent of that conditional. Thus the phenomenalist translation of that conditional must be of the form: if P were not the case, then if P were the case, then Q, and it is not, to say the least of it, clear that that is satisfactory.

If that cannot be made satisfactory, then phenomenalism cannot adequately represent in its terms a proposition which constitutes a basic empirical denial of mind-dependence; and will be thus a form of empirical idealism. But even if we dispose of that, phenomenalism will still be a kind of transcendental idealism. Suppose that we eliminate the antecedents of the phenomenalist sentences which merely hypothesise the existence of observers, and which are there just as a universal condition of the analysis; thus we make the so-called existence of observers a redundant condition on the occurrence of sense-data. Then genuinely empirical statements about the existence or non-existence of observers, such as the antecedent of the material object statement we considered just now, can be translated into the phenomenalist language: in some such form, presumably, as statements of the existence of Humean aggregations of sense-data. Then the sense-data which are the raw materials of the phenomenalist translations (including those sense-data aggregations of which constitute the empirical existence of observers) will not, as such, have a subject, and it is obvious from what has just been said why they cannot, as such, have a subject: for the only candidate for a subject recognisable to phenomenalism will be the empirical observer, but his existence has now been represented as the contingent aggregation of items which already, and even outside such an aggregation, have the character of sense-data. As Carnap said in the *Logische Aufbau*, '*das Gegebene ist subjektlos*', the given has no subject.

But it is still the *given*; and unless phenomenalism is to surrender its basically epistemological way of introducing one to these items, and its references to their being, or being related to, *observations*, they must remain items of which we have been given no adequate grasp unless they are in *some* sense mental. Neutral monism perhaps attempted to drop that implication, but to the limited extent that it progressed in that attempt, it seems not to leave one with any adequate bearings on the items in question at all. But then, while no form of mind-dependence of the world can be truly asserted *in* the phenomenalist language, the fact that its raw materials are of this character, and the fact that it is basically *the* language,[1] these facts *show* that the world is mental. We cannot say (except empirically and falsely) that the world is the world of experience; rather, its being the world of experience conditions everything we say. That is what it is for phenomenalism to be a form of transcendental idealism: a form which indeed is liable to the same objections as Wittgenstein, faced with solipsism, made to such things as the empiricist theory of meaning. Those objections are directed to starting with supposed first-person immediacies, and phenomenalism incurs them because that in terms of which it represents the world cannot be understood except in terms of first-person immediacies.

Thus phenomenalism is one or another form of idealism, and in either form is exposed, as much as solipsism, to the later Wittgenstein arguments. But, to turn away now from phenomenalism, must anything which could be called idealism have this character? Hacker, as I have mentioned, assumes that it is so. His reason for that emerges when he says (p. 216) that 'idealism in most of its forms' – that is his one qualification – is just a half-hearted form of solipsism which has not been thought through with the consistency of solipsism; thus also he refers (p. 71) to Schopenhauer's 'glib dismissal' of solipsism. Idealism is regarded just as a kind of aggregative solipsism; and that is indeed ridiculous.[2] But if the idea that the limits of *my* language mean the limits of *my* world can point to transcendental solipsism, then perhaps there is a form of transcendental idealism which is suggested, not indeed by the confused idea that the limits of *each* man's language mean the limits of *each* man's world, but by the idea that the limits of *our* language mean the limits of *our* world. This would not succumb to the arguments

[1] I shall not try to discuss how that second fact is to be understood. For the closely related point that the 'two languages' version of phenomenalism is not neutral about reality, cf. J. L. Austin, *Sense and Sensibilia*, pp. 60-1.
[2] Cf. Moore's objection to what he supposed to be a consequence of egoism in ethics: *Principia Ethica*, p. 99.

which finished off solipsism, for those arguments are all basically about the move from 'I' to 'we', and that, in this version, has already been allowed for.

I think that there is such a view implicit in some of Wittgenstein's later work. To see what such a view will be like, we can try to follow an analogy between this, first-person plural, view, and the first-person singular transcendental view which we have already touched on. First and most basically it is essential that the proposition that the limits of our language mean the limits of our world should be taken neither as a blank tautology, nor as an empirical claim. It would be a mere tautology if it meant something like: whoever are meant by 'we', it is going to be true that what we understand, we understand, and what we have heard of and can speak of, we have heard of and can speak of, and what we cannot speak of, we cannot speak of. Certainly. But the singular versions of those truisms were not just what was meant when it was said originally that the limits of my language meant the limits of my world. Nor, in that original case, did we intend an *empirical* thought, in which I both take myself as something in the world and make it depend on me: that is precisely what we left behind in distinguishing transcendental from empirical idealism. Now, we do not mean the plural analogue of that empirical monomania, either; and that is one way in which our statement is not an empirical statement.

There are other, and important, ways in which it is not an empirical statement. Thus the claim that the limits of our language mean the limits of our world might be construed empirically in this way, by taking *language* narrowly, to refer to one's system of communication, its grammatical categories, etc., and *world* widely, to mean how in general the world appears to one, the general framework of comprehension one applies to things, etc; and then, taking 'we' relatively to various linguistic groups, one would have the hypothesis, perhaps to be ascribed to Whorf, that the way things look to different groups profoundly depends on what their language is like. I shall come back to certain relativist questions raised by such theories; for the moment the aim is just the general one of illuminating by contrast the non-empirical character of an idealist interpretation of our slogan. If we are dealing with a genuinely empirical theory of this 'Whorfian' sort, then a given group's language should provide some sort of an empirical explanation, if only a very weak one, of its way of looking at the world; connectedly, we could explain some particular man's way of looking at the world, or some aspect of that, by reference to the language group he belonged to. But all that cancels the force of the essentially first-personal, even though plural, formulation we are dealing with. Nothing will do for an idealist interpretation, which merely puts any given 'we' in the world and then looks sideways at us. Under the idealist interpretation, it is not a question of our recognising that we are one lot in the world among others, and (in principle at least) coming to understand and explain how *our* language conditions *our* view of the world, while that of others conditions theirs differently. Rather, what the world is for us is shown by the fact that we can make sense of some things and not of others: or rather – to lose the last remnants of an empirical and third-personal view – in the fact that some things and not others make sense. Any empirical discovery we could make about our view of the world, as that it was conditioned by our use of count-words or whatever, would itself be a fact which we were able to understand in terms of, and only in terms of, our view of the world; and anything which radically we could not understand because it lay outside the boundary of our language would not be something we could come to explain our non-understanding of – it could not become clear to us what was wrong with it, or with us.

Here, in the contrast with a mere tautology and, very basically, in the contrast with an empirical view, we can begin to see an analogy between the plural view and the original first-person singular transcendental view. But still; why *idealism*? Enough reason, I think, is to be found in the considerations, rough as they are, which we have already put together, and which will serve also to tie those to certain identifiable concerns of the later Wittgenstein. Since the fact that our language is such and such, and thus that the world we live in is as it is, are, as presently construed, transcendental facts, they have no empirical explanation; anything that can be empirically explained, as that certain external features of the world are this way rather than that, or that we (as opposed to the Hopi Indians, or again as opposed to cats) see things in a certain way, or deal with things in one way rather than another – all these fall *within* the world of our language, and are not the transcendental facts. In particular, in the sense in which we are now speaking of 'our language', there could be no explanation of it, or correlation of it with the world, in sociological terms, or zoological, or materialistic, in any of the several current senses of that expression. Indeed there could not be an explanation of it which was 'idealistic', in the *explanatory* sense of that term often used, e.g. by Marxist writers, of an explanation given in terms of conditioning ideas or thoughts; for there are no ideas or thoughts outside it to condition it. However, while we could not explain it in any of those ways, we could in a way make it clearer to ourselves, by reflecting on it, as it were self-

consciously exercising it; not indeed by considering alternatives –
for what I am presently considering can have no comprehensible
alternatives to it – but by moving around reflectively inside our
view of things and sensing when one began to be near the edge by
the increasing incomprehensibility of things regarded from whatever way-out point of view one had moved into. What one would
become conscious of, in so reflecting, is something like: *how we go on.*
And *how we go on* is a matter of how we think, and speak, and
intentionally and socially conduct ourselves: that is, matters of our
experience.

As phenomenalism, regarded as a form of transcendental idealism,
gave everything in terms of something mental, though in the only
sense in which it could say that everything was mental, that statement was false; so *our* language, in this sense in which its being as
it is has no empirical explanation, shows us everything as it appears
to our interests, our concerns, our activities, though in the only sense
in which we could meaningfully say that they determined everything, that statement would be false. The fact that in this way everything can be expressed only via human interests and concerns, things
which are expressions of mind, and which themselves cannot
ultimately be explained in any further terms: that provides grounds,
I suggest, for calling such a view a kind of *idealism* (and not of the
stupid 'aggregative' kind). The history of post-Kantian philosophy
might in any case lead one to expect that there would be a place
for such a view.

3. RELATIVISM

We have here, in a vague sketch, the outline of a view. I have not
yet offered any grounds for the claim that Wittgenstein held it. In
fact, I am not going to claim anything as strong as that he held it;
it seems to me that both the nature of the view, and the nature of
the later Wittgenstein material, make it hard to substantiate any un-
qualified claim of that kind. I offer this model and its implied
connection with the earlier work as a way of looking at and assessing
that later material. But I will offer some considerations which
suggest that the influence of the sort of view I have sketched is to be
felt in the later work, and that reference to it may help to explain
some curious and unsatisfactory features of that work. In particular
it may help us to understand the curious use that Wittgenstein makes
of 'we'. To reach any understanding on that matter, we have to
approach it through the uninviting terrain of relativism.

In trying to distinguish a little while ago the transcendental version of 'the limits of our language mean the limits of our world' from an empirical version, I suggested one possible empirical version which I cavalierly labelled the Whorfian hypothesis, to the effect that language (narrowly construed) conditioned world-view (broadly construed). That was useful as an example (whether or not it represents the views of Whorf). It contains, we should now notice, three different elements. The first is that it takes language in a narrow sense, and the second is that it offers language in that sense as the explanation of the world-view. The third feature is that what are explained, or would be if there were a true such theory,[1] are various different world-views, held by different human sub-groups: there is more than one lot to call themselves 'we'. Now that of course follows from the first two points, since language in the narrow sense differs in the supposedly relevant respects between human groups. But, while still offering an empirical theory, one could drop the first point and keep the second and third: thus one would suppose that there were empirical explanations of differences in local world-view, but they did not lie in differences of language in the narrow sense.

Now as to the first point, I take it that Wittgenstein was not very interested, in these connections, in language in the narrow sense, and that he characteristically uses the term 'language' in a very extensive way, to embrace world-view rather than to stand in narrow and explanatory contradistinction to it. Hence his notoriously generous use of the expression 'language-game'; hence also, in the converse direction as it were, the tendency to use 'form of life' to refer to some quite modest linguistic practice: as Putnam[2] has justly said, '(the) fondness (of Wittgensteinians) for the expression "form of life" appears to be directly proportional to its degree of preposterousness in a given context'. The narrower sense of 'language' seems not to be an important factor in any explanations Wittgenstein would want to consider for variations of world-view between human groups. The question arises, then, of whether he is interested in any explanations at all.

I think in fact he is not basically interested in such explanations, and for a reason which I shall suggest ties up with our central question. Nevertheless at times he says things which would *prima facie* not rule out the possibility of explanation. At least, he thinks

---

[1] The references to the theory, like the references to Whorf, just function as a stand-in or dummy in the argument. I do not go into the difficulties that surround such a theory, such as that of independently characterising its explanandum.

[2] *Language, Belief and Metaphysics*, ed. Kiefer and Munitz (SUNY Press, 1970), p. 60.

that a different way of looking at and talking about the world might become comprehensible in terms of different *interests*:

> For here life would run on differently. – What interests us would not interest *them*. Here different concepts would no longer be unimaginable. In fact, this is the only way in which *essentially* different concepts are imaginable. (Z, 388)

Suggestions of a similar kind are to be found in the neighbourhood (378, 380), and in the preceding fragment a hint at a more specific kind of explanation might be detected (though hardly one which justifies what sounds like a tone of mild daring):

> I want to say an education quite different from ours might also be the foundation for quite different concepts. (Z, 387)

In the work *On Certainty*, again, we have the recognition that a 'language-game' changes over time (256), and the model of the river (96 seq.), in which some hardened propositions can form the bank, which guides other more fluid propositions, but over time new bits may accumulate and old bits be swept away – this offers the *fact* of diachronic change, and it does not exclude, even if it does not encourage, the possibility of explaining such change. Thus both over time and over social space, variety and change are possible, and, so far as this goes, presumably we might have some explanations of that variety and change. Other ways of seeing the world are not imaginatively inaccessible to us; on the contrary, it is one of Wittgenstein's aims to encourage such imagination. We can consider alternatives, as in the examples I have already mentioned – and there are of course many more in which he suggests how people with different interests and concerns might describe, classify, and see the world differently from us. Thus the different world-pictures, as so far introduced, are not inaccessible to one another; those who had one picture might come to see the point (in terms of interests, etc.) of another picture, and also perhaps come to understand why those who had it, did so. In that light, they could reflect also on their own world-picture, and understand, perhaps, something of why they had it. Thus in speaking of these various languages or world-pictures, it looks as though we are *not* speaking of things to which their subjects are, in terms of the idealism we have discussed, transcendentally related.

Now none of this yet implies anything about the *evaluative* comparability of different world-pictures. We have said that they are accessible to one another, to some extent, but that does not say anything, or anything much, about whether one could compare them with regard to adequacy. With regard, moreover, to those elements in the world-picture which purport to be truth-carrying, nothing has yet been determined about whether there is some objective basis from which one 'we' could come to recognise the greater truth of what was believed by another 'we'. But in fact, as is well known, Wittgenstein tends to say things which cast great doubt on that possibility, and not least in his last work. Thus *On Certainty* says (94):

> . . . I do not get my picture of the world [*Weltbild*] by satisfying myself of its correctness; nor do I have it because I am satisfied of its correctness. No: it is the inherited background against which I distinguish between true and false.
>
> 95. The propositions describing this world-picture might be part of a kind of mythology. And their role is like that of rules of a game; and the game can be learned purely practically, without learning any explicit rules.

And revealingly: *On Certainty*, 298:

> 'We are quite sure of it' does not mean just that every single person is certain of it, but that we belong to a community which is bound together by science and education.

There are the many remarks again which claim such things as that reasons can be given only within a game, and come to an end at the limits of the game (*PG*, 55), that our mode of representation is a language-game (*PI*, 50), that 'grammar' cannot be justified (*PB*, 7), and that the language-game is not reasonable or unreasonable, but is there, like our life (*OC*, 559). Nor is there any doubt that Wittgenstein included in the force of these remarks the kind of language-game which one human group might pursue and another lack. Thus in *On Certainty*, once more:

> 609. Suppose we met people who did not regard that (sc. the propositions of physics) as a telling reason. Now, how do we imagine this? Instead of the physicist, they consult an oracle. (And for that we consider them primitive.) Is it wrong for them to consult an oracle and be guided by it? – If we call this 'wrong' aren't we using our language-game as a base from which to *combat* theirs?
>
> 610. And are we right or wrong to combat it? Of course there are all sorts of slogans which will be used to support our proceedings
> . . .

612. I said I would 'combat' the other man, – but wouldn't I give him *reasons*? Certainly; but how far do they go? At the end of reasons comes *persuasion*. (Think of what happens when missionaries convert natives.)

Now none of this, nor its negation, will follow from the idea just of different human groups empirically co-existing with different world-pictures which are (in the earlier, unambitious, sense) accessible to one another. Nor does it follow from a view or set of views which I have not so far mentioned, but which I shall come back to briefly at the end of these remarks, namely the view which has been charted by Dummett in a number of articles to the effect that *truth* must be replaced by, or interpreted in terms of, the notion of *conditions which justify assertion*: this view I shall summarily call Wittgenstein's constructivism. While constructivism must bring enquiry and speculation to a halt in what we have been trained to perceive as an adequate ground, this entails nothing about what different human groups may or may not have been trained to perceive as such a ground, nor about what they could be trained to perceive as a ground, nor about what they would find it natural to do when confronted with conflicts with what they think they already know. Constructivism might tell us something about *human* knowledge, not about that of narrower groups.

The relativist elements which have been added to this scene are extra, and do not follow from the rest. But once they are there, they have a curious and confusing effect backwards (so to speak) on the rest. For it will be remembered that one consideration that I used in characterising a transcendental interpretation of 'the limits of our language mean the limits of our world' was that the features of our language, so conceived, were not a matter of empirical explanation; and hence, conversely, that when we were dealing with what could be empirically explained, we had no such transcendentally isolated item. But if we add the relativist views, it looks as though the question, whether something is empirically explicable or not, is itself relative to a language; for such explanation, and *a fortiori*, particular forms of scientific explanation, are just some language-games among others. Thus our view of another world-picture, as something accessible, and empirically related, to ours, may just be a function of our world-picture; as of course, may our supposed understanding of signs coming from the other group that they have the same feeling. Thus we lose hold at this level on the idea that they are *really* accessible. Once that alarm has broken out, we may indeed even begin to lose the hard-earned benefits of 'we' rather than 'I'. For if our supposed scientific understanding of the practices of other groups is to be seen merely as how those practices are *for us*, and if our experience of other forms of life is inescapably and non-trivially conditioned by our own form of life, then one might wonder what after all stops the solipsist doubt, that my experience which is supposedly of other individuals and the form of life which I share with them, cannot fail to be an experience only of how things are *for me*.

The point can be put also like this, that there is the gravest difficulty (familiar from certain positions in the philosophy of the social sciences) in both positing the independent existence of culturally distinct groups with different world-views, and also holding that any access we have to them is inescapably and non-trivially conditioned by our own world-view. For the very question from which we started, of the existence and relative accessibility of different world-views, becomes itself a function of one world-view. In fact what we have here is an exact analogue, at the social level, of aggregative solipsism.

So far as the social sciences are concerned, it is worth mentioning a certain view which is held by some followers of Wittgenstein, and which perhaps receives confused encouragement from the area we are considering. This is a view to the effect that it is possible to understand and at least piece-meal explain other outlooks, so long as the understanding is internalist and the explanation non-causal.[1] To suppose that that followed from general epistemological considerations at the level we are considering would be a muddle, representing something like aggregative solipsism (at the social level). For if relativist inaccessibility has taken over, then there are only two options: either one is submerged in, identical with an original member of, the other social system, in which case one has no explanations at all (except its own, if it happens to be self-conscious); or else one is necessarily bringing to it one's own conceptual outlook, in which case that will be no less so if what one is bringing is *Verstand* and Gestaltist redescription, than if one is bringing causal explanation. Of course, there may be other good reasons for preferring the former type of explanation; but the project cannot just follow from some relativist story about the plurality of human language-games, as seems sometimes to be supposed.

The relativist elements introduce a persistent uncertainty in the interpretation of 'we', which not only makes the application of Wittgenstein's views unclear, but makes it unclear what kind of

[1] Itself, of course, an idealist view, in what I earlier called the 'explanatory' sense of the term.

views they are. His references to conceptual change and to the different outlooks of different groups have a persistent vagueness which leaves it unclear how much room there is supposed to be for explanation. I earlier mentioned various cases in which Wittgenstein at least seemed to leave room for the possibility of explanation; but the range or determinacy of the explanations he left room for were, so far as the suggestions offered there went, exceedingly low – thus Wittgenstein referred sometimes in the weakest terms to what other people might find interesting, or related their practice in some broadly functional way to their interests. In some part, no doubt, these features of the work are owed to Wittgenstein's hatred of the cockiness of natural science, something which seems to me not easy in his case to distinguish from a hatred of natural science. His use of Gestaltist illumination can stun, rather than assist, further and more systematic explanation; to adapt a remark of Kreisel's,[1] when the child asks why the people on the other side of the world don't fall off, many would give an explanation in terms of gravity acting towards the centre of the earth; but Wittgenstein would draw a circle with a pin man on it, turn it round, and say, 'now *we* fall into space'.

Beyond that, however, the difficulties we have now run into raise the question of whether Wittgenstein is really thinking at all in terms of actual groups of human beings whose activities we might want to understand and explain. I think the answer to that is basically 'no'; we are not concerned so much with the epistemology of differing world-views, still less with the methodology of the social sciences, but with ways of exploring our world-view. We are concerned with the imagination; and vaguely functionalist remarks we noticed before are not the sketch of an explanation, but an aid to the imagination, to make a different practice a more familiar idea to us, and hence to make us more conscious of the practice we have. Seen in this light, the alternatives are not the sort of socially actual alternatives, relativistically inaccessible or not, which we have been discussing; nor are they offered as possible objects of any kind of explanation. Rather, the business of considering them is part of finding our way around inside our own view, feeling our way out to the points at which we begin to lose our hold on it (or it, its hold on us), and things begin to be hopelessly strange to us. The imagined alternatives are not alternatives *to* us; they are alternatives *for* us, markers of how far we might go and still remain within our

[1] G. Kreisel, 'Wittgenstein's Theory and Practice of Philosophy', *British Journal for the Philosophy of Science*, xi (1960) pp. 238-52. Kreisel's own use of the point goes further than anything suggested here, and in a rather different direction.

world – a world leaving which would not mean that we saw something different, but just that we ceased to see.

4. NON-RELATIVIST IDEALISM

Relativism, then, is not really the issue. While the 'we' of Wittgenstein's remarks often looks like the 'we' of our group as contrasted with other human groups, that is basically misleading. Such a 'we' is not his prime concern, and even if one grants such views as the 'justified assertion' doctrine, the determination of meaning by social practice and so on, all of that leaves it open, how much humanity *shares* in the way of rational practice. Nor is it just a question of a final relativisation of 'we' to humanity; for we cannot exclude the possibility of other language-using creatures whose picture of the world might be accessible to us. It must, once more, be an empirical question what degree of conceptual isolation is represented by what groups in the universe – groups *with* which we would be in the universe. If they are groups with which we are in the universe, and we can understand that fact (namely, that they are groups with a language, etc.), then they also *belong* to 'we'. Thus, while much is said by Wittgenstein about the meanings *we* understand being related to *our* practice, and so forth, that *we* turns out only superficially and sometimes to be one *we* as against others *in* the world, and thus the sort of *we* which has one practice as against others which are possible in the world. Leaving behind the confused and confusing language of relativism, one finds oneself with a *we* which is not one group rather than another in the world at all, but rather the plural descendant of that idealist *I* who also was not one item rather than another in the world.

But if that is the kind of *we* one is concerned with, it would, again, not follow (at least from this very general level of consideration) that any limit could be placed in advance on the scientific understanding of human practice and human meanings. For if we empirically differ from other groups in the universe with regard to the world-picture we have, then it might be possible to find an explanation of that difference, in terms of our differing evolution, our situation in different environments in the universe, or whatever. But if we could do that for ourselves (that is, humanity) if there turned out to be others to compare ourselves with, then it could not be impossible, though it might be harder, to do it for ourselves without our knowing of others, or without there being others. Even if we, humanity, were the only lot in the world, a transcendental idealism of the first-person plural could not rule out in itself the possibility of an empirical or scientific understanding of why, as persons who have evolved in a particular way on a particular planet, we have the kind of world-picture we have – even though such an explanation would, once more, have to lie within the limits of our language, in the only sense of 'our' in which they would mean the limits of our world. But if all that is possible, there is little left of the thought that those limits are *limits* at all: it might turn out with this sort of idealism, too, that 'when its implications are followed out strictly, it coincides with pure realism'.

Yet when that was so in the *Tractatus* case, the work itself, notoriously and professedly, tried nevertheless to go beyond it. I will end by suggesting that the later work may be seen also as trying to do that, or rather not preventing itself from doing that, with its own elements of a pluralised idealism. This concerns what I earlier called the 'constructivism'. This has many roots, particularly in the theory of knowledge, which I shall not try to say anything about. But a central thought it contains is one that can be put by saying that our sentences have the meaning we give them, and from that some important consequences are supposed to follow, with regard to their logic not being able to determine reality beyond, so to speak, what was put into it in the first place. Relatedly, the notion of 'truth' is to be replaced by, or interpreted in terms of, an appeal to the conditions which have been determined to be appropriate for the assertion of a given sentence.[1] But it is not easy to see, at least at first, how if this set of views is not a triviality, which has no important consequences at all, it can avoid having quite amazing consequences. For consider the following argument-schema, which I have discussed in a slightly different form elsewhere:[2]

> (i) 'S' has the meaning we give it.
> (ii) A necessary condition of our giving 'S' a meaning is Q.
> *ergo* (iii) Unless Q, 'S' would not have a meaning.
> (iv) If 'S' did not have a meaning, 'S' would not be true.
> *ergo* (v) Unless Q, 'S' would not be true.

It looks as though there should be something wrong with this argument, since any number of substitutions for Q in (ii) which relate to human existence, language use, etc., make it true for any 'S' one likes, and since (i) is supposedly true for any 'S', and (iv) for any true 'S', we can get the truth of any true 'S' dependent on

[1] See M. Dummett, 'Wittgenstein's Philosophy of Mathematics', *Phil. Rev.* (1959), reprinted in *The Philosophical Investigations, Critical Essays*, ed. Pitcher (New York: Doubleday, 1966).

[2] 'Knowledge and Meaning in the Philosophy of Mind', *Phil. Rev.*, lxxv (1966), reprinted in *Problems of the Self* (Cambridge, 1973).

human existence etc.; that is, prove unrestricted idealism. Now on some traditional views, there is no need to find anything wrong with the argument in order to avoid this, since (i) will be taken to be true just in case ' "S" ' names a sentence, and in that case (v) can be harmlessly true, as meaning 'Unless Q, "S" would not express a truth', and that of course will not entail: Unless Q, not S. But it is not obvious that for later Wittgensteinian views, and in particular for the theory of justified assertion, we can so easily drive a line between the sentence 'S' expressing the truth, and what is the case if S. Wittgenstein does indeed sometimes speak in these connections as though he were talking simply about the sentences of natural languages, and produces some very odd results, as at *PI*, I, 381:

> How do I know that this colour is red? – It would be an answer to say: 'I have learnt English'.

which is a translation of

> Wie erkenne ich, daß diese Farbe Rot ist? – Eine Antwort wäre: 'Ich habe Deutsch gelernt'.

But at least that is a case of someone's *knowing* something, and the difficulties, though revealing, are comparatively superficial. But if we are considering what would be true if . . ., and if we are to replace the notion of truth-conditions with that of assertion-conditions, and if we are to grant, what Wittgenstein surely holds, that for anything to have come to be an assertion-condition for a given sentence involves certainly a human practice, and perhaps a human decision; then something has to be done if we are to avoid even empirical idealism. The obvious thing to do is to regard talk about what would be the case if there were no human beings, language, etc., as talk about what *would* justify the assertion of certain sentences which we do understand (of which the assertion-conditions are fixed). That banishes the empirical idealism, since it removes any reference to convention-fixing from the hypothetical unpopulated scene, nor does it record any piece of convention-fixing. But it would give reason to reflect that any given supposition is determinate only because, on the theory, there is at some point a decision to count certain conditions as adequate for assertion. That reflection is more radical, and is meant to be more radical, than the banal thought in standing back from a sentence describing a non-human event, that if there were no human events there would be no such sentence. The point comes out rather in the thought that the determinacy of reality comes from what we have decided or are prepared to count as determinate:

> We have a colour system as we have a number system. Do the systems reside in *our* nature or in the nature of things? How are we to put it? – *Not* in the nature of things. (*Z*, 357)

The diffidence about how to put it comes once more from a problem familiar in the *Tractatus*: how to put a supposed philosophical truth which, if it is uttered, must be taken to mean an empirical falsehood, or worse. For of course, if our talk about the numbers has been determined by our decisions, then one result of our decisions is that it must be nonsense to say that anything about a number has been determined by our decisions. The dependence of mathematics on our decisions, in the only sense in which it obtains – for clearly there cannot be meant an empirical dependence on historical decisions – is something which shows itself in what we are and are not prepared to regard as sense and is not to be stated in remarks about decisions; and similarly in other cases. The new theory of meaning, like the old, points in the direction of a transcendental idealism, and shares also the problem of our being driven to state it in forms which are required to be understood, if at all, in the wrong way.

7

WITTGENSTEIN, SCHOPENHAUER, AND ETHICS[1]

A. Phillips Griffiths

WITTGENSTEIN always thought that he had not been understood, and indeed that it was very unlikely that many people ever would understand him. Russell not only failed to understand Wittgenstein's later work; according to Wittgenstein himself, Russell profoundly failed to understand even the *Tractatus*. Professor Anscombe[2] says even she did not understand him, and that to attempt to give an account of what he says is only to express one's own ordinariness or mediocrity or lack of complexity. Certainly, most people[3] acquainted with the *Tractatus*, when that work was Wittgenstein's only published book, gave it what now seems a quite crass positivistic interpretation. Wittgenstein's own preface to the *Tractatus*, despite its last sentence, does not help.[4] He does tell us that the whole sense of the work is that what can be said can be said clearly, and what we cannot talk about we must consign to silence: but this does not make it clear that what we cannot talk about is all that is really important. Even when one has realised all this, however, one is aware mostly of one's failure to understand; and that if one did get any distance in understanding the last sixth of the *Tractatus*, the process would be extremely difficult, and the results quite astonishing.

What most of us would take ethics to be about is how we should act, and what attitudes we should adopt to others and to our lives

---

[1] References in parentheses in the text of the form I. 25 or II. 25 are to the first and second volumes of Schopenhauer, *The World as Will and Representation*, trans. Payne (New York: Dover, 1969) followed by the page number.

[2] *LLW*, p. xiv.

[3] But not, I think, the composer Elizabeth Lutyens.

[4] 'What lies on the other side of the limit will be simply nonsense' (*TLP*, p. 27).

and to what happens to us. It cannot be radically divorced from politics, or perhaps one should say broad social issues. And it is no use, unless it can say something to this or that person in this or that condition, with this or that character or social place; it must speak to a man as he is in the midst of things. Wittgenstein said that the aim of the *Tractatus* was an ethical one;[1] yet the little he has to say about ethics at the end of the *Tractatus* is astonishing, in that for Wittgenstein ethics seems absolutely not to be about what most of us would take it to be about. In the *Tractatus* Wittgenstein says that ethics and aesthetics are one and the same (*TLP*, 6.421), and I think he really does mean identical, not merely the same in respect of being transcendental. But in the *Notebooks* he does make something of a distinction when he says 'The work of art is the object seen *sub specie aeternitatis;* and the good life is the world seen *sub specie aeternitatis.* This is the connection between art and ethics' (*NB*, 7.10.16; cf. I, 178). Here the object of aesthetics is the work of art, that of ethics, the good life. My attitude is an aesthetic one when the object, the work of art, is seen not 'from the midst' of objects but from outside. To see an object from the midst of objects, the usual way of seeing it, is to see it as at a certain distance from oneself, and in a changing relation to oneself and other things. To see it *sub specie aeternitatis* is to see it as placed in relation to the whole ('together with the whole logical space' (*NB*, 7.10.16)) and not in relation to some particular thing rather than another, such as oneself. My attitude is an ethical one when I look at the good life not as a possible life of this body with its history and its future and its individual wants and wishes, but as a life with no particular pre-eminence embedded in all life. Life and the world are one: so ethics and aesthetics are one. Life simply is the world as the object of will (*TLP*, 5.621), that will which is the bearer of ethical predicates (*NB*, 21.7.16). So what ethics is about is a will which is not in the world and therefore cannot be spoken about; it is not in any way about how we should act, what attitudes we should adopt to others and to our lives and to what happens to us; it does not speak to a man as he is in the midst of things.

But it may be objected that Wittgenstein surely is talking about what attitudes we should adopt. The attitude we should adopt to others and our lives and what happens to us is acceptance. He addresses the injunction 'be happy' to himself.

But this is not like any ordinary ethical injunction. It is nothing like a prescription of hedonism or eudaemonism. The world is

[1] *LLW*, p. 143.

independent of my will (*TLP*, 6.373); it is, as life, the object of a will alien to me (*NB*, 8.7.16). A man cannot make himself happy without further ado (*NB*, 14.7.16): indeed one wonders whether anything could count as a man making himself happy at all. It is not that one must set about doing anything, for example doing good. For that involves having particular attitudes towards particular persons. Yet in most people's conceptions of ethics, the attitudes it is about are to this person rather than that, to our and others' particular different lives and to what particularly happens, and our attitudes will be different according to the difference between the particulars. Whereas the attitude Wittgenstein is talking about is not an attitude to this or that but to the whole; it is not only the life of knowledge rather than action, it is the life of knowledge that is happy in spite of the misery of the world (*NB*, 13.8.16), because the misery is in so many particulars. The life that is happy has the right attitude to the world as a whole: it is the life which sees the world *sub specie aeternitatis* and is content, *whatever it might be*.

One might try to escape from thinking of Wittgenstein's view as so extraordinary by saying that when he speaks of ethics he is not talking about what we are talking about at all: that as it were we can go on thinking ethically, regarding Wittgenstein as dealing with something quite other, the mystical, recondite and irrelevant, leaving everything else as it is. But this would be a complete mistake.

When Wittgenstein says the ethical attitude is mystical (*TLP*, 6.45) he means, not that when he speaks of ethics he speaks of the mystical rather than ethics, but that the only ethics there can be is of the mystical. There *are no* ethics about what most of us would take ethics to be about.

In trying to grasp Wittgenstein's position it is worth while trying to retrace some of his steps toward it, and it may be helpful to do so by taking as Wittgenstein's starting point the Schopenhauerian position. There is plenty of justification for this (as will appear below) both in the *Notebooks* and in the *Tractatus*, for while there is only one reference to Schopenhauer by name[1] in the *Notebooks*, some of the remarks there, some of which are repeated in the *Tractatus*, are so exactly Schopenhauerian as to appear almost culled from the text.

Wittgenstein reports his own progress as follows. 'This is the way I have travelled: Idealism singles out men from the world as unique, solipsism singles me alone out, and at last I see that I too

---

[1] Engelmann seems to suggest that this was deliberate (*LLW*, p. 106).

belong with the rest of the world, and so on one side *nothing* is left over, and on the other side, as unique, *the world*. In this way, idealism leads to realism if it is strictly thought out' (*NB*, 15.10.16).[1]

At first sight Schopenhauer's idealism is not based on the uniqueness of man, but on the uniqueness of consciousness, which is common to man and beasts. Any world must be a world for consciousness and the world only comes into being when the first conscious eye opens. Nevertheless Man *is* unique, and for the world of natural science the first conscious eye must be a human one. Wittgenstein remarks that it is only from his consciousness that religion, science and art arise (*NB*, 1.8.16). For Schopenhauer too, it is only in man that consciousness makes religion, art and science, or indeed that philosophy within which idealism is grasped, possible. Only man can through his ideas grasp an object as an object of pure knowledge, as opposed to an object which is of interest only in so far as it satisfies or opposes a particular will, which is what all objects are for animals (I, 36ff). Only man has science, for only man has concepts (I, 39ff) and science is the attempt to provide general descriptions of the world in terms of organising concepts (a view reminiscent of Wittgenstein's in *TLP*, 6.342ff and particularly *TLP*, 6.371, though Wittgenstein does not make use of the notion of a concept here). The beasts have no notion of the past or the future. They remember, to be sure: that is, their present experience is modified by their past experience. But all that they are at any point aware of is their *present* experience. Man on the other hand has an awareness of past and future, and hence of the connection of past and future events. This is essential to science; but even so, it can lead to nothing more than the endless chase after such connections in the infinite past and unending future, with the danger of believing that we have found some ultimate explanations when we have merely come to an arbitrary stopping point: a common contemporary illusion inferior to the wisdom of the ancients (I, 119ff; II, 176; cf. *TLP*, 6.372). The beasts live only in the present; man lives in time, but only man can grasp that space and time are no more than the conditions of his consciousness, and thus reach the notion of the whole given world in time and space, that is nothing in itself: we grasp the Idea of the world as a whole, in that present which is eternity, and thus reach the level of the philosophical. And it is only at this level that we reach 'that disposition of the mind which leads to holiness and salvation from the world' (I, 274). At this philosophical level I grasp that the world is mere representation, a

---

[1] See also *TLP*, 5.64 and *NB*, 2.9.16.

world of past and future real only to me in the present. It is a world in which there were conscious trilobites, in which there were once only unthinking rocks, but it has being only because it is a world for a thinking subject in the present.

There is a thinking subject only because there is a world in evolution which at a certain point produced man. The world does not end with my death or begin with my birth, because there are others than myself who are the thinking subject. It is one and the same thinking subject for whom there is this one world in all men; yet I as subject am distinct from my neighbour. The world as representation requires the thinking subject, because only the structure of mind can supply relation and hence the multiplicity of the world. But this philosophical necessity requires no more than one thinking subject; so from the point of view of this philosophical necessity, all thinking subjects are one and the same. Yet, while the world is nothing but idea and idea for one thinking subject, I am undeniably not you. How then am I individuated?

Schopenhauer says that the truth of idealism was first enunciated by Berkeley (I, 3). Berkeley has the same problem. If all is either perceiver or perceived, why more than one perceiver? His answer is also Schopenhauer's: I am aware that some of my ideas are subject to my will, and attribute all others to other perceiving beings: in the case of Berkeley, other persons and God. Now Berkeley can try to refute solipsism by saying: you explain *some* of your ideas by your will: but since ideas themselves are inactive, those which are not explained by your own will must be attributed to another's. But this argument against solipsism was not open to Schopenhauer. Schopenhauer thinks solipsism cannot be refuted, though this does not matter because those who seriously believe in it are to be found only in lunatic asylums (I, 104). This is because while Schopenhauer can explain how it makes sense to individuate minds in terms of the notion of will, his notion of will is different from Berkeley's, and hence cannot be used to show that there are thinking beings other than myself.

Schopenhauer says 'Spinoza says that if a stone projected through the air had consciousness, it would imagine it was flying of its own will. I add merely that the stone would be right' (I, 126). Thus he turns Spinoza on his head: Spinoza thinks of 'acting of its own will' as an illusion of ignorance; Schopenhauer thinks everything acts of its own will. Determinism applies only to representation, not will: will is that which lies behind every particular fact, making it what it is, and we vainly try to explain what things are in terms of notions like force, where no explanation is possible: except that the will wills what it wills (cf. again *TLP*, 6.371 and 6.372). However, Man is again unique, and can form a concept of himself as an individual man, because only he is aware in himself of the same thing which is in the flying stone but of which the flying stone is not aware: his own action. To will is nothing but to act, to move. Willing is not something which precedes action or accompanies it: it is it (cf. *NB*, 4.11.16, p. 88), and the only difference here between myself and the stone is that I am immediately aware of my own action in a way that I am not immediately aware of the stone's, which I know mediately only as the stone affects my sensibility. This is sufficient to give me the notion of myself as an individual: I am that, distinct from other things, which I am immediately aware of as acting: I am that representation among all my other representations, my body. From this I can form the notion of other individuals like me, but unlike the stone, that is other individuals who also have this awareness. But nothing could prove any other being is such an individual, though if I seriously doubt this I will be a lunatic.

Solipsism, or theoretical egoism as Schopenhauer calls it, is he says like a small frontier fortress in the advance of philosophy (I, 104). The fortress is impregnable, but the garrison can never sally forth from it, and therefore we can pass it by and leave it without danger. Was it from this fortress that Wittgenstein sallied forth when he moved from idealism to solipsism in his journey to realism? Surely not: Wittgenstein did not think that all psychological facts were about himself. The truth of solipsism is connected for Wittgenstein with the thought that the limits of my language are the limits of my world. This language is characterised by Wittgenstein as 'the language which I alone understand' (*TLP*, 5.62). There has been some dispute[1] about whether 'alone' here qualifies 'which' or 'I', that is whether Wittgenstein meant 'the language only I understand' or 'the only language I understand'. Immediately after the observation 'The limits of my language are the limits of my world' (*NB*, 23.5.15) Wittgenstein remarks 'There really is only one world soul, which I for preference call my soul, and as which alone I conceive what I call the soul of others'. Oddly enough this remark presents the same difficulty of interpretation. He cannot have meant here that he, Wittgenstein, as opposed to any other human being, so conceived the souls of others. We must either say that Wittgenstein uses 'alone' to qualify not himself, but in the

---

[1] See G. E. M. Anscombe, *An Introduction to Wittgenstein's Tractatus*, 4th ed. (Hutchinson Home University Library, 1971), p. 167n.; Max Black, *A Companion to Wittgenstein's Tractatus*, p. 309; J. Hintikka, 'On Wittgenstein's Solipsism', *Mind*, LXVII (1958) p. 88.

former case the language he understands and in the latter case what he calls the souls of others; or assume that throughout 'I' refers to the thinking subject, in which case each interpretation comes to the same thing. In either case, it is surely clear that Wittgenstein is not in Schopenhauer's frontier fortress, thinking that the only soul is his, Wittgenstein's soul; but rather that the only soul is his and everyone else's soul. And this is of course Schopenhauer's position; he says '. . . the subject, does not lie in space and time, for it is whole and undivided in every representing being. Hence a single one of these beings with the object completes the world as representation just as fully as do the millions that exist. And if that single one were to disappear, then the world as representation would no longer exist' (I, 5). Wittgenstein's further remark (*NB*, 23.5.15, p. 46) that in describing the world completely, I never mention the thinking subject, is also a doctrine of Schopenhauer's, to the extent that the relations of time, space and causality which govern all objects cannot hold between the subject and those objects. But it is at this point that Schopenhauer and Wittgenstein diverge, and Wittgenstein takes his step to realism.

For Schopenhauer there *is* a reason in which if I am to describe the world completely I must mention the thinking subject; for the thinking subject has a nature which determines not that the world is, but how it is (I, 125). All objects stand in necessary relations to all others as determined and determining according to the principle of sufficient reason in time, space and causality. But these necessary relations, according to Schopenhauer, following Kant, are nothing but the forms of all knowledge lying within the thinking subject. But for Wittgenstein 'Empirical reality is limited by the totality of objects. The limit also makes itself manifest in the totality of elementary propositions' (*TLP*, 5.5561). The knowing subject supplies nothing which limits the world *a priori*; the forms of all objects do not lie within it. 'Whatever we see could be other than it is. Whatever we can describe at all could be other than it is. There is no *a priori* order of things' (*TLP*, 5.634). What objects, and what elementary propositions, there may be, is not given by logic, but by the *application* of logic (*TLP*, 5.557) to meaningful propositions, that is propositions which are the only ones I understand. Only that language I understand and is thereby my language can lead me through analysis to elementary facts and to the real substance of the world. Beyond this truth there is nothing that can be known about the world by any consideration of the metaphysical subject (so that is *how much* truth there is in solipsism). The attempts to draw limits *a priori* to what can be known or thought by a consideration of the nature of the thinking subject as in Kant or Schopenhauer is therefore totally misconceived. The thinking subject is not an object of experience, as Schopenhauer agreed, but it is not a limit on experience – on empirical reality – either. So the thinking subject does not exist; or, at least, emptied of its *a priori* forms it has shrunk 'to an extensionless point'; even the limited immanence allowed it by Schopenhauer is denied and it has become completely transcendental. But it shows itself, above all in aesthetics where the object is seen as surrounded by the world as an object of contemplation as a whole.

For Schopenhauer Man, in knowing himself as a thinking subject, does not know himself as he is in himself. He knows himself as he is in himself in being conscious of his will. But this is to be conscious of an aspect of that blind will which gives rise both to the thinking subject and to empirical reality. The thinking subject is *in* the world which is the manifestation of will. For Wittgenstein, the thinking subject is not a part of the world, but its limit: it is now as metaphysical, as real or unreal, as the will. For Wittgenstein now aesthetics and ethics can be one in a way that they cannot for Schopenhauer.

For Wittgenstein, the disappearance from the world of the thinking subject does not of course mean the disappearance of thoughts or thinking from the world. Wittgenstein's book, *The World as I Found It* would contain psychological propositions (e.g. *TLP*, 2.1). Also he says that it would contain 'a report on my body, and should have to say which parts were subordinate to my will, and which were not etc.' (*TLP*, 5.631). This would be 'a method of isolating the subject or rather of showing that in an important sense there is no subject'. Now according to Schopenhauer, the human individual individuates himself as a willing, rather than a thinking subject, as having a will which is opposed to other wills. But for Wittgenstein the disappearance of the willing subject is also the disappearance of the individual will; his book would have to report that no parts of his body were subject to his will. In Wittgenstein's book there are still thoughts and thinking (if not thinking subjects (*TLP*, 5.542, 5.5421)) but not willing. There is an illusion of will in the notion of free will: that I can do this or that in future contingencies (*TLP*, 5.1362, 6.374). It is an illusion that I can bring anything about. The world is the totality of elementary facts, and there is nothing in any one fact to explain another (which could do for the will). The will therefore cannot be attached to any particular object in the world; to speak of my will can only be to speak of the world will, which wills that this is how things stand.

As the transition from solipsism to realism robs any particular facts of pre-eminence ('Whoever realises this will not want to procure a pre-eminent place for his own body or the human body. He will regard humans and animals quite naively as objects which are similar and which belong together.' This must not be taken as an attempt to raise the status of our feathered friends. '. . . a part of the world among others, among animals, plants, stones, etc., etc.' (*NB*, 2.9.16)) so the realisation that the will does not exist in the world robs every particular fact of any pre-eminence of value; indeed of any value, for the will is indifferently related to each of the totality of facts. Thus everything has value, but not this or that. Schopenhauer says 'Every knowing individual is therefore in truth, and finds himself as, the whole will-to-live, or as the in-itself of the world itself, and also as the complementary condition of the world as representation, consequently as a microcosm to be valued equally with the macrocosm' (II, 332). For Schopenhauer this is the principal source of suffering, and on a right view neither has value; but for Wittgenstein the value of the macrocosm remains.

At the beginning of his extended and tortuous consideration of will in the *Notebooks* Wittgenstein asks 'What really is the situation of the human will? I will call will first and foremost the bearer of good and evil' (21.7.16). The world will, of which it is impossible to speak, is what, in *Tractatus*, 6.423, is the bearer of ethical attributes. Yet in 6.43 Wittgenstein speak of good and bad acts; and it seems clear that Wittgenstein wants it to be possible at least in some sense for me to think ethically in relation to myself, even in such a way that an ethical law 'Thou shalt' can be addressed to me, so that my acts merit punishment or reward (*TLP*, 6.422). Again in the *Notebooks* (8.7.16) he speaks of fear in the face of death as the sign of a false, i.e. bad will. The world will cannot be a will of that which can fear; he must be speaking here of a man's will. Again in the last entry of the *Notebooks* (10.1.17) Wittgenstein speaks of what might be allowed or not allowed, and of sin; though nothing is not allowed if suicide is not allowed, and a doubt is expressed that suicide is either good or evil.

Indeed from what Wittgenstein has already said such a doubt is surely in place. For so far as suicide is an event in the world, it is a fact among facts, and no fact explains any other fact: it just is. That the facts are the facts, is the product of the alien will, but the alien will wills the world as a whole, not some particular thing in it such as my not killing myself. If I am to kill myself, then I can contemplate this *sub specie aeternitatis* with the same acceptance as everything else. That I want to die, and die, and this is somehow connected with its being suicide rather than simply death, cannot be relevant. My wanting is a psychological state in the world alongside others, and anyway has no necessary connection with what happens. Wittgenstein has earlier marked the possibility (*NB*, 29.7.16) that one can want and yet not be unhappy if the want does not attain fulfilment: that is, one can contemplate the want and its non-fulfilment with acceptance. And if that is possible, one can want to kill oneself and kill oneself, or want not to kill oneself and kill oneself, or want to kill oneself and not kill oneself, or want not to kill oneself and not kill oneself; and, whichever it turns out to be, one can accept. There is also of course the further possibility of neither wanting, nor not wanting, to kill oneself, and either killing or not killing oneself. Wittgenstein asks whether perhaps in general that is best: that is, whatever one does or happens, not wanting at all. But immediately afterwards he says he is making crude mistakes (*NB*, 29.7.16). And he surely could not maintain this, because wanting is an experience, a fact, among facts, and a fact in the world willed as a whole.

Perhaps we should not be surprised that a philosopher who made it a cardinal point that nothing ethical can be said, fails to provide us with things we can ethically say. But something is supposed to be shown, and though as I said at the beginning Wittgenstein would be surprised if he succeeded in the case of ordinary persons such as oneself, it is worth persisting in the effort to grasp what it is that has been shown. The attempt is necessarily self-defeating since as soon as one articulates something it cannot be right; nevertheless Wittgenstein himself thought that such pseudo-propositions could be elucidatory. Something is supposed to be shown to us as individuals; not merely that the common conception of ethics is an illusion, but something of what the ethics that cannot be spoken of is like. Just as the disappearance of the thinking subject from the world means that I can have no synthetic *a priori* knowledge of the world, so the disappearance of the will from the world means that I can have no synthetic *a priori* ethical laws to direct me in the world. Yet it is still somehow as if I can be aware of the sphere of the ethical applying to myself. I shall first attack the question of how this can begin to be possible, and afterwards deal with some more particular ethical questions and how Wittgenstein's remarks connect with more common conceptions.

In the *Tractatus* (6.433) Wittgenstein suggests we can speak or not speak of the will in two ways: first, in the way we cannot speak, of the world will; second, of this or that man's will, which is of interest only to psychology. He does so in the last explanation attached to 6.42 'And so it is impossible for there to be propositions of ethics'.

The will which would be the subject of ethical propositions cannot
be spoken of. On the other hand, this or that man's will, regarded
as a fact in the world, cannot be the subject of ethical attributes;
for (*TLP*, 6.4). 'All propositions are of equal value'. All that happens
is accidental, meaningless; hence if anything is to have value or
meaning it must lie outside the world as of course the higher will
does.

Now consider 6.43:
If good or bad acts of will do alter the world, it can only be
the limits of the world that they alter, not the facts, not what
can be expressed by means of language.
In short their effect must be that it becomes an altogether
different world. It must, so to speak, wax and wane as a whole.
The world of the happy man is a different one from that of the
unhappy man.

Wittgenstein seems to be saying what would have to be the case
if we were to make acts the subject of ethical attributes: that is,
how it would be if it were possible for a man to think ethically in
relation to himself, that is with respect to his own acts. From the
Notebooks it is clear that Wittgenstein thinks that the will has to have
an object. If we speak of willing in the world, then the object of
that will is the intended action itself (*NB*, 4.11.16). Now, does the
will in so far as it is the will of a particular individual have to be
with respect to only part of the world as its object? He says that it
looks as if this is so: 'as if one part of the world were closer to me
than another (which would be intolerable)' and again 'the will
would not confront the world as its equivalent, which must be
impossible!' Now what is impossible, is that the higher will should
not confront the world as its equivalent. But that one part of the
world should be closer to me than another is not impossible, but
intolerable: and this surely means ethically intolerable.[1] Wittgenstein never explicitly answers the question as to whether my will
must always be directed to the particular, but it seems clear that he
does not, in a certain sense, think so. How could it be otherwise?
Well, in a particular person the object of the will is the intended
action itself. Now the intended action must be determined by the
agent's description of it; so the intended actions available to me
are limited only by the descriptions available to me. Now suppose I

[1] Cf. Wittgenstein in a letter to Engelmann: '. . . I am in a state of mind that is
terrible to me. I have been through it several times before: it is the state of *not
being able to get over a particular fact*' (*LLW*, p. 33).

intend to eat an egg. My description of what I am doing need refer only to a small part of the facts. But what if I propose to eat an egg *sub specie aeternitatis*? That is to say, if I see myself eating an egg not just in relation to a few facts, but seeing my eating an egg as simply one, and no pre-eminent one, of the limited totality of facts. If in aesthetics it is possible to regard the object together with the whole of logical space, then it should equally be possible in ethics so to regard my action. My attitude then is not just to the egg, or the satisfaction of my own hunger, but to the totality of facts: my will now confronts the world as its equivalent. I do God's will because my will and God's will are now identical.

The trouble with this is that this description of my intended action is not really available to me at all: for I cannot refer to the limited totality of facts; I cannot stand outside the world and talk about it. However, the higher will, which is the subject of ethical attributes, cannot be spoken about: so, if there is any way of imagining myself characterising my own acts ethically, it will be to the degree that I cannot speak about my own will either.

But for the moment, continuing to speak as we cannot speak, it seems that it is only in this way that one could make one's own will the subject of ethical attributes. My acts then will be good or bad, but in relation to the world and not any particular facts. They will be conceived of as making a difference to the world as a whole: to its limits rather than to any part of it. But how on earth could I, by a particular act, alter the limits of the world? I can try to understand what Wittgenstein says here only by making some very radical assumptions: what I now say is no more than a speculation which has only the very dubious backing that I cannot personally think of anything else.

So far as acts are good or bad, their effect must be that the world becomes altogether different. 'It must, so to speak, wax and wane as a whole.' Well, how *is* this 'so to speak'? In the *Notebooks* Wittgenstein explains this waxing and waning 'as if by accession or loss of meaning' (5.7.16). To wane is to lose meaning. The meaning of the world is what it says; and of course part of the problem is that the totality of facts have nothing other than themselves to say anything about (but in so far as it has meaning it must say something beyond itself: because the meaning is not to be found in the whole of the natural sciences). At any rate, by my good or bad acts the world means more or less to me, and is different for me in the way that the world of the happy man is different from the world of the unhappy man. What I have said so far suggests something very unplausible: that Wittgenstein thought that the meaning of the world could have a

E

degree, which is quite incompatible with everything else he says concerning meaning. Perhaps part of this implausibility could be removed if I were to make the following radical and quite bold, not to say unfounded, assumption: that here Wittgenstein is talking about the world *for a man* or *for me* in a radically subjective sense, quite different from the objective real world which is found in the truth of solipsism. Ethical attributes properly apply to the higher will: how then can I apply them to my, subjective will? The meaning of the world is the meaning of the higher, objective world. If my world is *the* world it has *its* meaning; if it is not it has less meaning. It is my subjective world which must wax and wane.

If ethical attributes apply to the higher will, then they can only be such attributes as 'good', 'perfect', etc. The higher will cannot be bad. The higher will is God's will, and Wittgenstein might have said, as he later indeed did say,[1] that God's will is good because it is God's will, not because there is something good which God wills. God's will is good, whatever it is. My will is good in so far as it is like God's will, willing the object of God's will, whatever it is. In so far as it is not good, the world has less meaning for me.

All this would appear to rule out any answer to the ethical questions a man 'in the midst of things' might ask. Nevertheless in the *Notebooks* Wittgenstein does raise some specific issues. I shall look at two of these in the light of what has so far been said, and in passing suggest that ordinary ethical attitudes can be to some extent accounted for from Wittgenstein's position. But first I shall digress to consider the relation between Wittgenstein's and Schopenhauer's ethics, for this will allow us to throw some light on what follows.

For Wittgenstein, the world and life are one (*TLP*, 5.621) and life is the object of the higher will, to which ethical attributes apply: and the only ethical attribute which could apply to the higher will is 'good'. Schopenhauer thought life is evil, and if there is any good for me it is to escape it. Mere suicide is valueless: life still goes on. It seems a man must seek a personal Nirvana, when life, not just the will in him, would become nothing. How different Wittgenstein's position is from Schopenhauer's may be seen from the fact that Wittgenstein's prescription is to live happily, while only he who lives not in time but in the present is happy (*NB*, 8.7.16). Schopenhauer says '. . . just as life, the will's own phenomenon, is certain to the will, so also is the present, the sole form of actual life. . . . Therefore whoever is satisfied with life as it is, whoever affirms it in every way, can confidently regard it as endless, and can banish the

---

[1] See R. Rhees, 'Some Developments in Wittgenstein's View of Ethics' *Philosophical Review*, LXXIV (1965) pp. 17–20.

fear of death as a delusion.' But Schopenhauer is far from *recommending* this attitude: no phenomenal being *can* be satisfied with life as it is. There nearly always is great pain for man, and the only alternative is boredom. The higher the being in the animal kingdom, the greater its pain; in man, because he has knowledge, it is greatest. To escape it is to become less than human. Schopenhauer says of any 'theory that the greatest *wisdom* consists in enjoying the present and making this enjoyment the goal of life, because the present is all that is real and everything else merely imaginary' that 'you could just as well call this mode of life the greatest *folly*: for that which in a moment ceases to exist, which vanishes as completely as a dream, cannot be worth any serious effort.'[1]

Despite this ultimate difference between them, it is obvious that Wittgenstein was tremendously influenced by Schopenhauer in these matters, as the example I have just given shows. Indeed a great deal of Schopenhauer's ethical thinking seems to have been incorporated almost unchanged into Wittgenstein's thought. Much that Schopenhauer gives in concrete detail as the practice of goodness seems to have been fulfilled (though of course I have no right to say followed) by Wittgenstein. Indeed, from the little I know of Wittgenstein and the much less I know of Schopenhauer, Schopenhauer's account of the good man on the way to holiness looks much more like Wittgenstein than like Schopenhauer himself: who both by his own standards and mine seems to have been an absolute bounder. I think then that Wittgenstein followed Schopenhauer in these matters quite a long way, though certainly not all the way; and I shall therefore think it reasonable to interpret what Wittgenstein might have said in the light of some things Schopenhauer does say.

To live in accordance with the will of the world is to live happily. What then of the malicious misanthrope, who delights in the misery of the world, for though he shares in it he can more than merely *console* himself with the misfortunes of others? He is the happiest man about. Is he then a better man?

For Schopenhauer, such a man is the worst: because what he is doing is locking himself within his own individuality. Other people's happiness or unhappiness is important only in so far as it affects him: others are instruments to him. The philanthropist on the other hand, who is happy because things are going well for others, is to some extent escaping his own individuality, seeing others as others like himself, and this is an attitude of sympathy which can gradually

[1] Schopenhauer, *Essays and Aphorisms*, trans. Hollingdale (Penguin Books, 1970) p. 52.

extend to the whole of life. The nobility of mind of such a man on the road to goodness is a form of knowledge, but not one that can be expressed in propositions; it is a 'knowledge that, just because it is not abstract, cannot be communicated, but must dawn on each of us. It therefore finds its real and adequate expression not in words, but simply and solely in deeds, in conduct, in the course of a man's life' (I, 370). It is conduct itself which constitutes ethical knowledge, and those acts which we characterise as just or right from an external point of view are no more than the signs of this inner knowledge. 'The highest degree of this justice of disposition, which, however, is always associated with goodness proper, the character of this last being no longer merely negative, extends so far that a person questions his right to inherited property, desires to support his body only by his own powers, mental and physical, feels every service rendered by others, every luxury, as a reproach, and finally resorts to voluntary poverty' (I, 371). (I cannot forbear observing, though perhaps I should, that Schopenhauer, who adds to this list of signs of goodness sexual abstinence – a man must 'castrate himself from sin' – most spectacularly failed to exhibit them himself.)

For Wittgenstein, too, the malicious man is not happy in the ethical sense: he is not happy with the world, but with himself: and this is shown by what would happen if the world changed, and turned out not to be as hideous as it is. He would not be happy with the world *whatever it was*. On the other hand we must see the corollary to this: the philanthropist who has concern for other men or even men and animals is not in much better case, for to him some objects are more important – closer – to him than others, and this is intolerable. In the first place, one is powerless. But in the second place, philanthropy is possible only because there is misery in the world; and to be happy is to be happy despite the misery of the world. It is to love the world as it is whatever it might be: and that is the life of knowledge. (One is reminded here of the Intellectual Love of God.)

Now it would probably be that anyone who lived Wittgenstein's life of knowledge and detachment from the 'amenities of the world' would show what we commonly take to be the signs of a good man: malice, selfishness, greed, dishonesty, luxury, lust, despair, and so on, would be foreign to him so far as he lives his life *sub specie aeternitatis*, and is not concerned with this or that particular, and in particular not himself. I am not sure that he would thereby exhibit *all* the signs of what we would commonly call a good man (for example one might expect him to exhibit only the more passive civic virtues) but be that as it may, it is clear that for Wittgenstein these would be no more than the *signs* of a good will. The position is reminiscent of those who defended the doctrine that salvation is by faith not works. Can the man who has faith then be saved, if all he does is evil? There is no such man: he who has faith will not do evil. But it is his faith that saves, and his goodness is only a sign of that faith, not that which is rewarded by salvation. So for Wittgenstein the goodness of the will – which is its own salvation, its own reward (*TLP*, 6.422) – will depend not on the consequent virtues a man will exhibit, but on his attitude to the world as a whole.

In dealing with this issue Wittgenstein says that what matters is not *what* one wants but *how* one wants (*NB*, 29.7.16). There can be nothing good or bad about wanting as such. 'What happens' – and my wanting is a *fact* of psychology – 'whether it comes from a stone or my body is neither good nor bad' (*NB*, 12.10.16). Nor does he think one can do anything about the fact that one wants this rather than that. The kind of detachment he seeks is not sheer asceticism, in Bentham's[1] sense of the word: it is not seeking pain, or beating certain wants out of oneself. (Whereas for Schopenhauer, the next post on the road to salvation is precisely that: but only because the world is evil and must be escaped, which Wittgenstein totally rejects.) The wants are there as a fact: and hence there are those things which fulfil them and those which do not and hence, from the point of view of wanting, a sort of good and bad. So there really are *amenities*. 'The only life that is happy is the life that can renounce the amenities of the world. To it the amenities of the world are so many graces of fate' (*NB*, 13.8.16). Wittgenstein is not saying 'Learn not to want a warm bed' but 'Of course you want a warm bed, but learn to be content to want one and not have one'. As one might say, 'I wish that so and so, but Thy Will be done'.

At the end of the *Notebooks*, we have seen, Wittgenstein expresses the doubt that suicide itself may be neither good nor evil. To fear death is the sign of a bad will; but to seek death, he beforehand suggests, is the surest sign of a bad will. Schopenhauer's condemnation of suicide – which is in the end equally severe – is based on similar considerations to his condemnation of malice. A man who wills to kill himself is thereby hopelessly locked in his own individuality. He is concerned with his own pain to the exclusion of everything else, and concerned only with ending his own pain by ending himself: for after his death the evil world of conflicting will, which must anyway throw up another example of himself, is unchanged. Even the man who kills himself through an excess of sympathy, to

[1] Jeremy Bentham, *Principles of Morals and Legislation*, chap. II. Cf. also Calvin's essay 'On Christian Liberty' in his *Institutes of the Christian Religion*.

blot out of existence a consciousness racked by the spectacle of the pain and misery of the world, acts under a delusion at best; for once he is dead the pain and misery of the world is as great as ever (for Schopenhauer there is a principle of the conservation of agony). Nothing in itself is changed, for he has removed only a representation, nothing real. Wittgenstein could no doubt see badness in the particularity of a will directed to self-destruction also. But for him there is a further consideration which makes suicide the paradigm of evil, the 'elementary sin'. Even to investigate it has dangers, for it is like investigating mercury vapour to comprehend the nature of vapours: using the most pre-eminently poisonous vapour to find out about others (*NB*, 10.1.17). To seek death is to reject life (or if it is not, is it really suicide?) and this is fundamentally different from the other futile bad strivings of a particular will. For in death the world does not change, but ceases to exist (*NB*, 5.7.16; *TLP*, 6.431). In all other sinning we fail to accept the world whatever it is – we would not have it as it is. In suicide we would not have it at all. We desire not merely a different meaning but no meaning: no God.

Mr Pears ends his discussion of the mystical in the *Tractatus*[1] by saying that Wittgenstein has priced his ethical theory out of this world. Wittgenstein has priced ethical *propositions* out of this world: but he was the last to deny that there were attitudes which must be treated with respect, which cannot be argued about or even articulated, but which show themselves and can be grasped. And it is not as we have seen entirely removed from everyday attitudes: if the stuff of goodness is in a place ordinary men find too high for them, some of its signs are in the place they would commonly be thought to appear. However, it is surely true that ethics so conceived is far from being ethics as it is commonly conceived, as I conceive it to be as a common person. Yet some of the ideas developed by Schopenhauer and Wittgenstein have (at least a kind of negative) compulsion.

Here is a world of bodies related in all sorts of contingent ways, associated with various psychological facts. Among these are certain wants of mine; but having noticed that, what more is there to say? I want what I want and that is that. But where is there a place for thinking about what I ought to do, ought to want? There are certain states of mind now associated with this body, but why should they involve concerns with the future states of mind associated with this body, or with some other body, or with other states of mind at all, except that they just happen to? What seems to happen here is that

---

[1] David Pears, *Wittgenstein* (Fontana/Collins, 1971) p. 91.

this kind of reflection seems to make some of these actual states of mind themselves irrational in some way. I ask 'Well, what's so special about anything?' and am told 'It's special if you're concerned about it'. I want to reply 'If there's nothing special about it how am I concerned about it?' My present toothache *must* bother me and I must be concerned about it. But why should the thought that tomorrow I will suffer infinitely greater agony concern me any more than does my discovery, perhaps from reading an old medical report, that I suffered some very severe pain forty years ago, which I have completely forgotten? Why should I fear what I will not regret? Equally (not, however, still more) why should the fact of someone else's severe pain be of concern to me? Why should anything have any significance for me other than present amenities, the immediately felt pain or pleasure? Pain is undoubtedly painful, but only to him who suffers it at the time he suffers it.

It is important to realise how radical such scepticism about value can be. It is not one that allows us to rest, as some so-called ethical sceptics do, in a denial of all 'moral values' in favour of sheer selfishness. For whether selfishness, egoism, involves a moral attitude or not, there is no doubt that it presupposes values which go far beyond the immediately present want. The selfish man has some notion of himself as of value, at least to himself; but there seems no non-arbitrary way of discriminating between future states of his own body and psychical states which will be associated with it, from the present or future, or for that matter past, states of bodies or psychical states associated with those bodies, so that it makes any sense to attach a different value, or indeed any value, to them. The selection of the future states of my body and future psychical states associated with my body as the self that I value seems entirely arbitrary. It is not in *every* way arbitrary; but it is arbitrary as a ground for the attribution of value.

When does a caterpillar die? Immediately it enters the chrysalis? Slowly, in some transition within the chrysalis? Or when the emerged butterfly drops after its brief fluttering? Biologically there is every reason to identify the single organism with the caterpillar-butterfly; for it is a notion required if we are to theorise about and explain certain phenomena, such as the reproduction of caterpillars and butterflies. But why should this way of individuating an entity, which happens to be convenient for certain scientific purposes, be of any concern to the caterpillar? How could we show the caterpillar it had made some kind of mistake if it regarded itself as meeting death in the chrysalis, so that if it could it would delay the process into the autumn, with the certainty of grave damage to the future butterfly?[1] The way biologists want to chop up the world, or put it together, has nothing whatever to do with what I am concerned about, says the caterpillar. I am a caterpillar, and butterflies are nothing to me. But of course the caterpillar is still being arbitrary: why worry about the psychical states which might be associated with this body in the autumn, even if they will be those typical of a caterpillar? Why be more concerned for such states than those typical of a butterfly? Why be more concerned about them than states associated with other caterpillars, or butterflies, or for that matter ichneumon flies? Why does the caterpillar think he dies when he enters the chrysalis, rather than every hour, every moment?

'Where *in* the world is a metaphysical subject to be found?' (*TLP*, 5.633). Unless there is a living soul that is one through all the changes of my body from womb to grave, where is the self that I value? I no more than Wittgenstein can find such in the world. Where then, in the world, can we find anything which has meaning or significance for judgments of value? If there is such meaning or significance, it must lie outside the world. But how can it? For Schopenhauer, I believe, value cannot be found anywhere. There is only the present complex of wants and aversions, pleasure and pain, which at every point in time for every individual adds up to intense suffering. Outside the world of individuals, of representation, is only the will, a blind striving in eternal conflict with itself. Anything that is, is either evil to the individual or *sub specie aeternitatis* indifferent; and if in ourselves the will can recognise its own inner nature, through knowledge of its mirror or objectification, the world of phenomena, it will annul itself, leaving – nothing. Nothing has value; value lies not outside the world but nowhere. On the other hand, for Wittgenstein it can lie outside the world: to believe in God is to believe that the world as a whole has meaning and hence value. But what is one to say who does not believe in God, who does not believe the universe as a whole has any meaning or significance any more than has the sea, or copper sulphate? Even Wittgenstein could not at times bring himself to believe in this meaning; he respected those who did or who sought it, but sometimes said of himself that his inability to come to terms with things was a result of his lack of faith. To find oneself in such a position is to be beyond even despair. It is also to find oneself in a philosophical predicament: for if one to any degree approaches the mean sensual man, so long as one is not a sheer psychopath or a hermit driven mad by his own metaphysical speculations – one has ineradicable concerns which

---

[1] This and other very hard ethical issues are brilliantly and imaginatively dealt with by Naomi Mitchison in her *Memoirs of a Spacewoman*.

one cannot but stick to, but which one recognises to be utterly unintelligible: not something beyond speaking about, but such that one must say are sheer incoherent nonsense. The mean sensual man finds deep significance and importance in himself and in other persons; and also in some other things: in some animals, and in particular objects he calls works of art, not seen against a background of the universe but in art galleries (and, *pace* Schopenhauer and possibly also Wittgenstein, in art which is not *contemplation sub specie aeternitatis*, but the manifestation of his own individual and free will, in his singing and dancing and painting and writing). Yet he finds this in a world in which there is no reason to distinguish himself from others, or men from other animals, except for the purposes of natural science, which is quite irrelevant to any of these concerns.

I cannot find these things in the world. It turns out that some things I thought of the greatest significance to me, of dignity and worth beyond price, are arbitrary constructions out of facts which could be put together in different though equally arbitrary ways. Not only myself, but those I thought closest to me, lose all pre-eminence and become like the dead, roll'd round in earth's diurnal course with rocks and stones and trees. (Cf. *NB*, 2.9.16, 15.10.16.). Where, indeed, did I get this idea of myself or an *alter*? Other than the notion of the seeing eye, the knowing subject which disappears into an extensionless point, there are only bodies and the succession of psychological states, related to each other by the 'laws' of natural science. The solipsistic predicament in which I am the only consciousness confronting the world has resolved itself into a realistic predicament. From the uniqueness of man I pass to seeing him as one and merely one of the objects of natural science. From the self-centredness of subjective idealism I pass to total self-alienation.

*   *   *   *   *

The predicament is, I think, inescapable, and the questions I have been led to ask unanswerable, within the philosophical tradition leading to Schopenhauer and the early Wittgenstein. It is one of the streams which flowed through the work of Kant. The individual who is all-in-all to himself in the works of Hobbes and Locke must already begin to deny his empirical nature in Kant; he comes to sheer self-hatred in Schopenhauer, and at least self-contempt in Wittgenstein. It is a tradition which looks for the principle of individuation in inner sense, so that the self is either like a lost ghost only externally related to anything else, or it disappears altogether leaving only the alien world of biology. It cannot find a place for our common interpersonal concerns, because it never considers persons as internally related to others, and thereby constituted by such a system of relations. It treats the social dimension of man, not as an essential element in, but as a contingent consequence of, his nature.

8

HOW TO READ WITTGENSTEIN

Renford Bambrough

In the Michaelmas Term 1968 I gave a course of lectures on the *Philosophical Investigations*. Until then nobody had lectured at Cambridge specifically on that book, though it had been in print for fifteen years and must by that time have been lectured on in nearly every other philosophy department in the English-speaking world. One reason why we were so slow is suggested by a remark that John Wisdom made after hearing Max Black give a lecture on the *Tractatus* in the early fifties. As we came out of the lecture room he said to me 'That was a strange experience. I have a clear memory of all that from my early years in Cambridge. And yet in some ways it was like hearing a lecture on Spinoza.'

Some of the same ambivalence is evoked in some of us – and is liable to be evoked in anybody who heard or took part in any of the conversations that grew into the *Investigations* – by the grinding of the mills of scholarship and philosophical commentary on the *Investigations* and *The Blue and Brown Books*.

It is not that the *Investigations* is or seems as remote as the *Tractatus*. The later Wittgenstein is a controversial figure in death and in print as he was in life and in talk or typescript. He has disciples and detractors, and there are so many of each, and they are so hungry for recruits, that he is in danger of being neglected by those who are neither.

When I had been in America for just a few weeks on my first visit, the Chairman of a philosophy department in California said to me 'I expect you've been here long enough to know how philosophy in this country is being ruined by this Wittgenstein fad'. Another philosopher said to me in California on a later visit, 'So you're here to spread more of this Wittgenstein poison'. At the other and equally deplorable extreme we find remarks of which one might say (as Mr Anthony Quinton said of the remarks by Dr R. C. Marsh that are interleaved between the articles in Russell's *Logic and Knowledge*) that they are like the captions put on the placards beside Epstein's statues when they are exhibited at Blackpool.

It is difficult to be matter-of-fact about Wittgenstein (as about Freud or Leavis or Popper or Namier or Oakeshott).

That list of names suggests that the difficulty may have something to do with a particular sort of distinction and originality, with the breaking, for good or ill, of some of the familiar moulds of our thinking. And the fact that most of us would have serious reservations about the value of the work of one or more of these writers underlines the point rather than weakens it. It may also be significant that they are all men who appeal or have in their time appealed to the young, and have been unpopular with professors. As Socrates says in the *Apology*, young people can be expected to gather round a man who criticises conventional ideas: ἔστι γὰρ οὐκ ἀηδές – it is rather entertaining.

My concern with *how to read* Wittgenstein, by its reminiscence of Ezra Pound's *How to Read* and *An ABC of Reading*, makes a useful link between the reading of philosophy and the reading of other species of literature. Like Pound, I tell you that which you your-selves do know, and tell it to you because you sometimes forget it. And one thing that you know but may forget is that much of Wittgenstein, like much of Plato, is literature as well as philosophy, and so calls for kinds of reading at which philosophers do not always keep in practice.

No book was more deliberately designed than the *Investigations* to be 'a machine to think with'. In the Preface Wittgenstein writes: 'I should not like my writing to spare other people the trouble of thinking. But, if possible, to stimulate someone to thoughts of his own.' (In the Preface to the *Tractatus* he had written: 'Perhaps the book will be understood only by someone who has himself already had the thoughts that are expressed in it – or at least similar thoughts'.)

A book written with such an unusual purpose cannot be read as a textbook or treatise or standard classic of philosophy is read, any more than *Ulysses* (let alone *Finnegans Wake*) can be read as Trollope or even Jane Austen or George Eliot can be read. You may know how to read *The Prelude*, but still have to learn how to read *The Waste Land*.

The main difficulty comes from the main difference. Wittgenstein does not present a philosophical system or series of doctrines. He rarely summarises or signposts his work, and when he does so it is done in an epigrammatic and aphoristic style that is so close to what is being summarised that the same problem is liable to recur. An American woman once said to me at the end of a lecture: 'Will you please tell me what you have said? I find that I can't pay any attention to the content when I am listening to that wonderful English accent.' Of course I had to refer her to somebody else, because if I had given her a summary I should inevitably have done it in the same wonderful English accent.

Again in the Preface, Wittgenstein explains that his method of presentation is required by the nature of his questions and the substance of his answers. Above all the form of his philosophical remarks is prompted (and he thinks *dictated*) by his conception of the nature of philosophical questions and answers. He had at first tried to go against the grain of his thinking and to produce an orderly book, one that would proceed naturally and logically from one topic to another. In the end he had had to be content with scattered 'remarks', with offering 'only an album' or, at the best, 'what might be called the fragments of a system' (*PI*, II, xi, p. 228).

The differences between Wittgenstein's later work and the work of his predecessors and contemporaries, including his own earlier work, *are* very great, and he makes the most of them. Though he continued to speak of his researches as *philosophical* investigations, he also described his activity as 'one of the heirs of the subject that used to be called philosophy'. It is as though he had set out to contradict every cliché and platitude about philosophy. His paradoxes about the nature of philosophy are individually startling. If we put them together they amount to such a travesty of philosophy as it has usually been conceived that it is not surprising that his disciples, his detractors, and Wittgenstein himself have sometimes been disposed to deny that what he was doing was philosophy at all.

Philosophy, he says, does not call for subtlety, for the making of fine distinctions. The traditional ideals of exactness and precision are 'requirements' that we try artificially to impose on our thought rather than standards that it ought to be expected to meet. Our craving for generality, our contemptuous attitude towards the particular case, must be mortified and transcended if we are to achieve any answers to our philosophical perplexities. It is not the business of philosophy to advance any kind of theory or to build any system of ideas or propositions. We must not seek the foundations of knowledge, but offer to ourselves and others reminders of what we have always known. Philosophy is not the search for truth and knowledge or a struggle against ignorance and error. It is a battle against the bewitchment of our intelligence by means of language. Our search is for a cure for mental cramp. When we criticise the systems and 'theories' of other and earlier philosophers we are demolishing houses of cards built in the skies of Spain. Philosophy leaves everything as it is. The philosopher must not offer or aspire after a positive grasp of how things stand. His problems have the form 'I don't know my way about'. When he remarks that 'this is what we *call* a justification here' or that 'this game is played', another philosopher may object that he is shutting his eyes against doubt. He will reply only: 'They are shut'. Philosophy, he goes on, must abjure all explanation, and description alone must take its place. He 'holds no opinions in philosophy'. If we were to offer theses in philosophy, everyone would accept them.[1]

These remarks are all false, though they have truth in them. A consideration of them can best begin by applying them to themselves, since they are themselves typically philosophical remarks.

The *Tractatus* Preface had offered *solutions* to *problems*. Wittgenstein now renounces all such claims, and with them the conception of philosophy as consisting of a set of standing questions to which rival answers may be given. The conception to which he now opposes himself is one that he had shared with Russell and Ramsey and Moore, and which is embodied in the philosophical tradition that philosophy is the pursuit of *truth*, the attempt to arrive at definite and true answers for which convincing, even if not conclusive, reasons can be given.

Ramsey described Russell's theory of descriptions as 'a paradigm of philosophy'. Russell said that logic was the essence of philosophy. Moore was the supreme exponent of philosophy as the attempt to establish that certain propositions were *true*, and others *false*.

Wittgenstein rejects their conception and their mode of expressing it. Or at least he purports to reject it, though (and here we begin to see more clearly the application of Wittgenstein's remarks to Wittgenstein's remarks) he is in fact almost as clearly aware of the continuities between his own problems and techniques and those of Russell and Moore and Ramsey (and Leibniz and Hume and Plato) that justify him in calling his work 'philosophical' as he is of the differences between his own techniques and theirs that prompt him to say that he offers no theories, answers no questions, and engages only in an activity that is an *heir* of philosophy.

The literal claim not to be doing *philosophy*, or not to be concerned with traditional questions or doctrines, is in any case implicitly

[1] See *PI*, I, 107–9, 118, 123–9, 486, 654–5; *Blue Book*, pp. 17–18; Norman Malcolm, *Ludwig Wittgenstein: a Memoir*, p. 50.

contradicted by the character and outcome of the philosophical investigations of which the book consists. It is not just that there are direct references to some of the traditional doctrines (Idealists, Solipsists, Realists, *PI*, I, 402; Nominalists, 383; Behaviourism, 308). These are few and could all be dispensed with without affecting the course or destination of any of Wittgenstein's philosophical excursions. What is more important is that throughout the work there is the implicit claim to be throwing light on matters that had been left obscure by earlier philosophers, and the fact that the misunderstandings against which Wittgenstein's remarks are directed are recognisable, with or without their traditional labels, as theories or theses that had been held and assumptions that had been made by philosophers of earlier times, and were and are still held by many of Wittgenstein's contemporaries and successors.

Now the denial of a thesis is a thesis. And though one may deny a theory without affirming an alternative theory, the rejection of a theory, like the rejection of a thesis, is the adoption of a thesis. Wittgenstein rejects all theories and many theses, so Wittgenstein cannot be allowed to hold the philosophical opinion that he holds no opinions in philosophy.

Here we need to step back to consider for ourselves some questions about the nature of philosophical questions, and some questions about how such questions are to be answered. For it is to these questions that Wittgenstein is offering unorthodox answers when he says that he is not offering any answers of any kind to any questions of any kind. When we see what such questions are like and that and how they can be answered we can also see how Wittgenstein came to say that they were not *questions* and/or that they could not be *answered*. We can then see that Wittgenstein's mistakes fall under his own rubric about philosophical mistakes (e.g. 'not a *stupid* prejudice' *PI*, I, 340; see also *Zettel*, 460: 'Philosophical mistakes contain so much truth') and hence that his remarks about the nature of philosophy are among the clearest illustrations that could be given to show the justice of his remarks about the nature of philosophy.

These contortions are typical of the strains to which language is subjected if it is used in an attempt to express Wittgenstein's meaning in general and theoretical terms. One reason why Wittgenstein deliberately abandoned such an attempt, and why his loyal followers abide by his decision (Malcolm: 'An attempt to summarise the *Investigations* would be neither successful nor useful' – *Philosophical Review*, 1954) is that every remark made in the course of such an attempt is misleading and needs immediate qualification.

It is not an accident that it is in trying to present Wittgenstein's thoughts in a more systematic form that Wisdom performs somersaults like these:

> I have said that philosophers' questions and theories are really verbal. But if you like we will not say this or we will say also the contradictory. (*Philosophy and Psycho-analysis*, p. 37)

> See also the excellent articles by Dr. Glanville L. Williams in the *Law Quarterly Review*, 'Language and the Law', January and April 1945, and 'The Doctrine of Repugnancy', October, 1937, January, 1944 and April, 1944. The author, having set out how arbitrary are many legal decisions, needs now to set out how far from arbitrary they are – if his readers are ready for the next phase in the dialectic process. (*Philosophy and Psycho-analysis*, p. 157)

That last phrase is the key to the understanding that we need. To recognise the dialectical or conversational character of philosophical enquiry is to see both why Wittgenstein and others have thought that it could not be conducted in general and systematic terms and also that Wittgenstein himself here succumbs to a misunderstanding of just the kind that his renunciation of systematic exposition was meant to save us from.

First we may illustrate these points in Wittgenstein's own way, by examples. But it will turn out that the underlying logic of philosophical dialectic, and therefore of philosophical paradox and platitude, allows of a statement more general and systematic than Wittgenstein and most of his followers have recognised or acknowledged.

I have discussed elsewhere[1] some typical examples of Wittgenstein's habit of saying what he does not mean when that is the best way of saying what he does mean or (every case is debatable) his habit of saying what is false under the pressure of his recognition of a truth whose literal expression conflicts or seems to conflict with the literal expression of another truth that is more generally recognised. He said that he wanted his reader not to think but to look when what he wanted from him was a kind of thought that he might not get if he called it thought. He is like the coach who says, 'Stop trying so hard' when he wants more and better effort than the pupil will give if he is told to try harder.

These examples are typical in their structure (and the first is

---

[1] Mainly in 'Objectivity and Objects', *Proc. Arist. Soc.*, LXXII (1971–2).

typical also in its content) of what peculiarly characterises a philosophical dispute, and it can be expressed in more general terms by going back to my suggestion that every remark made in the course of any attempt to summarise Wittgenstein's philosophy is bound to be *misleading*. Wittgenstein himself repeatedly uses topographical metaphors (*PI*, Preface, I, 18, 203, 525, 534, etc.) and he remarks that a philosophical problem has the form 'I don't know my way about' (*PI*, I, 123; see also 108). A remark is misleading if it suggests what is false, even if it does not say what is false. A remark is incurably misleading if it suggests what is false and there is no modification of the remark that will remove the misleading suggestion without introducing a new one. When a remark is incurably misleading its negation is usually also incurably misleading. Most philosophical remarks are incurably misleading.

It is misleading to say that this or that enquiry will go better if you stop *thinking* and misleading to say that your drive at golf will improve if you stop *trying*. Each of these remarks falsely suggests that you may sensibly and usefully leave the enquiry or the stroke to take care of itself. But if I say instead that you must think harder or try harder I may also mislead you, for I may prompt you to persist in a mode of effort or a mode of thought that is inappropriate to what you are trying to achieve.

When it is misleading to say that *p* and it is also misleading to say that not-*p* we may try to say what we need to say without saying either that *p* or that not-*p*. Wittgenstein preaches this method and he often practises it. When he 'assembles reminders for a particular purpose' (*PI*, I, 127), when he abjures explanation (*PI*, I, 109) and allows what used to be called 'aseptic' description to take its place, he is doing his best to escape from the standard philosophical forms of words precisely because he has noticed that they are incurably misleading, that to deny what is expressed by one of them is as misleading as to assert what is expressed by it.

But there is a consequence of this situation that Wittgenstein's theory does not adequately allow for, though his practice sometimes implicitly recognises it: and that is that if an expression is incurably misleading then the denial of it can be used to express something that is not misleading, even if the denial is *also* incurably misleading. If what is expressed by '*e*' is some truth and some falsehood, when I say 'not-*e*' I shall be denying some truth but also denying some falsehood and hence also asserting some truth. And the same goes for saying '*e*' in opposition to 'not-*e*'.

In practice Wittgenstein sometimes does adopt this alternative method. Instead of asserting neither *p* nor not-*p* he asserts both, and thus incurs some at least of the odium and obloquy to which people (especially philosophers) are liable when they want to have it both ways:

> Many philosophers, therefore, when they admit a distinction, yet (following the lead of Hegel) boldly assert their right, in a slightly more obscure form of words, *also* to deny it. The principle of organic unities, like that of combined analysis and synthesis, is mainly used to defend the practice of holding *both* of two contradictory propositions, wherever this may seem convenient. In this, as in other matters, Hegel's main service to philosophy has consisted in giving a name to and erecting into a principle, a type of fallacy to which experience had shown philosophers, along with the rest of mankind, to be addicted. No wonder that he has followers and admirers. (Moore, *Philosophical Studies*, pp. 15–16)

Wittgenstein takes these risks when he says in one place that we do not require a foundation for language and in another that its real foundation is not what we think it is (*PI*, I, 124, 129). He takes them again in the *Remarks on the Foundations of Mathematics* when he both denies that a mathematical proposition can be believed and explains what it is to believe a mathematical proposition. (The whole discussion (*RFM*, I, 106-12) is a good example of Wittgenstein's internal duologue; see also p. 91 of Norman Malcolm's *Memoir* as well as II, xi, p. 203 of the *Investigations*.)

A characteristically philosophical form of words is always capable both of expressing something true and of expressing something false, and when such a form of words is used the speaker may mean by it only what is true or only what is false or *both* what is true *and* what is false in what the expression is naturally capable of expressing. Correspondingly, somebody who denies an assertion made with such an expression may intend to deny the false content of the assertion, or the true content, or both. (This paragraph is itself a most misleading philosophical remark.)

It follows that a philosophical remark that is misleading may do good as well as harm. And though there are no rules for telling when a misleading remark will do good, the metaphor of leading and misleading itself has some help to offer us here: whether you guide a man to one destination or another when you point in a certain direction depends not only on the direction in which you point, but also on the direction or directions in which you and he happen to be facing, and on what you and he believe or know and what you have said to each other before on this and on other occasions.

On one occasion I may point due north and be pointing straight at Piccadilly Circus. On another occasion I may point straight at Piccadilly Circus and be pointing due south. There is also the case in which we must get the man to start off in a southerly direction if he is to find his way to Piccadilly Circus, even though Piccadilly Circus lies due north of where he and we are standing when we give him our directions. (Remember how often on French roads one meets the sign '*toutes directions*'.)

These remarks have application far outside our immediate concern with how to read Wittgenstein. They have to do with how to read philosophy, and how to understand a lot that is said in a more or less philosophical manner by people who, and about things which, have nothing to do with philosophy.

The first Impressionists would not have been contradicting themselves if they had sometimes defended their work by asking 'Why should we always try to give a realistic, naturalistic representation of nature and man?' and sometimes by insisting that Impressionism was the true realism or the true naturalism.

Understanding of these points is necessary not only for making sense of Wittgenstein and the relations between his work and that of his predecessors, but for the understanding of any philosophical conflict that cuts across differences of idiom, style, age or continent.

You will not be able to read Wittgenstein if you cannot read philosophy and you cannot read philosophy if you have never learned to read.

If you can read and can read philosophy and can read Wittgenstein you will be able to see that what he says about other philosophers applies also to himself. Not even his own philosophical words can be taken at their face value, not even when they express his theory about the nature and effects of philosophical theories.

He is right to hold that the traditional theories are all dangerously and demonstrably false. And since the demonstration takes the form of showing by description that instances of our familiar knowledge do not have the character that the theories require them to have, it is not surprising or unreasonable that Wittgenstein, whose recognition of these facts is unprecedentedly clear, should have held the philosophical theory that all philosophical theorising must be renounced. He chose to undercut the theorising that led to so much confusion and distortion, and the patient descriptions that he offers instead of theorising do achieve what they aim at, provided that they are followed with the patience that went into their compilation.

Such extreme patience is too much to expect of most philosophers, who are by nature and tradition interested in the large view and the generality of statement that Wittgenstein opposed. Fortunately he provided all the materials for a larger view and a more general statement than his explicit account of his aims and methods allows him to countenance, and they can be expressed with what I believe to be a negligible loss of accuracy in a form that rivals the scope and grasp of the traditional metaphysical theories that Wittgenstein strove to supersede. In any case, accuracy is not the only philosophical value. There are occasions on which some accuracy and literalness may reasonably be at least temporarily sacrificed in exchange for the benefits of perspective and synopsis. An aerial photograph from 30,000 feet cannot focus on a shrub, but it can show the great rivers and the mountain ranges that are invisible on a six-inch ordnance survey map.

Once when I showed a paper of mine to John Wisdom he complained that it represented a return to 'the old dogmatic idiom'. He was using the word 'dogmatic' to describe any mode of philosophical writing, however many and strong reasons it might invoke, in which theses were stated and defended. Such modes were to be contrasted with the use of the dialectical idiom, the conversational exchange that is directly presented by Plato, and whose pattern of suggestions and qualifications is closely followed in the superficially continuous prose of Aristotle and Wittgenstein. This idiom is designed to minimise the dangers of misrepresentation that are otherwise the almost inevitable consequence of that slipperiness and duplicity of philosophical forms of words on which I have remarked. When Wisdom himself wrote the sentences that I quote on p. 122 he was exploiting to an extreme degree the capacity of dialectical exchanges to contribute to a unified apprehension by the adumbration and resolution of conflict between one misleading philosophical remark and another.

Misrepresentation is otherwise *almost* inevitable, but not quite. There is another idiom in which philosophy may fitly be conducted and presented, and which combines many of the advantages of the dialectical method with some of the advantages of that sustained and continuous exposition that Wittgenstein in the Preface to the *Investigations* says that he had despaired of achieving.

This third idiom might be called the *legal* idiom, because of its structural kinship with the operations of lawyers in the 'adversary system', where advocacy of the claims of opposing parties is followed by summing up and judgment. In this idiom each side is allowed a longer and more sustained development of its submissions before its exaggerations are corrected by the other. The structure of dialectical discussion is preserved, but the unit of discourse is larger. The legal idiom is dialectic on a longer wavelength. It preserves many of the advantages of detailed dialectic and has some advantages of its own. In the legal idiom it is possible to undercut the traditional theories as Wittgenstein wished to do, and yet to benefit from the scope and range that they provide, and which is lacking in many more accurate presentations of the detailed character of concepts and kinds of knowledge.

Even if there had been no hints in Wittgenstein's text that he had himself aspired after such an overall perspective I should still wish to offer it, and to offer it as in considerable measure a re-statement of the results of his own investigations. In fact he gives many signs of his desire for such a development, and not only in the sentences of the Preface to which I have already referred. Some of the signs are explicit and unmistakable: others are more indirect but cumulatively powerful. All the signs taken together amount to a strong case for rejecting the assumption of Rush Rhees, Norman Malcolm, and in general of the majority of Wittgenstein's closest disciples, that he could consistently and would necessarily have been shocked by any attempt to transpose his work into the legal idiom and so to extend it in new directions without altering its central content or being alienated from its temper and spirit.

When a symphony is transcribed for two pianos there is necessarily (by a *logical* necessity) a great loss in instrumentation, orchestral colour and texture, but the bones of the underlying structure can be more clearly displayed. A teacher or critic who uses such a transcription has not necessarily forgotten that bones are meant to carry flesh. Accuracy of transcription may be defended or assessed by reference to the full score on which it is based, and the score itself may be freely quoted as evidence and in response to challenge. And that is another way of saying that the dialectical and legal idioms are applicable to the exposition and criticism of works of philosophy and works of art as well as to the systematic study of philosophical problems. Those who complain that a particular reading or presentation is partial show by their complaint that they think it possible to envisage a single presentation that is balanced and complete. One who presents a particular and partial view may be well aware that it takes more than one part to make a whole and that only by way of many particularities can we hope to arrive at a unified apprehension:

Verbal description of everything, however, must remain infinitely distant from the thing itself, overstatement and understatement sometimes hitting off the truth better than a flat assertion of bare fact. (Anthony Powell, *The Kindly Ones*, pp. 14–15)

The explicit indications of Wittgenstein's interest in a systematic and general treatment of the problems of philosophy are found in his references to traditional philosophical theories, and especially in some remarks of the widest possible scope that he makes at *PI*, I, 402:

> When as in this case, we disapprove of the expressions of ordinary language (which are after all performing their office), we have got a picture in our heads which conflicts with the picture of our ordinary way of speaking. Whereas we are tempted to say that our way of speaking does not describe the facts as they really are. As if, for example the proposition 'he has pains' could be false in some other way than by that man's *not* having pains. As if the form of expression were saying something false even when the proposition *faute de mieux* asserted something true.

> For *this* is what disputes between Idealists, Solipsists and Realists look like. The one party attack the normal form of expression as if they were attacking a statement; the others defend it, as if they were stating facts recognized by every reasonable human being.

In other places he refers to the traditional theories with which his readers will be most likely (and with most excuse) to identify his own accounts:

> 'Are you not really a behaviourist in disguise? Aren't you at bottom really saying that everything except human behaviour is a fiction?' If I do speak of a fiction, then it is of a *grammatical* fiction. (*PI*, I, 307)

> We are not analysing a phenomenon (e.g. thought) but a concept (e.g. that of thinking), and therefore the use of a word. So it may look as if what we were doing were Nominalism. Nominalists make the mistake of interpreting all words as *names*, and so of not really describing their use, but only, so to speak, giving a paper draft on such a description. (*PI*, I, 383)

The implicit signs of the same aspiration vary in degree of indirectness. Some of the most striking are the aphorisms of enormous generality that stand out from the background of detailed consideration of detailed examples: 'What is your aim in philosophy? – To show the fly the way out of the fly-bottle' (*PI*, I, 309). 'A philosophical problem has the form "I don't know my way about" '

(*PI*, I, 123). In these and similar sentences we see surviving in the *Investigations*, *Zettel*, and in the oral tradition from his later years, the Wittgenstein who distilled from the more diffuse and informal *Notebooks* the systematic pregnancies of the *Tractatus*.

Many of these aphorisms are specially concerned with the nature of philosophy. Here I am more interested in the indications that Wittgenstein would have been prepared to countenance an attempt to re-state his substantive epistemology in the more formal and more general terms customarily used by philosophers before, during and after his own time, but these meta-philosophical remarks are highly relevant to my search. For again we need to attend to the misconceptions of the nature of philosophical questions that led Russell and others to clothe their enquiries in mathematical or scientific dress, and to the lingering misconception in Wittgenstein that led him to think that in rejecting their misconceptions he must cast off all the clothes that they had worn. If we firmly grasp the nature of philosophy as he conceived it, and do not allow our choice of idiom to cause us to backslide into confusion about our objectives, in putting on a more formal dress we shall be doing no more than respect the spirit of Wittgenstein's own recognition (*PI*, I, 48) that avoiding misunderstandings in any particular case is more important than insisting that one or other of two or more ways of expressing a point is the right or best way of expressing it. This is just one of many junctures at which loyalty to the verbal detail of Wittgenstein's remarks is liable to involve a betrayal of what he rightly thought more important.

But what I most rely on would still be there if Wittgenstein had deleted all his aphorisms: the patterns and structures that are exhibited by his mosaic of examples and remarks. What I have said and shall say about particular philosophical topics and about the dynamics of philosophical dispute can largely be mined from seams that run right through the *Investigations*, linking one example and one topic with another, causing us to approach the same topic repeatedly from different angles (Preface again). That the pattern as I have outlined it is partly traced by the explicit generalities I have quoted is a welcome but unnecessary confirmation of what can be made obvious by tracing some of the threads on which the beads are strung.

The test of an interpretation of a philosopher, like the test of a philosophical theory, lies in the details of what it compendiously lays down or sums up. One of my purposes here is to ask you to notice in the other lectures of this series and in the rest of your reading of Wittgenstein and about Wittgenstein that his work exhibits the structural solidity and the relevance to current and traditional philosophical conflicts that I have attributed to it. Another aim is to reveal that his own work employs the shifts and devices which he diagnoses in the work of his predecessors. Both purposes will be advanced if I give the rest of my time and space to his treatment of one topic of the first importance on which it is possible even in a narrow compass to show his method at work and to show how different it is from what he said his method was. In Part II, xi, of the *Investigations*, p. 222, he writes:

> I can know what someone else is thinking, not what I am thinking. It is correct to say 'I know what you are thinking', and wrong to say 'I know what I am thinking'.

Here (he adds) we have 'a whole cloud of philosophy condensed into a drop of grammar'.

In the cloud from which the drop was condensed are all the controversies about mind and body, solipsism, dualism, materialism, behaviourism and the problem of other minds from which Wittgenstein was trying to escape but to which his remarks here and in so many other places are decisively relevant. When he calls the cloud a cloud of *philosophy* he confirms what should in any case be obvious, that his remarks take their meaning and their point from the context of history and doctrine which includes Descartes and Hume and Russell and the sceptic about other minds. The shafts are directly aimed at these targets. The medicine in the bottle is more familiar than the label leads us to expect.

But it is not enough to see through the obliqueness and obscurity of the expression to the kinship of Wittgenstein's themes with those of his predecessors. His methods and modes of expression are also akin to theirs, as they must be if his denials are to have any bearing on their assertions.

The traditional sceptic and the traditional dualist hold that I can know what I am thinking and cannot *know* what someone else is thinking. They say or imply that it is correct to say 'I know what I am thinking' and wrong to say 'I know what you are thinking'. They insist that there can be knowledge only where there cannot be doubt.

Wittgenstein is right to reject the traditional impulse to place such restrictions on the scope of knowledge. It *is* correct to speak of my knowledge of your mind. I *can* know what someone else is thinking. But while we are agreeing with Wittgenstein's denials of the familiar paradoxes of the dualist and the sceptic, we may fail to notice that the form and content of his denials is as paradoxical and false as the form and content of their assertions. He meets their paradoxes with counter-paradoxes, and not merely with the reassertion of familiar truths.

I can know what I am thinking and I can know what you are thinking.

It is correct to say 'I know what you are thinking' and also correct to say 'I know what I am thinking'.

That what Wittgenstein says is false can be shown by an example. Suppose that a group of us are subjects in a psychological experiment in which we are asked to hold electric terminals in our hands and to report whether we do or do not feel pain when the current is switched on. One of us serves as reporter and writes down on a pad how many of us feel the pain on each occasion. The others hold up their hands if they feel the pain. The reporter does not hold up his hand, but simply writes down a number on his pad after he has counted the hands. Now the reporter knows how many people feel the pain and nobody other than the reporter knows how many people feel the pain. But the only case known to the reporter and not known to the others is the reporter's own case. Therefore it is possible for the reporter to know whether he feels pain and correct for him to say that he knows that he feels pain.

The kinship between Wittgenstein and his opponents goes deeper still. It is not just that he uses as a stylistic device in his rejection of the old paradoxes the paradoxical form in which they clothe their paradoxical content. His argument for his paradoxical conclusion is of the same kind as the arguments of the sceptic and the dualist for their paradoxes, and is of just the kind that Wittgenstein so often warns us not to countenance. (But of course he never claims that his studies of methods of exorcism had made him immune from the bewitchment of his own intelligence by means of language.)

The familiar sceptical argument is that there cannot be knowledge where there can be doubt. Wittgenstein's argument is that there cannot be knowledge where there cannot be doubt. The sceptic claims that it cannot make sense to speak of knowledge where there is any possibility of error. Wittgenstein argues that it cannot make sense to say 'I know that p' unless it makes sense to say 'I suspect that p' or 'I suppose that p'.

It obviously makes sense to say 'I think he is in pain but I may be mistaken' so the sceptic says I cannot *know* that he is in pain. It obviously does not make sense to say 'I think I am in pain but I may be mistaken' so Wittgenstein says that it does not make sense to say that I know that I am in pain.

Though Wittgenstein has therefore made a mistake it is naturally not a stupid mistake. It is a mistake with a point. And its point is not very different from the point of the traditional mistake against which Wittgenstein's argument is directed. Wittgenstein is protesting at the imposition of a *requirement* (*PI*, I, 107) for the application of the word 'knowledge'. He is insisting that there can be knowledge where there can also be doubt. But when he reacts to the opposite extreme of suggesting that there cannot be knowledge except where there can also be doubt he is himself imposing a requirement that must be resisted by any philosopher whose purpose is 'to *accept* the everyday language-game, and to note *false* accounts of the matter *as* false' (*PI*, I, xi, 200).

The sceptic or dualist rebels against the application of the word 'knowledge' to my knowledge of your mind because my knowledge of your mind is so different from your knowledge of your mind or my knowledge of mine. Wittgenstein points out that the presence of the possibility of doubt, suspicion, conjecture or opinion is not fatal to the possibility of knowledge. But he himself goes on to emphasise the very difference that his opponent was concerned to emphasise – the difference between third-person knowledge of a mind and first-person knowledge of a mind. The difference deserves the heavy stress that both sides give to it. But if we stand above the conflict we can see, as Wittgenstein, who set such store by *differences*, by the recognition in so many contexts that 'there are many cases here', ought to have been the first to see, that both sides are suffering from 'a craving for generality' and 'a contemptuous attitude towards the particular case'. The fact that I cannot suspect that I am in pain is a reason for holding that there are cases of knowledge which do not allow for doubt or suspicion. It is not a reason for denying, in the interests of any *a priori* picture of the nature of knowledge or the use of the word 'knowledge', that I can know that I am in pain.

What is most important in Wittgenstein's thesis and argument can survive the demonstration that what he says is false; just as what is most important in the theory and argument of the dualist or sceptic can survive the demonstration that what he says is false. Wittgenstein had always known this, even if he sometimes forgot it. There is no finer text on which to preach this sermon than his own remark in the *Tractatus* that 'What the solipsist means is of course correct'.

What is most important in Wittgenstein's later work, including his warnings against the dangers of systematic philosophy, can survive the recognition that his fragments are fragments of a system.

9

WITTGENSTEIN ON PERSONS AND HUMAN BEINGS

Jenny Teichman

I. 'PERSON' AND 'HUMAN BEING'

THE last part of Wittgenstein's *Blue Book*[1] consists of a discussion of Solipsism. In the course of that discussion there occur several remarks (extending over about a page-and-a-half) which are explicitly concerned with the concept of a *person* and with the criteria of personal identity. This section is replaced in the *Philosophical Investigations* by half a sentence which reads: '. . . there is a great variety of criteria for personal "*identity*" '.[2] Wittgenstein has italicised the word 'identity', and has placed it in inverted commas: I don't quite know why he does this, but it might be a hint to the effect that there is something slightly suspect about the notion of personal identity.

On the other hand, the *Philosophical Investigations* contains at various points a number of remarks about human beings. These remarks are all quite new, and have no parallel in either the *Blue Book* or the *Brown Book*.

Now, it is plain that the notion of a *person* and the notion of a *human being* are different from each other. But in spite of that, one might be tempted to explain away the dissimilarities between the *Blue and Brown Books* (on the one hand) and the *Philosophical Investigations* (on the other) which are referred to above, by saying that they are at the least merely verbal, and at the most, merely a matter of emphasis. For the *Blue Book* and the *Brown Book* were composed in English, whereas the *Philosophical Investigations* was written in German. Now, the word 'person' occurs far more frequently in English than the word *Person* occurs in German. In English, a

[1] *BB*, pp. 58–74.   [2] *PI*, I, 404.

lot of humdrum work is done by the word 'person', work which in German falls to (for instance) the words *man*, *er*, *der*, *jeder*, etc. and which *could* be done, though clumsily, by the English equivalents 'one', 'the one', 'the one who . . .' and so forth. As well as that, it can occasionally, though certainly not always, be appropriate to translate the German word *Mensch* (= 'human being') as 'person'.

I do not think, though, that the change from talking about persons to talking about human beings is a mere accident; it is not to be explained in terms of the change from writing in English to writing in German. This becomes obvious enough if we look at what Wittgenstein actually says about persons and about human beings. The change, the difference, is significant; it has the effect, too, of illuminating a number of problems, including, oddly enough – or perhaps on second thoughts not so oddly – the problem as to how to give a correct philosophical account of the concept of a *person*.

2. WITTGENSTEIN ON 'PERSON'

In the *Blue Book*[1] Wittgenstein makes the following observations about persons and personal identity.

Firstly he says that there are many characteristics which we use as the criteria of personal identity. *Secondly*, he says that these criteria usually coincide, i.e. give the same results as each other (otherwise, no doubt, they would not count, or not all count, as criteria in the first place). Wittgenstein writes: 'Our actual use of the phrase "same person" and of the name of a person is based on the fact that many characteristics which we use as the criteria for identity coincide in the vast majority of cases'. *Thirdly*, he says that an individual is as a rule recognised by the appearance of his body. The body changes very gradually, and this is also true of the voice, and of habits. Wittgenstein writes: 'We are inclined to use personal names in the way we do, only as a consequence of these facts'. If the facts were different, we would give names in a different kind of way. Thus: 'Imagine that all human bodies which exist looked alike, that on the other hand, different sets of characteristics seemed, as it were, to change their habitation among these bodies. Such a set of characteristics might be, say, mildness, together with a high-pitched voice and slow movements, or a choleric temperament, a deep voice, and jerky movements, and such like.' He goes on: 'Under such circumstances it would be possible to give the bodies names but we should perhaps be as little inclined to do so as we are

[1] *BB*, pp. 61–2.

to give names to the chairs of our dining-room set. On the other hand, it might be useful to give names to the sets of characteristics.' *Fourthly*, he says that the present ordinary use of the word 'person', taken together with some possible change in the world, would not force upon us any one particular change in the use of the word. For, he says, the present ordinary use is a composite use suitable under ordinary circumstances; in such a case 'the term "personality" hasn't got *one* legitimate heir only'. Wittgenstein denies, for instance, that Locke's imagined example of the man whose memories are separated into those of odd days and those of even days *has* to be described as a case of two persons inhabiting one body, though it *could* be. The description, he says, 'is neither right nor wrong'.

In brief: Wittgenstein claims that the ordinary use of the word 'person' is composite: the elements of the composition are the appearance of the body on the one hand, and 'sets of characteristics' on the other. These sets of characteristics include both physical and psychological properties and dispositions.

3. THE PHILOSOPHICAL NOTION OF A PERSON

The philosophical notion of a person has for some centuries at least been inextricably mixed up with Dualism, and with Dualistic accounts of the nature of consciousness. Twentieth-century attempts to rescue the concept of a person from Cartesian entanglements themselves sometimes incorporate traces of the doctrine they attack. So that contemporary discussion of the concept of a person can still take place against a sort of dualistic backdrop. Strawson, for instance, in his book *Individuals* feels when he is engaged on an analysis of the idea of a person that he has to divide, not indeed the stuff of the world, but certainly its predicates into two, presumably basic, varieties: the corporeal and the psychological. Even Wittgenstein, as we have just seen, wants, in the *Blue Book* at least, to endow the notion of a person with two aspects, namely, the bodily appearance, and the 'sets of characteristics'; and seems convinced, for reasons which are perhaps rather slender, that the ordinary use of the word is 'composite'. You might as well argue that the ordinary use of the word 'table' is composite. Taken overall, the ordinary use of the word 'table' exemplifies the substance-quality distinction: but that hardly seems a reason for saying it is *composite*.

Allowing a 'basic' division into matter and consciousness is like pushing Humpty-Dumpty off the wall: it's extremely difficult to get the pieces together again. When the idea of consciousness is completely separated from, abstracted from, humanity and human life philosophers develop two typical syndromes: firstly, a dire suspicion that anything at all might be a subject of consciousness, and secondly, the fear that nothing (except oneself) is such a subject.

The problem of Solipsism is associated with the concept of a *person*, not with that of a *human being*. Not many philosophers have in fact written about the notion of a human being: it apparently does not strike philosophers as interesting. Perhaps part of the reason is that *human being* names members of a natural species. Although the expression is for all that somewhat honorific in tone (understandably enough perhaps) still its ordinary use is to some extent governed by the fact that it belongs alongside other species-terms: words, that is to say, such as 'dog', 'cat', 'horse', 'worm', 'flea', etc.

The word 'person' in its ordinary use is in fact very closely associated with the ordinary use of the expression 'human being', though philosophers tend to ignore this. To take some examples: *Descartes* tells us that a person or self is 'a conscious being'. *Locke* says that *person* stands for: 'a thinking intelligent being, that has reason and reflection, and can consider itself as itself . . . which it does only by that consciousness which is inseparable from thinking'. *Strawson* writes: 'The concept of a person, is the concept of a type of entity such that both predicates ascribing consciousness, and predicates ascribing corporeal characteristics, are equally applicable to a single individual of that single type'. (Note the emphasis on the *single individual*.) *Pucetti* says: 'There is an intimate connection between person-predicates sharing an intellectual character, and those sharing a moral character . . . the former are a necessary condition of the latter . . . and any entity qualifying as a "moral agent" [his quotation marks] would be a person'. None of these definitions mentions humanity.[1] It is almost as if the authors believed that *being human* is only *accidentally* associated with being a person. They speak rather as if they thought that it would be perfectly possible to grasp notions like 'consciousness', 'thinking intelligent being', 'person-predicates', 'predicates-having-an-intellectual-character', 'predicates-having-a-moral-character', etc. without having any notion of what a human being is like. This may sound a little carping. After all, no author (or reader either) could as a matter of fact be totally ignorant about human beings, because

---

[1] I feel that Pucetti should be partially exempted from any criticism implied in this paragraph. The first chapter of his book *Persons* is in fact called 'Human Persons': and the first sentence of the book is: 'Any discussion of persons should begin with human persons'. For all that, the first chapter is not actually about human beings. The chief topics of this chapter are (*a*) the concept of God, and (*b*) P. F. Strawson's account of the concept of a person.

as a matter of fact all authors and readers are themselves human beings. I don't think, though, that this is a reasonable excuse for overlooking the important status of the concept of a human being in any correct analysis of the idea of a *person*. In most writings on the notion of a *person* the status of the concept of a *human being* is at best that of an unacknowledged paradigm.

4. THE ORDINARY USE OF THE WORD 'PERSON'

What *is* the ordinary use of the word 'person'?[1] Well, in ordinary life we mostly carry on as if the extension of the term 'person' and the extension of the term 'human being' were identical. Mostly, but not invariably. In the Law, for instance, persons are divided into two sorts, the natural and the artificial. In Theology, persons are classified as either human or divine (spiritual). Both Law and Theology, it seems to me, take the human being as a kind of starting-point or paradigm. Lawyers I imagine, would agree that artificial persons are persons in a derivative sense of the word. It is, I daresay, less likely that theologians would regard spirits as being persons in a derivative sense.

Natural Persons. The only natural persons we come across in real life are in fact human beings. But the existence of other varieties of natural persons is a logical possibility; that is to say, the intension of the word allows for this possibility. There might be non-human natural persons living on planets in other galaxies for all we know. Creatures who don't look like us and who could not breed with human beings would count as persons, non-human but natural, if they lived just in the way we live. Living in *just* the way we live would certainly be a *sufficient* condition of the members of some other natural species counting as persons (what the *necessary* conditions are is of course much harder to say).

Spiritual Persons (Spirits) include gods, angels, fallen angels and possibly elves or fairies.

The distinction between natural and spiritual is rather blurred in some myths, perhaps in most. The gods of some myths behave as if they were members of a natural biological species: they eat and drink and have children and so on. Sometimes they go on as if they shared membership of *our* species!

The OED defines elves as 'supernatural beings' and fairies as '*small* supernatural beings'. Since fairies are small they must have bodies, so *supernatural* does not in this context imply that the beings in question are spirits. Perhaps in this context *supernatural* merely

---

[1] It is not possible to describe the *whole* use in two pages.

means 'able to play magic tricks'. For elves and fairies are described in most stories as having eyes and ears and arms and legs and (green) blood. They feel anger and benevolence and can speak to each other and perhaps also to us. I myself think they are best regarded as members of an imaginary natural species, rather than as spirits. The fact that they are called 'the Little People' shows that they are in a way thought of already as a natural species (albeit a non-existent one). For the word 'person' has two plurals, 'persons' and 'people': the first of these is used in the case of the artificial and the divine or spiritual: the second is reserved for natural beings. We may say (for instance) that the Governing Body of the College and the Students Union are two separate legal persons: not two separate legal people. We do not speak of the Three People of the Trinity. (After all, the *singular* term 'people' means a tribe or nation of men.)

In general, the status *qua* persons of imaginary or fictional creatures is often somewhat unclear. Pickwick, Snodgrass and Winkle are fairly obviously supposed to be men: Tinkerbell is a fairy: Peter Pan, though, is no ordinary boy: and it is not clear (to me at any rate) whether beings like Thoth and Jiminy Cricket and the Valkyrie are supposed to be spirits or bodily individuals or what. No doubt it is sometimes the case that the creators of such beings have inadvertently left the question open.

Artificial Persons. (1) In the Law, artificial persons are such entities as Government Departments and Trade Unions and Colleges and so on. That is to say, they are corporate bodies which are empowered within a system of law and custom to make decisions of various sorts, and which under that system are said to have certain duties, rights, obligations and responsibilities.

(2) The term 'artificial intelligence' suggests the possibility of another variety of artificial person, namely, computers or other similar machines.

5. PERSONS AND HUMAN BEINGS

The term 'person' in its ordinary use as sketched above is not like the name of a *genus* having species and sub-species. It is certainly not the name of a natural *genus*; it is not analogous to, say, 'vertebrate'.

The reason why it will not do to call it a *genus* at all, is that its supposed species belong to different categories of being from each other. By that, I mean that *the manner of existence* of any one kind of person is radically different from the manner of existence of either of the other two. For instance: an artificial (legal) person such as a College, can exist for a while, then as it were lapse out of existence, then be re-founded or re-constituted and begin to exist once more. Natural beings, including human persons, cannot have intermittent existence of this kind. It is easy to imagine a law which would require artificial persons to renew their existence annually, perhaps by payment of a tax. Natural creatures, including human persons, cannot renew themselves in *this* way. Again, natural persons are alive, whereas spirits are not; nor are they dead either, of course. Divine beings do not live, they exist. They are indeed sometimes incorrectly *spoken* of as being alive.

The concept of a person is certainly not formed by the abstraction of a common feature (such as consciousness, say) or set of common features, or even, from a set of overlapping resemblances. It is not abstracted from examples of (respectively) natural, artificial and divine persons. When the word is actually taught and learnt, it is treated as if its extension were identical with that of 'human beings' – even, as if its intension were identical too. Someone who had never heard of gods and angels and elves and Santa Claus and the persons of legal fiction could still count, it seems to me, as one who had an adequate, though not of course a complete, concept of *person*. He would not be like an individual who, having never come across any animals except cats, and having not thought about the possibility of other kinds of animals, always speaks as if all animals are cats and all cats are animals. This latter individual would not have anything like an adequate conception of *animal* and his notion of what a cat is, would also be defective. *His* notions would be of no use to him if he was suddenly confronted with an elephant, say, or a sheep. Whereas the man who unthinkingly takes it that all persons are human beings and *vice versa* has enough of the concept of a person to help him deal with any elves or Martians he might meet – enough, too, I would think, to enable him to cope (intellectually) with any manifestations of the divine which he might experience. Legal fictions are more tricky: but these persons are persons in a very obviously derivative sense, as the word 'artificial' clearly implies.

It appears that, for any X, we need a reason for calling X a person, *unless X is a human being*. There are reasons why Trade Unions are legal persons while the group which meets at the Mitre every Friday night is not. In general, an artificial person is called a person because the role it plays in society is analogous in important respects to roles played by individual human beings. The gods are persons because like human beings they issue commands, make things, give advice, punish and reward, and can be addressed (e.g. in prayer).

F

The reason why one needs a reason to call X a person differs as between the artificial and the divine, on the one hand, and possible non-human but natural persons on the other. The only reason one would need a reason, in the case of Martians, say, supposing we should one day meet some, is that these beings are and would be entirely unfamiliar to us, and their ways entirely unknown. But if it turned out that their ways were exactly like our ways, that would be a sufficient reason, not only to call them persons, but to regard them forthwith as persons in the primary and central sense of the word. Non-natural persons, however, are persons in a derivative sense or senses and could not through an increase in familiarity, come to count as persons in a primary or paradigmatic sense.

The reasons for calling some entity a person always refer back to the behaviour or (as Wittgenstein might say) to the natural history of human beings. Conversely, it would be ludicrous to be asked to give one's reasons for supposing that human beings are persons. If human beings are not persons, then, one is inclined to say, there can be no such things as persons at all.

The ordinary use of the word 'person' is, furthermore, such that *all* human beings count as persons. Various legal arrangements take note of this, but the matter itself is more than a mere legal fiction. Immature, defective, sick, and dying human beings all count as persons not only in Law, but in the way we talk. Anyone who wishes to deny *personhood* to what are in fact human beings (for instance to foreigners, or to people in coma) invariably[1] denies *humanity* as well. Thus some foreigners are sometimes described as 'sub-human' and some people in coma are sometimes described as 'merely vegetable'. (I don't by the way wish to defend this way of talking about people.) No doubt it is the slightly honorific tone of the adjective 'human' which allows such denial: for no one ever called a sick giraffe a 'mere cabbage': and whoever heard of a *sub-frog* or a *sub-elephant*? The thought behind these denigrations is: 'If not a person, then not a human being', and this surely tells us something about what should be included in a correct account of the ordinary use of 'person'.

The most obvious difference between natural, i.e. paradigmatic, persons on the one hand, and artificial persons and spirits on the other hand, is that natural persons have bodies. Following Strawson one might here conclude that the primary sense of the term 'person'

---

[1] The human embryo is a special case. Its status (as a possible person) is *sui generis*, chiefly, I think, because of the fact that during its existence *qua* embryo it changes a great deal, and very rapidly. Compare here the *Blue Book* observations on persons cited on pp. 134-5, above.

is as referring to individuals to which both corporeal and psychological predicates can be applied. On these principles there is no particular reason why one might not suppose that a parrot is thinking deep thoughts, or that a computer is conscious, while at the same time harbouring grave doubts about whether one's best friend had the *right* psychological predicates, or *enough* of them, to count as a person. I should prefer to argue that the application of the term 'person' in its central, primary, and most ordinary sense requires not only that the referent is/has a material body, but also, that it is/has a living biological body, i.e. is a member of a particular species: either the human species, or one like it. This way of thinking rules out parrots as persons on the grounds that they belong to a species of the wrong sort and it rules out computers as persons on the grounds that they are not living creatures at all. On this way of thinking, a decision to call a computer a person would be no more daring or mystifying than a decision to call some artificial (legal-fictional) persons persons. It would not incorporate any temptation to suppose that machines can be *conscious*: but would simply record the fact that the computer was playing a certain sort of role similar to one of the roles played by individual human beings.

I have said that the notion of a *person* is inclined to incorporate dualistic assumptions. This is especially true of philosophical accounts of persons, but it is also to some extent true even of the ordinary notion of a *person*. For although the ordinary notion of a *person* is derived from a certain paradigm, namely, the human being, this fact about it is perhaps not a very conspicuous fact.

We must now ask firstly: why should it be supposed anyway that the notion of a human being is less likely to lead us into problems (such as the other-minds problem) than the notion of a person? And secondly: what reason is there to believe that the notion of a human being is of any philosophical interest at all?

I will answer these questions (or at least try to) by describing certain aspects of Wittgenstein's account of consciousness as it appears in the *Philosophical Investigations*. Much of what he says about consciousness involves reference to human beings, and these are the references I want to concentrate on.

6. WITTGENSTEIN ON CONSCIOUSNESS AND HUMAN BEINGS

i. *Thinking and language both belong to the natural history of human beings*

Wittgenstein writes at *PI*, I, 466: 'What does a man think *for*? . . . We are not interested in causes – we shall say: Human beings do in fact think'. At *PI*, I, 467 he continues: 'Does a man think because he has found that thinking pays? (Does he bring up his children because he has found it pays?)' At *PI*, I, 25 he says: 'Commanding, questioning, recounting, chatting, are as much a part of our natural history as walking, eating, drinking, playing'.

2. *Certain forms of thinking and consciousness presuppose the existence of language*

On page 174 (*PI*, II, i) Wittgenstein writes: 'One can imagine an animal angry, frightened, unhappy, happy, startled. But hopeful? And why not? A dog believes his master is at the door. But can he also believe that his master will come the day after tomorrow? – And *what* can he not do here? . . . Can only those hope who can talk? Only those who have mastered the use of a language. That is to say, the phenomena of hope are modes of this complicated form of life.'

Hope, of course, is not to be taken as the only instance of a kind of consciousness which requires language. Calculating, predicting, long-range planning, and much of believing are all of them impossible to beings which have no language. A being without language could not entertain the thought encapsulated in Descartes's *Cogito*: nor indeed the doubts expressed by a Solipsist.

Now, to regard thinking, language and consciousness as part of our natural history already makes it a bit difficult to pose the other-minds problem. The term 'natural history' itself suggests the existence of tribes, kinds, varieties, or, at the very least, of pluralities of some sort or other. In this part of Wittgenstein's account, thinking, via reference to language, is designated as one of the natural activities of an existing plurality, viz., the human race.

To regard thinking, consciousness and language as part of the natural history of the human race makes it difficult to pose the problem of solipsism: but it cannot make it actually impossible, unless thinking, language, etc. are to be regarded as *essentially* the activities of a plurality of beings. Now, is the description of thinking, language, consciousness, as 'part of our natural history' supposed to be an *essential* description? (I leave aside the question as to whether such a description would be a *correct* description.)

There is some evidence, I think, that Wittgenstein intended the above account of language and thinking to be taken as an essential description. But the evidence is not, so to say, overwhelming. On the other hand, there is not much evidence in the other direction.

Let us examine some more of Wittgenstein's remarks on this topic.

3. *A living human being is a kind of paradigm of a conscious being*

Thus at *PI*, I, 281 Wittgenstein writes: 'Only of a living human being and what resembles (behaves like) one do we say that it has sensations: it sees; is blind; hears; is deaf; is conscious or unconscious'. Again, at 360 there is a very similar remark: 'We only say of a human being and what is like one that it thinks'.

Concerning consciousness, Wittgenstein says:

4. *We cannot attribute consciousness to anything we like*

Indeed, there are not many things at all to which we can attribute consciousness. Furthermore, what can be imagined in this context turns out to be not *thereby* logically possible.

At *PI*, I, 284 he writes: 'Look at a stone and imagine it having sensations . . . How could one so much as get the idea of ascribing a *sensation* to a *thing*? One might as well ascribe it to a number! – And now look at a wriggling fly, and at once these difficulties vanish and pain seems able to get a foothold here when before everything was, so to speak, too smooth for it.'

Now here, surely, an objection could be raised. Surely having acquired the notion of consciousness from wherever we do acquire it, we can then ascribe it to all sorts of things, not necessarily truthfully, but at least meaningfully? For can it be said of anything presented in experience that it is as it were logically incapable of consciousness? If that were so, how could there be such things as fairy stories, in which pots and kettles can speak and think?

Wittgenstein's answer to this objection may or may not be right, but I think it is possible to be confident about what it actually *is*. He says that such imaginings are 'of no use to us'. Thus, at *PI*, I, 390 he asks: 'Could one imagine a stone's having consciousness? And if anyone can do so – why should that not merely prove that such image-mongery is of no use to us?' A similar point is made at *PI*, I, 351 where he compares the statement: 'The stove is in pain' with the statement: 'It is 5 o'clock on the Sun', and also with the statement 'The Northern Hemisphere is above the Antipodes'.

The fact that I can picture in imagination, a clock on the Sun with its hands pointing to 5 o'clock, is neither here nor there. Given what we know of the nature of the Solar System, the fact that someone can imagine clocks on the Sun cannot suffice to give any sense to saying that it *is* 5 o'clock on the Sun. Similarly, the fact that in drawing a picture of the Earth, or in making a model of it, I can, and indeed I must, place or draw some bits of the Earth above other bits, and some bits below other bits: that fact does not suffice to give sense to the statement that, *in reality* (as compared with *in a map*) the Antipodes are below or above the Northern Hemisphere. That there are fairy-stories in which pots and kettles think and speak does not, after all, make a thinking speaking kettle into a logical possibility.

5. There are many suggestions throughout the *Philosophical Investigations* that language and the 'forms of life' with which it is associated, or of which it is part, require the existence of *several* human beings.

(i) For instance, the language-games described in the early part of the book are all of them games for two or more players. The 'forms of life', the structured activities of which the language-games form a part, are all social activities, not solitary ones. It is possible that this is an accident, not intended by the author: but rather unlikely I think. The parallel, and much longer, passages in the *Brown Book* also describe only social or tribal activities or games.

(ii) The celebrated passage which begins at *PI*, I, 244 and which is sometimes called 'the private language argument' certainly asserts (does it not?) that a private language of sensation is an impossibility. There is no reason to suppose that Wittgenstein, all the same, thought that some *other* kind of private language – a private language so to say about things which are *not* sensations – *is* a logical possibility!

(iii) There are at various places suggestions that *meaning* is a notion which can be understood only in relation to the existence of *common* human behaviour. (And of course, *language* requires *meaning*.) Thus, at *PI*, I, 206 Wittgenstein says: 'Following a rule is analogous to obeying an order. Suppose you came into an unknown country with a language quite strange to you. In what circumstances would you say that the people there gave orders, and understood them, obeyed them, rebelled against them, and so on? *The common behaviour of mankind is the system of reference by means of which we interpret an unknown language*' (my italics).

(iv) At *PI*, I, 242: 'If language is to be a means of communication there must be agreement, not only in definitions, but (queer as this may sound) in judgments'.

(v) At *PI*, I, 355 he says that all language is founded on *convention*.

(vi) At *PI*, I, 207 he says that a language must be 'regular': this 'regularity' includes *common* reactions to training, to orders and commands, etc. Without common reactions, he seems to suggest, we would have no right to call these or those sounds 'orders', 'commands', 'training', etc. – 'There is not enough regularity for us to call it "language" '.

(vii) Finally: at *PI*, I, 344 Wittgenstein asks: 'Would it be imaginable that people should never speak an audible language but should still say things to themselves in imagination? "If people always said things only to themselves then they would merely be doing always what as it is they already do sometimes" – So it is quite easy to imagine this: one need only make the easy transition from *some* to *all*.' He sarcastically compares this last move to another, saying that it is like: 'An infinitely long row of trees is simply one that does not come to an end'. Now, when he speaks here of an 'inaudible' language, he doesn't mean, of course, any kind of deaf-and-dumb speech. 'Inaudible' must be taken to embrace 'invisible' and indeed 'undetectable'. He seems to be saying, that is, that a language which cannot be used in communication is not a language at all (any more than infinity is a number).

Although human beings both at work and play sometimes become involved, up to a point, in common activities which include animals (especially dogs and cats and beasts of burden) and although in these cases the human beings could be said to be communicating with the animals in a primitive sort of way, still, common activities, common responses and reactions, common judgment, in short common 'forms of life' depend by and large upon the fact that the human race is a (one) biological species.

The overall conclusion which I am tempted to draw from these various considerations is this. Language, and therefore the higher forms of consciousness, depend, logically, for their existence on the possibility of common 'forms of life'. Hence, also, they depend, as an empirical matter of fact, on the existence of human beings regarded as members of a (fairly gregarious) species. To assert the existence of *such* forms of consciousness is in part to assert the existence, not of a single person, nor even of several separate persons, but rather, of people, that is to say, of groups of individuals having not only common characteristics but also common (mutual) responses, interactions, etc.

If this conclusion, which is about the essence of language and thought, is a true conclusion, then it means that solipsistic doubt, and the other-minds problem have disappeared.

POSTSCRIPT

I said earlier (p. 142) that although there are good reasons to place this interpretation on Wittgenstein's writings, the reasons are not, so to say, *overwhelming*. And there is in fact at least one passage in the *Investigations*, the gist of which appears (at first glance anyway) to

run counter to the suggested interpretation. This passage is at
PI, I, 243: it is interesting to compare it with *PI*, I, 344 which I
have already quoted (p. 145).

PI, I, 243 reads as follows:

> A human being can encourage himself, give himself orders,
> obey, blame, and punish himself; he can ask himself a question
> and answer it. We could even imagine human beings who spoke
> only in monologue; who accompanied their activities by talking
> to themselves. An explorer who watched them and listened to
> their talk might succeed in translating their language into ours.
> (This would enable him to predict these people's actions correctly,
> for he also hears them making resolutions and decisions.)

(Here follows the celebrated section on 'private languages'.)

The difference between the 'language' described in *PI*, I, 243
and the 'language' described in *PI*, I, 344 is of course that the latter
is inaudible. The 'language' of 344 *cannot* be used in communication,
whereas the 'language' of 243 is *not in fact* used in communication, ever. It seems that if Wittgenstein allowed such a 'monologue
language' as a possibility then the interpretation offered in this
paper has been somewhat undermined.

PI, I, 243 is puzzling in two ways. Firstly, it is puzzling because it
appears to contradict what could perhaps be called the general
tendency of the whole book; and is indeed hard to square with many
particular paragraphs. Secondly, it is puzzling in itself, for the case,
the example, is 'under-described'. It is not really clear just what sort
of set-up Wittgenstein here envisaged.

One question that comes up is this: how did the people who
speak the audible 'monologue language' ever come to learn it?
If their language is *never* used in communication, then learning and
teaching are impossible. The learning and teaching of language are
themselves a kind of communication and the language being taught
and learnt is *itself* an element in that communication.

If we avoid this difficulty by supposing that the people of 243
acquired their language 'in a flash' and/or as the result of the
agency of a supernatural power, we then have to square this
solution with those passages in the *Investigations* whose apparent
purpose is to repudiate and refute so-called 'solutions' of just
that type. Thus, we will have to square the solution with *PI*, I, 346,
which reads: '. . . couldn't we imagine God's suddenly giving a
parrot understanding and its now saying things to itself? – But
here it is an important fact that I imagined a deity in order to
imagine this.'

Now, are the people who speak always in audible monologue similar to the parrot? Is it *important* that we cannot conceive of them teaching each other, but must suppose that their language comes from the intervention of an all-powerful being? Or is it *non-important?*

Another question that comes up is this: if the people of 243 do not teach each other their language, how is it that there is in their tribe or group just *one* language? For Wittgenstein says the explorer might come to understand *the* language of the place. I suppose this too would have to be explained by reference to a deity or some such. And again: would Wittgenstein regard this as an 'important' fact, or not?

A third difficulty which *I* feel is this: by what right does the explorer (or Wittgenstein) decide that the people in the example *are* in fact speaking in monologue all the time? And we must remember that 'monologue' means, here, 'speech addressed to oneself'.

If a man is alone, and is speaking a language known to us, we have some right to say, on the basis of *that* description, that he is speaking to himself. But not invariably, of course: if he is whispering into a microphone, or directing his words at a dictation machine, the case is altered. If a solitary man utters sounds that even so much as *sound* like a language, we have *some* right to say that he is speaking, and speaking in monologue, i.e. speaking to himself.

Consider now the explorer of *PI*, I, 243. Let us suppose he one day finds himself in what looks like a work-group, or at a party, or in some gathering or other. The other people present are uttering sounds which seem to be part of a language: of *one* language. These sounds 'accompany their activities'. The explorer (and Wittgenstein) know, however, that the language being spoken on this occasion is being spoken as a number of separate monologues. But *how* could this be known? Suppose that some of the activities were joint activities, like sharing out the peanuts and olives, or distributing spades, pick-axes, trowels, and the like. Let us remind ourselves of what was said in *PI*, I, 206 (already cited, p. 144: 'The common behaviour of mankind is the system of reference by means of which we interpret an unknown language') and now ask *by what right, for what reason*, the explorer *rejects* as translations of the sounds uttered on such occasions such bits of dialogue as: 'Have some celery', 'No thanks', 'Bring that brick', 'OK', 'Here's your shovel, mate', 'But I wanted the one with the square handle!'? Part of the imaginative exercise referred to as possible at *PI*, I, 243 would be like this: it would have to be the imagining of groups and collections of 'people' (or beings) which did not *in fact* engage in co-operative ventures, or alternatively, of groups or collections of beings which, when they did engage in co-operative ventures in fact did not utter any sounds or make any significant meaningful gestures: reserving their sounds and gestures for occasions on which they were alone or virtually alone.

Such a feat of the imagination is in a way possible, of course. (Octopi might go on like this for all I know.) But now we have to square this bit of 'imagine-mongery' with, for example, *PI*, II, xi, p. 223: 'If a lion could talk we could not understand him'. Is it really true that the explorer of *PI*, I, 243 could translate the language of the people he meets there? What is his system of reference?

My present view of 243 is as follows: it does not, after all, in any way undermine the interpretation of Wittgenstein's writings in the *Investigations* on the topics of consciousness, language, and human beings which has been put forward in this paper.

For, in the first place, it runs counter to the general tendency of the *Investigations* as a whole, and cannot easily be squared with individual paragraphs therein which concern the same topics.

In the second place, the situation described in 243 is in fact *underdescribed*. We just do not *know* what Wittgenstein would have said in answer to such questions as: 'Do these folk ever engage in co-operative ventures? How far is their life-style like that of any known race or tribe of human beings? How do they learn (or acquire) their language? How far are they similar to the parrot of *PI*, I, 346, or to the lion of p. 223 (*PI*, II, xi)? Do they for instance rear their children in a way which is roughly similar to the way in which real human beings are reared?' (etc.)

In the third place, the paragraph which is causing all this trouble for my interpretation does in fact occur immediately before the section on 'private languages'. It seems possible, and indeed probable, that in *PI*, I, 243 Wittgenstein was as it were making a *maximum concession* to any readers who might be attracted to the idea of a 'private language theory' of the origins of language and meaning. This maximum concession, however, consists of an atypical and under-described example, from which no real positive conclusions ought to be drawn. I think, therefore, that my interpretation can stand.

10

OTHER MINDS

Godfrey Vesey

1. INTRODUCTION

THERE is a passage in Wittgenstein's *Philosophical Investigations*[1]
in which he compares an answer that may be given to a philosophical
question about someone else's pain with an answer that may be
given to a question about the meaning of 'It is 5 o'clock on the sun'.
Wittgenstein does not compare other answers that may be given to
the two questions. And he does not compare the questions themselves
in respect of what lies behind them – making them ones which we
can, or cannot, easily 'see through' – or in respect of how they
should be answered. Yet there is material in what he says elsewhere
in the *Investigations* and in other of his later writings[2] for a many-
sided and, I think, useful development of the comparison. Anyway,
that is what I shall attempt in this lecture.[3]

2. AFTERNOON ON THE SUN

Consider the question 'How can I mean anything by "It's afternoon
on the sun"?'

[1] *PI*, I, 350: ' "But if I suppose that someone has a pain, then I am simply
supposing that he has just the same as I have so often had." – That gets us no
further. It is as if I were to say: "You surely know what 'It is 5 o'clock here'
means; so you also know what 'It's 5 o'clock on the sun' means. It means simply
that it is just the same time there as it is here when it is 5 o'clock." '

[2] Particularly *PE*, pp. 275–6, 281, 290, 295–6, 301–3, 312–20; *BB*, pp. 46–9,
55–7, 103–5; *PI*, I, 244, 256–8, 261, 264, 268–9, 273–4, 283–4, 293, 304, 307–8,
350–1, 357, 363, 572–3, 580, 582, 585–7, II, i, ix, xii; *Z*, 78, 170, 469, 487, 532–4,
537, 540–2, 545–51.

[3] I am grateful to Rush Rhees and Peter Hacker for comments on an early
draft of this lecture.

To see what lies behind it, ask "What is the explanation of the meaning of "It's afternoon"?"

We know very well what the correct explanation is. I shall call it the fact-presupposing explanation. The fact presupposed is that the earth revolves on its axis so that places on the earth have varying positions relative to the sun. Were it not for this fact of *nature* we wouldn't have our time-of-day language. But, having it, it is a fact of *grammar* (in Wittgenstein's sense) that it is afternoon at a place on the earth when at that place the sun is past the zenith but not yet over the horizon. Knowing that this is the explanation of the meaning of 'It's afternoon' we can see how we might use the term 'afternoon' on another planet, such as Mars. Mars takes a bit longer to revolve on its axis than the earth, so a Mars afternoon would be a bit longer than an earth afternoon.

We can imagine the following situation. A space-craft lands on Mars. The never-ending dust-storms prevent the space-travellers from knowing, by looking out of their space-craft port-holes, whether it is a Martian day or night. The outlook is equally black. Nevertheless they note that the temperature regularly rises and falls, and they suppose that, as on Earth, when it is warmer it is day-time. Knowing the *meaning* of 'It is day-time on Mars' they have used an argument from analogy to settle a question of *fact*, the question whether or not it is day-time on Mars.

Knowing the fact-presupposing explanation of 'It's afternoon' we can see through the question 'How can I mean anything by "It's afternoon on the sun"?' That is, we can see that the answer we should give is 'You can't, short of giving an entirely new meaning to "It's afternoon", and why should you want to do that?' We can see why we can extend the use of 'afternoon' to Mars but not to the sun. The sun can't be past, or not past, the zenith on the sun.

Suppose, now, that a different sort of explanation of the meaning of 'It's afternoon' had been given. I shall call it an *experiential* explanation, because it is in terms of our experiences. We can imagine someone saying: 'We understand "It's afternoon" from our own case, i.e. from our experience on earth of, for example, seeing the sun more than half-way across the sky as we recline in our garden chairs after lunch. What is to stop us from generalising? Can't we at least *suppose* that we might have the same experience on the sun?'

If someone who said this was asked 'But what do you *mean* by "It's afternoon on the sun"?' he might say 'I mean just the same as I mean by "It's afternoon" on the earth'.

Challenged to explain how he could mean the same, since he

couldn't conceivably experience the sun in the sky on the sun, he might, but very implausibly, produce the following justification for the generalisation of time-of-day language to the sun. On the earth there is regularly more evaporation – effusions of water-vapour from the surface – by day than by night. But on the sun there is something analogous. There are, regularly, outbreaks of solar-flare activity. (The composition of the sun and the earth being what they are it is natural that the effusions on the sun should be of fiery matter whereas those on the earth should be of water-vapour.) In view of the analogy it is reasonable to suppose that there are sun-days and nights, and a sun-afternoon when the solar-flare activity is past its peak but not yet entirely over.

If it were again put to him that he couldn't conceivably experience the sun in the sky on the sun, he might, even more implausibly, say: 'That is why I said "suppose". I agree, of course, that the supposition can't be verified.'

To this it might be replied that it is not simply the case that the evaporation/solar-flares analogy is not sufficiently strong an analogy to justify our using the term 'afternoon' on the sun; it is *no justification at all*. The situation is quite different from the one in which we say 'It's afternoon' on Mars. On Mars the time-of-day language-game is practically the same as on earth, and, given the language-game, we use an argument from analogy to settle a question of fact that arises within the language-game. The fact that day-time and warmth are merely contingently related, provided it is a reliable contingent relation, does not affect the validity of the argument from analogy. But when it comes to saying 'It's afternoon' on the sun the evaporation/solar-flares analogy is being advanced, not in order to justify an answer to a question of fact that arises within the language-game, but in order to justify an extension of the language-game we have on earth to the sun. And we can easily see that an external contingent relation, no matter how regular a contingent relation it is, won't do the trick. We can see this because we are in no doubt as to the fact-presupposing explanation of the meaning of 'It's afternoon'. As I said, the sun can't be past, or not past, the zenith on the sun.

We are not tempted to give an experiential explanation of the meaning of 'It's afternoon', or beguiled by answers to the 'Afternoon on the Sun' question like 'We mean the same by "It's afternoon on the sun" as we mean by "It's afternoon" on the earth'. So in the way in which there is an 'Other Minds' problem in philosophy there is not an 'Afternoon on the Sun' problem. We can see through the questions and answers about 'Afternoon on the Sun'. That is why it is useful to compare questions and answers about 'Other Minds' with questions and answers about 'Afternoon on the Sun'. It is useful because our aim is to see through questions and answers about 'Other Minds'.

3. OTHER MINDS

Consider the question 'How can I mean anything by "There exist pains I don't feel, pains in other minds"?', and compare it with the question about afternoon on the sun.

What immediately occurs to us is not a fact-presupposing explanation of the meaning of pain-language. It is two, opposed, experiential explanations – one in terms of 'the feeling of pain itself', the other in terms of people looking, sounding, etc., as if they are in pain ('pain-behaviour'). The first of these is the more compelling. We think: surely we learn concepts by having experiences, and surely the experience that matters in the case of the concept 'pain' is the pain itself. But since the pain I have to experience to learn the concept is necessarily *my* pain, this explanation leads to our asking ourselves the question 'What possible reason could I have to think that other people ever have what I mean by "pain"?' – a question which invites the answers, 'None' (solipsism) or, alternatively, 'An argument from analogy'. But solipsism is intuitively unacceptable; and nobody seems to be able to come up with an argument from analogy that will do the trick. Hence our perplexity, the 'Other Minds' problem.

Wittgenstein's contribution to 'dissolving' the 'Other Minds' problem has two sides to it: one negative, an attack on the experiential explanation of the meaning of pain-language in terms of 'the feeling itself'; and one positive, a fact-presupposing explanation of the meaning of pain-language.

The fact that the negative side receives very much more attention from him than the positive side, and that the attack is pressed home on only one of the two experiential explanations, has had the unfortunate result that Wittgenstein can be mistakenly thought to be giving the alternative experiential explanation, in terms of behaviour. But to read Wittgenstein as a behaviourist is to ignore the many passages in which he explicitly disavows that he is attacking one experiential explanation only to embrace another,[1] and to ignore his own fact-presupposing explanation of the meaning of pain-language.

Since it is only by understanding his own fact-presupposing

---

[1] *PE*, p. 296; *PI*, I, 244, 281, 304, 307.

explanation of the meaning of pain-language that we can hope to see through questions and answers about 'Other Minds', let us consider the positive side of his teaching first.

4. WITTGENSTEIN'S OWN EXPLANATION OF PAIN-LANGUAGE

The fact-presupposing explanation of the meaning of 'It's afternoon' is in terms of certain things which happen naturally, such as the earth's revolving on its axis. Were it not for these things there would not be the possibility of the time-of-day language. Similarly, Wittgenstein's fact-presupposing explanation of the meaning of pain-language is in terms of things that happen naturally. People moan and cry when they are in pain. And other people react to their moaning and crying by tending the part that has been hurt.¹ This is something that happens naturally. There are, we might say, natural or primitive 'expressions' of pain. Wittgenstein says that a child learns to use pain-language 'to replace its moans'.² The linguistic expression 'stands for', 'is a substitute for', the natural expression.³ In my ordinary use of words to stand for sensations my words are 'tied up with my natural expressions of sensation'.⁴ If people did not naturally groan, grimace, etc., 'then it would be impossible to teach a child the use of the word "toothache" '.⁵ 'The game we play with the word "toothache" entirely depends upon there being a behaviour which we call the expression of toothache.'⁶ 'The language-games with expressions of feelings are based on games with expressions of which we don't say they may lie.'⁷

But to see what this talk of the linguistic expression 'replacing' the natural expression really means we must consider, in order to reject, the prevalent notion that if someone says 'It hurts' or 'I'm afraid', and they are not lying, then what they say must be justified by some observation. It is not justified by an observation of their own behaviour. Therefore, it is thought, it must be justified by something

---

¹ *Z*, 540–5; cf. *PI*, II, ii: 'My attitude towards him is an attitude towards a soul. I am not of the *opinion* that he has a soul.'

² *PE*, p. 295. See also *PI*, I, 244.

³ *PE*, p. 301.　　　⁴ *PI*, I, 256.

⁵ *PI*, I, 257.　　　⁶ *PE*, p. 290.

⁷ *PE*, p. 293. Some of these quotations might be interpreted as endorsing the experiential explanation of the meaning of pain-language in terms of behaviour. But (*PE*, p. 296) Wittgenstein writes: ' "Do you mean that you can define pain in terms of behaviour?" But is this what we do if we teach the child to use the expression "I have toothache"? Did I define: "Toothache is such and such a behaviour"? This obviously contradicts entirely the normal use of the word!'

else – an inner feeling of pain or fear.[1] They 'introspect' the feeling, and then 'express' it in language.[2] When Wittgenstein says that the linguistic expression is a substitute for the natural expression, and that there is no sharp line between the linguistic and the natural expression of a feeling,[3] he is attacking the notion that in the relation between saying 'It hurts' and being in pain there must be a justifying element of reflecting on how one feels (a 'ground' for the utterance), an element which doesn't come into the relation between moaning and being in pain.

Consider the following sentences:

(*a*) He had difficulty keeping his eyes open.

(*b*) He said 'I think I could do with a strong cup of coffee' (to keep awake).

(*c*) He spoke irritably.

(*d*) He yawned.

(*e*) He said 'I expect you've got a busy day tomorrow' (as a hint to the guest that he should go to bed).

(*f*) He made an elaborate pretence of yawning (as a signal that it was bed time).

(*g*) He stretched, sighed, and said 'Oh, I'm so tired'.

(*h*) He thought for a while, then said 'You know, I think I'm getting a bit tired; I think I need a holiday'.

The words 'because he was tired' could be added to each of them. What would it mean in the case of (*g*)? Is the speaker in (*g*) *describing his feelings*? (In (*b*) is he *describing his thoughts*?) Or is saying 'Oh, I'm so tired', although it is a learnt, and not an involuntary, expression of tiredness, as natural a part of the tiredness-syndrome for someone in our linguistic community as yawning? Is saying 'Oh, I'm so tired' natural tiredness-behaviour for us, in spite of the fact that 'I'm tired', unlike yawning, even pretence yawning, can be said to be true or false?

I think Wittgenstein's answer to the last two questions would be

---

[1] *PE*, p. 319.

[2] *PE*, p. 312: 'The idea is here that there is an "expression" for everything, that we know what it means "to express something," "to describe something". Here is a feeling, an experience, and now I could say to someone "express it!" But what is to be the relation of the expression to what it expresses? In what way is this expression the expression of this feeling rather than another?! One is inclined to say "we *mean* this feeling by its expression," but what is meaning a feeling by a word like? Is this quite clear if, e.g., I have explained what "meaning this person by the name '*N*'" is like?'

[3] *BB*, p. 103.

'Yes'. I think he would say that 'because he was tired', added to
'He said "Oh, I'm so tired"', serves to distinguish the case in
question from ones in which someone is, say, play-acting, or
lying; but that it would be a mistake to regard saying this as an
endorsement of the experiential explanation, in terms of feelings, of
the meaning of tiredness language. He writes, not of tiredness but of
toothache, as follows:

> Now what makes a 'natural form of expression' natural? Should
> we say 'An experience which stands behind it'?
>   If I use the expression 'I have toothache' I may think of it as
> 'being used naturally' or otherwise, but it would be wrong to say
> that I had a *reason* for thinking either.[1]

> 'I don't just *say* "I've got toothache", but *toothache makes me say
> this*.' (I deliberately didn't write 'the feeling of toothache', or 'a
> certain feeling'.)
>   This sentence distinguishes between, say, saying it as an example
> of a sentence, or on the stage, etc., and saying it as an assertion.
> But it is no explanation of the expression 'I have toothache', of
> the use of the word 'toothache'.[2]

It is important to see, here, that Wittgenstein is not denying that
people do have toothache (that it really aches!),[3] or even that
people sometimes reflect on their feelings and describe them, as in
(*h*).[4] What he is asserting is that 'I have toothache' has meaning in
virtue of pain-language taking the place of moaning; and what he
is denying is that saying this commits him to an experiential explanation of the meaning of pain-language. For moaning is not describing,
hence it is not the description either of behaviour or of feeling. And
so the verbal expression 'I have toothache', that replaces it, is not a

---

[1] *PE*, p. 313.

[2] *PE*, p. 315. See also p. 319.

[3] *Z*, 487 (in terms of joy).

[4] *PI*, I, 585–7 and, especially, II, ix. But note that in *PI*, I, 290–2 Wittgenstein
says that describing my state of mind is not like describing my room, that 'thinking
of a description as a word-picture of the facts has something misleading about
it', and that you should not 'always think that you read off what you see from the
facts'. In *PI*, II, ix he says: 'I can find no answer if I try to settle the question
"What am I referring to?" "What am I thinking when I say it?" by repeating the
expression of fear and at the same time attending to myself, as it were observing
my soul out of the corner of my eye. In a concrete case I can indeed ask "Why
did I say that, what did I mean by it?" – and I might answer the question; *but
not on the ground of observing what accompanied the speaking*. And my answer would
supplement, paraphrase, the earlier utterance.' (My italics.)

description either – either of behaviour[1] or of feeling.[2] It is, itself, behaviour.[3] We might even say that to call it a *statement* is misleading.[4]

In the light of this fact-presupposing explanation of the meaning of pain-language, Wittgenstein can answer the question 'How can I mean anything by "There exist pains I don't feel, pains in other minds"?' as follows. The question arises only because you think of having learned the meaning of the word 'pain' by some sort of internal ostensive definition. You insist on giving an experiential explanation of the meaning. But that is a mistake. A child grows up in a community in which people moan and cry when they are in pain (as he does himself); in which they also use expressions like 'I'm in pain' and 'I've got toothache'; in which others react sympathetically to their linguistic, as to their non-linguistic, expressions of pain; and so he comes to use the linguistic expression himself in the place of the natural expression. All this gives the word 'pain' the meaning it has.[5] In its absence we wouldn't even be able to understand the question 'What possible reason could I have to think that other people ever have what *I* mean by "pain"?', let alone the answers that have been given to it.

5. COMPARISON

I said that Wittgenstein paid more attention to the negative side of his teaching, his attack on the experiential explanation of the meaning of pain-language in terms of feelings, than to the positive side, his own explanation in terms of 'It hurts' replacing moaning. There are two sides to his attack on the experiential explanation. The first is an attack on the main element in the experiential explanation. This is the idea that all words have meaning by being names of things referred to by them, and that learning the meaning of a word is a matter of finding out what thing it refers to, what thing bears the name in question.[6] (The subsidiary element is the idea that since 'pain' is evidently not the name of a material object

[1] *PI*, I, 244: ' "So you are saying that the word 'pain' really means crying?" – On the contrary: the verbal expression of pain replaces crying and does not describe it.' Also, *PI*, I, 357: 'I do *not* say it from observation of my behaviour. But it only makes sense because I do behave in this way.'

[2] *PE*, p. 319: 'One wishes to say: In order to be able to say that I have toothache I don't observe my behaviour, say in the mirror. *And this is correct*, but it doesn't follow that you describe an observation of any other kind. Moaning is not the description of an observation. That is, you can't be said to *derive* your expression from what you observe.' See also *PI*, I, 357; *Z*, 78, 487.

[3] *PI*, I, 582, II, i; *Z*, 545.   [4] *Z*, 549.   [5] *Z*, 532–4.
[6] *PE*, pp. 276, 290, 296, 312; *PI*, I, 244, 257, 264, 268, 274, 293, II, ix; *Z*, 545.

it must be the name of an aethereal one, a personal experience.[1])
The second is what might be described as a pathology of the positions
(solipsism, etc.) adopted by those philosophers who accept the
experiential explanation.[2] Since it is an exposition of the second
part that is aided by a comparison with the 'Afternoon on the Sun'
question and answers, I shall devote my remaining time to it. I have,
in any case, written on the first part elsewhere recently.[3]

Now for the comparison.

In section 2 I said that we can imagine someone saying: 'We
understand "It's afternoon" from our own case, i.e. from our
experience on earth of, for example, seeing the sun more than
half-way across the sky, etc. What is to stop us generalising?
Can't we at least *suppose* that we might have the same experience
on the sun?'

Similarly, we can imagine someone saying: 'We understand pain-
language from our own case, i.e. from our experience of pain.
What is to stop us generalising? Can't we at least *suppose* that others
have the same experience?'

In section 2 I said that if someone were asked 'But what do you
mean by "It's afternoon on the sun"?' he might say 'I mean just
the same as I mean by "It's afternoon" on the earth'.

Similarly, if someone were asked 'But what do you *mean* by
"Someone else is in pain"?' he might say 'I mean just the same by
"pain" when I say someone else is in pain as I mean when I say
"I'm in pain" '.

In section 2 I said that challenged to explain *how* he could mean
the same, since he couldn't conceivably experience the sun in the
sky on the sun, he might produce an argument from analogy to
justify the generalisation of time-of-day language to the sun.

Similarly, challenged to explain *how* he could mean the same
by 'pain' in 'Someone else is in pain' as in 'I'm in pain', since he
couldn't conceivably experience someone else's pain, he might
produce an argument from analogy to justify the generalisation of
pain-language to others.

It would go like this: 'I've noticed that I regularly groan when
I'm in pain. Other people sometimes groan. Surely it is reasonable
to suppose that they have the same feeling as I have when they
do so.'

If it were again put to him that he couldn't conceivably experience

---

[1] *BB*, p. 47.

[2] *PE*, pp. 281, 319; *BB*, pp. 46, 48–9, 55–6; *PI*, I, 283, 293, 350; *Z*, 537, 542,
545–7.

[3] *Other Minds?* (The Open University Press, 1973).

other people's pain, he might say 'That is why I said "suppose".
I agree, of course, that the supposition can't be verified.'[1]

Now, although the idea that whenever we see that someone is
in pain we make an inference from behaviour to feeling is about as
mythical as the idea that at some time in the past we made a
Social Contract,[2] the 'argument from analogy' line of reasoning
seems much less implausible here than in the 'Afternoon on the
Sun' case. Although it does not in fact provide a justification, we
are much less inclined to say that it does not. Why is this so?

There are a number of reasons. Let me briefly mention just three
of them.

The first is that we are not so tempted to think of the word
'afternoon' as having a meaning for us in virtue of being the name
of an object, as we are to think of 'pain' as having a meaning for us
in virtue of being the name of an object. We are much more ready
to accept a fact-presupposing explanation of the meaning, in
terms of the earth's revolving on its axis, and so on, than to accept
what Ryle would call a ' "Fido" – Fido' explanation. In the case of
pain, on the other hand, it seems to us to be a substantive and yet
not to be the name of a material object.[3] And so we come under the
spell of Descartes, for whom, since the mind is distinct from the body,
a pain must be a mental, a private, object.

The second relates to what I said about the evaporation/solar-
flares analogy being an *external* relation. There is no connection
between effusion, as such, and the time-of-day language. But there
is a connection between moaning and the pain-language – namely,
the one for which Wittgenstein argues, that 'I'm hurt' *replaces*
moaning. Since there is a connection it is understandable that we
should think there is. But this doesn't explain why we should think
it is the sort that is invoked in an argument from analogy.

The third reason relates to the fact that whereas it doesn't make
sense to say 'It's afternoon' on the sun, it does make sense to talk of
other people's feelings. The reason why it makes sense is not
because of an argument from analogy. But since it does make sense

---

[1] *PE*, p. 281: ' "So if I say 'he has toothache' I am supposing that he has what I
have when I have toothache." Suppose I said: "If I say 'I *suppose* he has toothache'
I am supposing that he has what I have if I have toothache" – this would be like
saying "If I say 'this cushion is red' I mean that it has the same colour which the
sofa has if it is red." But this isn't what I intended to say with the first sentence. I
wished to say that talking about his toothache at all was based upon a supposition,
a supposition which by its very essence could not be verified.'

[2] *PE*, p. 281; *Z*, 537, 542. See also *PE*, pp. 303, 313, 318.

[3] *BB*, p. 47; *PI*, II, ix: 'We ask "What does 'I am frightened' really mean,
what am I referring to when I say it?" '

we can employ arguments from analogy to answer factual questions that arise within the language-game. For example, I can say that Jones is behaving just like Smith did, and we now know that Smith behaved as he did because he had feelings of being persecuted, so it is possible that Jones has feelings of being persecuted, too. In short, whereas there is not the possibility of using an argument from analogy to answer factual questions about time on the sun, there is this possibility when it comes to people's feelings, and so, being predisposed by the second reason to think that there is *some* sort of connection between moaning and the pain-language, we naturally fall into the trap of confusing valid fact-establishing arguments from analogy with invalid meaning-establishing ones, and produce the well-known argument that I am, in general, justified in applying 'mental' language to other people by the fact that they behave as I do when I'm in a certain state of mind. It takes a Wittgenstein to pull us up with a jolt, by saying that this is like translating a chair – not the word 'chair', but a chair – into French.[1]

6. CONCLUSION

In conclusion, is there anything of a general nature that can be said about Wittgenstein's treatment of the 'Other Minds' problem?

I think there is. It illustrates, I think, three elements in his later philosophy of language. The first is his idea that language is not a thing apart from the rest of life, and related to it only via what goes on in the mind of the language-user.[2] The second is that the components of language do not have meaning for us in virtue of standing for objects, of various ontological kinds, with which we become acquainted through some kind of ostensive definition. The third is the application of the second to concepts like 'pain': words like 'pain' do not have meaning for us in virtue of standing for

---

[1] *Z*, 547: 'So he is having genuine pain, and it is the possession of *this* by someone else that he feels doubt of. – But how does he do this? – It is as if I were told: "Here is a chair. Can you see it clearly? – Good – Now translate it into French!" ' This is connected with the remark (*Z*, 548): 'In order to doubt whether someone else is in pain he needs, not pain, but the *concept* "pain" '. See also *PI*, I, 283, 383–4.

[2] *PI*, II, i: 'And do you mean to tell me he doesn't feel it? How else does he *know* it? – But even when he says it as a piece of information he does not learn it from his sensations. For think of the sensations produced by physically shuddering: the words "it makes me shiver" are themselves such a shuddering reaction; and if I hear and feel them as I utter them, this belongs among the rest of those sensations. Now why should the wordless shudder be the ground of the verbal one?' See also *PE*, pp. 313, 318; *BB*, p. 103; *PI*, I, 304, 363, 585, II, ix; *Z*, 78, 170, and, especially, 545.

objects with which we become acquainted through an internal ostensive definition. If all this had to be summed up in one sentence I suppose it would have to be that Wittgenstein's treatment of the 'Other Minds' problem is an extended illustration of a point in philosophical logic: namely, that the *meaningfulness* of some of the things we say is dependent on contingent facts of nature – such as that the earth revolves on its axis, and that we moan with pain and react as we do to others who moan. One reason why the 'Other Minds' problem was so important for Wittgenstein was because he could not dissolve it without revising the view he had taken on this point when he wrote the *Tractatus*.[1]

The expression 'facts of nature' is one which Wittgenstein himself uses.[2] But I think I should, finally, draw attention to a difference between what might be called facts of physical nature and facts of human nature. Wittgenstein uses the expression 'form of life' in the latter connection.

That the earth revolves on its axis is, of course, a fact that has very important implications for our lives. But it is not itself a fact of our lives. That we moan with pain and react as we do to others who moan, on the other hand, is a fact of our lives. Wittgenstein writes:

> The concept of pain is characterized by its particular function in our life. Pain has *this* position in our life; has *these* connexions. (That is to say: we only call 'pain' what has *this* position, these connexions.)
>
> Only surrounded by certain normal manifestations of life, is there such a thing as an expression of pain. Only surrounded by an even more far-reaching particular manifestation of life, such a thing as the expression of sorrow or affection. And so on.[3]

We can imagine forms of social life which don't provide the necessary backing for sorrow and affection. Jean-Luc Godard's film 'Alphaville', is about this. In Alphaville a child is unlikely to see its father. Natasha, the heroine, 'speaks of her father as if being his child was a theoretical, not sentimental, relationship'.[4] A man who is so abnormal as to weep at the death of his wife is said to be behaving illogically.[5] They don't have the word 'weep'. Nor do they have words like 'tears', 'tenderness', or 'love'. When the hero,

---

[1] *TLP*, 2.0211–2.   [2] *PI*, II, xii.   [3] *Z*, 532–4.

[4] From the 'original Treatment' in *Alphaville, a film by Jean-Luc Godard*, English translation and description of action by Peter Whitehead (London: Lorrimer Publishing, 1966) p. 89.

[5] Cf. *Z*, 383.

Lemmy, tells Natasha he loves her, she says 'Love . . . love . . . what is that?' He says 'This' and caresses her. But she says 'No . . . that's something I know all about . . . that's sensuality'. But eventually his loving concern for her evokes a response. It reminds me a bit of Wittgenstein's account of how a child might be trained in the practice of 'narration of past events':[1]

> NATASHA: You're looking at me in a very strange way! I've the feeling that you expect me to say something to you?
> LEMMY: Yes.
> NATASHA: I don't know what to say. At least I don't know the words. I was never taught them. Please help me . . .
> LEMMY: Impossible, Princess. You've got to manage by yourself, and only then will you be saved. If you can't . . . then you are as lost as the dead in Alphaville.
> NATASHA: I . . .
> . . . love . . .
> . . . you . . .
> I love you.[2]

In the Original Treatment it says: 'Natasha tells Lemmy that she loves him, but pronounces it as a child speaks its first words'.[3]

To say that Natasha has discovered how to *express* love is to miss the point. It is the possibility of love itself that the film is about. The *logical* possibility.

---

[1] *BB*, pp. 104–5.　　[2] *Alphaville*, p. 75.　　[3] Ibid, p. 97.

11

WITTGENSTEIN ON THE SOUL

İlham Dilman

1. IT is sometimes said that a human being has a soul, whereas animals and lifeless things do not. The distinction made is of significance probably for most religions. Although it sets man apart and places him in a unique category, it should not be taken to imply that there is no difference between what is alive and has sentience, apart from man, and what is lifeless and unconscious. This was Descartes' error. For he ran together several distinctions and equated the soul with consciousness.

If we are to appreciate the nature and religious import of this distinction we must begin by asking what the existence of the soul amounts to and why it is only human beings who are said to have souls. It is very difficult not to think of the soul as a substance – 'something subtle like air or fire or aether (as Descartes puts it) mingled among the grosser parts of the body'. Those who denied its existence have very often done so just because they thought of it as a substance and could not find any evidence for its existence – in J. B. Watson's words: 'No one has ever touched the soul, or seen one in a test tube, or has in any way come into a relationship with it as he has with other objects of his daily experience'.[1]

Wittgenstein opposed this picture, and he helped us to appreciate what the existence of the soul amounts to without thinking of it as a substance. 'The human body is the best picture of the human soul' he wrote in *Philosophical Investigations* (II, iv). And again: 'If one sees the behaviour of a living thing one sees its soul' (*PI*, I, 357). Part of what is being said here is that we can see what state of soul a man is in – whether, for instance, he is joyful or depressed,

[1] J. B. Watson and W. McDougall, *The Battle of Behaviourism* (Psyche Miniatures General Series) p. 13.

hopeful or in despair – in his behaviour. I shall not discuss the problems connected with this part of Wittgenstein's contention. He is also saying that the reality of the soul, i.e. the *possibility* of joy and sorrow, love, grief, hope and despair, depends on the life of those capable of these things, and can be seen in human behaviour.

But this is not like seeing a man's anger or distress in his words, face and deeds. For when on a given occasion what a man says or does convinces me that he is angry or hurt, the possibility remains that I may be wrong. Whereas there is no question for me whether he has a soul – unless this means whether he has lost his soul and stopped caring about the depravity into which he has sunk. My point is that the very conception I take of him when I talk of what he *says* and *does*, when I use the personal pronoun in referring to him, when I address him in the way I do, precludes the possibility of giving sense to the words 'He has no soul'. But if that has no sense, then neither do the words 'He has a soul'.

Thus if, under ordinary circumstances, I were to point to someone and say that he has a soul it would not be clear what I was saying. Am I drawing attention to something you are likely to forget? Could you be under some misapprehension which I might wish to correct? (See *PI*, II, iv – 'He isn't an automaton'.) Contrast with: 'He has feelings, you know' – said to someone who is treating him callously. The point remains that in the absence of such special circumstances I might still be *trying* to say something, even though what I come out with does not make sense as it stands. For I might be a philosopher fighting against those who wish to deny the existence of the soul.

What is in question is not so much a belief I have about this person in particular, or about human beings in general, as a conception within the framework of which I may hold different beliefs – for instance, that my friend is in pain:

'I believe that he is suffering.' Do I also *believe* that he isn't an automaton? (*PI*, II, iv)

Compare with:

I have a telephone conversation with New York. My friend tells me that his young trees have buds of such and such a kind. I am now convinced that his tree is . . . Am I also convinced that the earth exists? (*OC*, 208)

Wittgenstein would say that the latter proposition belongs to my frame of reference: What could stand upright if that were to fall?

Could I, for instance, have a telephone conversation with a friend in New York?

Similarly, if I believe that he is suffering then I am necessarily taking a certain conception of what is before me. We do not have a second belief here that can be open to doubt or question. Of course, during a visit to Mme Tussaud's, I may doubt, for a moment, whether what seems to be an attendant is really an attendant and not one of the wax figures to be found there. And my friend may whisper: 'I believe he is one of the attendants'. My doubt, short-lived as it is, has a specific basis: Is he a live human being or only a wax imitation? Suppose that it moves and begins to talk. This will remove my doubt. I see that he is one of the attendants, a live human being. This discovery changes my whole attitude to what is before me. If a moment ago I had thought of it as a wax figure then I could not have intelligibly supposed that he might be hungry or bored. There would have been no logical room for me to hold this belief.

It could, of course, be said that first I *believed* one thing, namely that what is before me is a wax figure, and that soon after I came to *believe* something else, namely that all the time I was looking at one of the attendants. But this is different from the case where I first *believe* that he is in pain and then come to see that he was pretending. In the former case Wittgenstein speaks of an 'attitude':

> Our attitude to what is alive and to what is dead, is not the same. (*PI*, I, 284)
>
> My attitude towards him is an attitude towards a soul. I am not of the *opinion* that he has a soul. (*PI*, II, iv)

Having this attitude means reacting to people in certain ways – for instance, resenting what they say, being insulted, hurt, angered or irritated by their words and deeds, being grateful for what they do, pitying them, feeling embarrassed in their presence, and so on. This attitude, these reactions are a pretty basic feature of the life we live. Without them it is hard to think what human life would be like and whether we would be human at all. They form part of the framework in which we attribute various emotions, intentions, plans and aspirations to human beings, hold them responsible for what they do, praise, blame, criticise, try, and punish them. These 'language-games', as Wittgenstein would call them – thanking, cursing, greeting, praising, judging, etc. – are based on these matter-of-course reactions which constitute our 'attitude towards a soul'. Wittgenstein speaks of them as a 'special chapter of human behaviour' (*Z*, 542). He says that they are a proto-type of a way of thinking

(Z, 541) and that the language-games in question may be regarded as extensions of this mode of response (Z, 545). My relation to what I react to in these ways is part of my concept of a human being (Z, 543). Thus to think, for instance, that 'we tend someone else because by analogy with our own case we believe that he is experiencing pain too' is 'putting the cart before the horse' (Z, 542). The horse is our natural reaction to someone who has hurt himself and is crying; and the mistake of putting the cart before the horse lies in the sceptic's idea that unless such a reaction is based on reason and can be justified, it is irrational. Wittgenstein would say that if that stands in need of justification then none of our beliefs and conjectures about our friends and acquaintances can be justified.

We see that there is no direct way of stating or affirming the reality of the human soul. The words 'Men have souls, whereas animals and lifeless things don't' do not express a truth we can be ignorant of unless we are insane. If we know what is being contrasted in these words, if we have the concept of a human being, then we do not need these words, and if we do not understand the contrast in question, such words cannot possibly help us. Certainly they do not say something that can be established by investigation, by a closer scrutiny of men, animals and lifeless things. They are meant to bring into focus a whole dimension of our life and speech to which it is difficult for us to conceive an alternative we can make sense of. What is at issue is the difference between the terms in which we think and talk of human beings, make sense of human behaviour, and those in which we talk about and study animal behaviour and also different types of physical phenomena. Of course, there are no sharp lines between men and animals, and between what is alive and what is not. Certainly there is an overlap between human and animal behaviour, the extent of which varies from one animal to another. Still, much with which we are familiar in human life has no place at all in animal life: 'One can imagine an animal angry, frightened, unhappy, happy, startled. But hopeful? And why not?' (*PI*, II, i).

Why can we not intelligibly say of a dog or an infant that it is hopeful? Or of a stone that it is in pain? (*PI*, I, 283). Why can we not say that a computer calculates? Wittgenstein asked this last question in the course of his considerations of the formalist view of mathematics (*RFM*, IV, 2).

A computer can reel out unimpeachable answers to the questions we feed into it. It may be tempting to think that here is exemplified the kind of competence that makes us speak of thought and intelligence in a mathematician. If the mathematician differs from the computer in *other* respects why should that undermine the similarity in their mathematical performance? Certainly if a man or a child writes down the answer to a mathematical problem this, *in itself*, does not prove that he has intelligence. To think of him as having mathematical ability we want him to be able to solve *other* mathematical problems. Whether or not his present performance exhibits ability and intelligence depends on what he does on *other* occasions. But when we call a man who solves a wide range of difficult mathematical problems intelligent, we take it for granted that the symbols, formulae and simple operations he uses have meaning for him, that he understands them. We cannot take this for granted in the case of the computer. Merely responding to the problems fed into it with the correct answer does not show that the computer understands what it prints. If it understands the symbols in question, if their combinations mean anything to it, it must be able to use them, e.g. it must be able to count, to measure, to compare. But if it is to count, it must be able to point to or look at the objects it counts. Supposing it had a metal rod that shot out from its side and it turned in the direction of the objects it was meant to count. For this to be pointing it would have to point to things in various *other* situations and follow it up in the appropriate ways. It would have to respond to people pointing to things and places in ways that would show that it understood them. There would have to be occasions in which there is some point in pointing to things for its benefit. Holding the arm horizontal with the index finger straight is pointing *only* in the traffic of human life. What is true of the activity of calculating, then, is equally true of counting, measuring and pointing: each requires the complex surroundings of human life.

In short, if the computer is to calculate it would have to have something like the human body, with arms, face, eyes, and enter into various activities in which the symbols and formulae it prints play a role. It is their role in these many activities, in shopping, measuring, accounting, engineering, that gives them the sense they have. Without this role mathematics would be little more than 'a wallpaper pattern'. A person who cannot use mathematical symbols in their civil roles does not understand them. If a man responded to mathematical questions with the quickness of a computer and always came up with the correct answer, if he could carry out complicated formal transitions, work out involved mathematical proofs, but were 'otherwise perfectly imbecile' then he would be 'a human calculating machine' (*RFM*, IV, 3). No more. A person who produces such answers, whether in words, writing or print, is performing an activity in which thought and intelligence are displayed *only* if he lives a life in which this activity has point and a bearing on other things he does, *only* if he has other interests – interests independent of producing these answers. In the absence of such a life even a being who is alive is not a human being. At best he is a human offspring. And the activity we imagine him to carry on, in analogy with the computer, is not what it is in a life which gives it the kind of connections calculating has in our life.

Philosophers had been so preoccupied with trying to find something covert behind the overt activity, that when they came to recognise that they had been wrong they jumped to the conclusion that if a machine imitates a mathematician overtly it must be calculating, since the sequences in time, actual and possible, are what adds up to the intelligent activity of carrying out a calculation. I have argued that without the wider surroundings of a human life they cannot do so. For these surroundings and the kind of connections the sequences in question have in those surroundings are logically relevant to what kind of activity they constitute. What it makes sense to say about them depends on their surroundings. As Wittgenstein would put it: If there is anything behind the calculations which human beings carry out, anything over and above my utterance of a formula when I have a flash of understanding, it is these circumstances and connections (*PI*, I, 154). It is these which the behaviourist neglects, just as the formalist neglects the civil life of mathematical symbols and formulae.

What is true of calculating is certainly true of speaking, hoping, grieving, pretending and rejoicing. Rush Rhees once said that if a creature speaks and can understand you then it should be the kind of creature that can be insulted by what you say, that can laugh at your jokes, and which can cry too. It must be capable of lying, pretence and deception. 'Otherwise I say things into it because I want to get certain information out. I do not take it for granted that it *understands*, in the sense in which I assume this of a human being when I am talking to him' (Swansea, 1962). That he gives me 'prosaic information' in words that belong to a language I understand does not in itself show that he is speaking, or that he understands my questions. What do the words he utters mean *to him*? Indeed, what *could* they mean, if he has no interest himself in the kind of information he gives, if he doesn't carry out any investigations to obtain results that play a role in *his* life, results that make a difference to what he does in various situations, if he does not care to obtain correct results, show regard for the truth, if he is indifferent to whether or not others lie to him, if he has no feelings for those with whom he speaks or for anything else?

If he is *saying* anything to me in words which convey some information which I can use, though he is indifferent to it, there must be other occasions when he cares what he tells people. And if there are such occasions then he is a being with desires, fears, hopes and interests, and the words he utters now have a role in connection with these or are related to other words which do. There must be other contexts in which he expects things of people and responds to their demands on him, contexts in which he enters into relation with people in conversation. His saying something to me on this occasion, his understanding my questions, cannot be divorced from such numerous occasions where words play a role in *his* life and where he responds to other people's utterances – with laughter, pity, sorrow, anger, irritation, indignation, fear, gratitude. If he is giving me some information now in words that I understand, he must be the kind of being who can himself ask questions, entertain doubts, and who has something to say. If he is not just repeating words parrot-wise he must live a life in which there is a place for concern, joy, anger, sorrow, fun, danger, desire and interests, to which the words he utters now have a relation, directly or indirectly through other words.

On the other hand, the kind of life in which these things are possible is unimaginable apart from language; he could not have grown into that kind of life if he did not speak a language, if he did not live with people who do. That is, the language we speak makes our lives what they are; it makes us the kind of beings we are. This is the point behind Wittgenstein's question whether we can imagine a dog or an unweaned infant hopeful or in despair (*PI*, II, i). He answers that only those who have mastered the use of language can hope or know despair. How can anything that a suckling does be an expression of hope? How can the smile of an unweaned infant be pretence? (*PI*, I, 249). The surroundings that are necessary for anything he does to amount to an expression of hope are not yet present. In the surroundings of the infant's life there is no room for the distinction between a genuine expression of feeling and a feigned one: 'A child has much to learn before it can pretend' – or before he can conceal his feelings (*PI*, II, xi, p. 229). Pretending too, like grief and hope, are 'special patterns in the weave of our lives' (*PI*, II, i, xi, p. 229). These phenomena are modes of the kind of life we live with language (*PI*, II, i).

We see that one cannot make sense of what it is to speak, to make an inference, to calculate, if one leaves out the kind of life that surrounds people's utterances, the activities in the weave of which inferences are made and calculations carried out. Equally, one cannot make sense of what it is to form intentions, keep resolutions, fall a prey to emotions, hope, grieve, rejoice and despair, if one does not consider the kind of surroundings in which these things take place. These phenomena of human life are logically intertwined in the sense that the possibility of any one of them presupposes much of the rest. For if it is to be possible for a creature to hope or feel remorse, to deliberate before acting or to carry out a calculation, he must live the kind of life in which he exhibits a wide range of affective reactions in particular situations, a life which he lives with others like him who share these reactions and with whom he comes into contact in the various activities of such a life. It is in this dimension that what makes us the kind of creatures we are is to be found; not in some additional substance or medium in which certain elusive activities go on. We have no clear idea of what such a substance would be like, and neither is it possible that we should – given the way we separate it from every activity in which we enter as embodied beings. But if the soul is not such a substance or medium, this is not to say that the soul is unreal.

The Cartesian idea of the soul as a substance is largely rooted in the attempt to grasp the soul's reality in separation from what underlies the possibility of human joy and suffering, love, hope and despair, kindness and cruelty, good and evil. It arises when 'language is like an engine idling'. But this is not always true where people have talked of the body and the soul as two different substances. When, for instance, Socrates in the *Phaedo* speaks of a purification which 'consists in separating the soul as much as possible from the body' he speaks in terms of an imagery in which the soul and the body figure as two different substances. Yet there is nothing incoherent in this idea of the soul which belongs to a language that has a long and respectable ancestry and to which Plato has contributed in the way he has *used* that language to deepen the kind of understanding possible within its framework. The Platonic picture of the soul, as opposed to the Cartesian, is not a *philosopher's* picture, for it belongs to a language which men have used for centuries in sizing up their lives and sifting their moral reactions to it. It is this language we must turn to if we wish to understand what it means to speak of the soul, though I should add that not everyone means the same thing by 'soul'. I shall consider *one* strand in what is meant by this word.

2. I have argued that what is presupposed by the reality of the soul underlies our identity as human beings and that to speak about a man's soul is to speak about the man, though in a certain way.

The terms 'soul' and 'human being' are certainly not equivalent. A spiritual life is *one* dimension of human life – and I do not mean one compartment. It is possible for a person's life to lack this dimension or for a human being to turn away from it – Alcibiades in the *Symposium*: 'He (Socrates) compels me to realise that I persistently neglect my own interests by engaging in public life. So against my real inclination I stop up my ears and take refuge in flight.' The true interests in question refer to Alcibiades' soul.[1] Conversely, when someone who has lived a life of pleasure discovers a limit to it in coming to care for others and he condemns his previous life, we say that he has found his soul – Dmitry in *The Brothers Karamazov*: 'What do I care if I spend twenty years in the mines? I am not a bit afraid of that – it's something else I am afraid of now: that that new man may leave me'. The new man is the man who has found a new life, a life of the spirit.

People often speak of the soul when they wish to bring into focus those aspects of a person's life in which he is most truly himself. I shall qualify this presently. To see a man's soul is to see what he is really like – the fears behind the exterior assurance, the loneliness and the need for affection drowned in a busy public life, the callousness behind a façade of respectability, the kindness or the remorse in a heart caught up in a life of vice. Take the words: 'His soul rebelled against his own arguments and deeds'. What is in question is Raskolnikov's moral reaction to his own deeds and arguments. But the deeds condemned are as much 'his' as the moral reaction to them. Hence Dostoyevsky is not merely interested in those aspects of Raskolnikov's life in which he is most truly himself. If he had simply said that *Raskolnikov* rebelled against his own arguments and deeds he would not have said the same thing.

Not every time that our interest centres around what a man is really like is our vision directed to his soul. It is only when we are interested in making certain moral judgments that our concern to see the reality behind appearances brings a man's soul into focus. Thus when on hearing Raskolnikov's confession Sonia exclaims, 'Oh, what have you done to *yourself*!' she is concerned with Raskolnikov's soul. She pities him and calls him unhappy most of all because of the crime he has committed. Even if Raskolnikov had not been wretched she would have called him unhappy and she would have pitied him all the more – much as Socrates pities Archelaus, the Macedonian tyrant, and calls him unhappy.

People sometimes say that when it comes to death we are all

---

[1] See Dilman and Phillips, *Sense and Delusion* (Routledge, 1971) pp. 82–4.

the same, and whether we are clever or not, rich or poor, loved or
forgotten counts for nothing. The only thing that counts is whether
we have lived well or badly. Again, the measure of what we are
like in the eyes of death, and so of what belongs to the soul, is a
moral one. This is clear in Plato's image of nakedness at the end of
the *Gorgias*. Socrates says he believes that when living men are
tried by living judges the judgments are often bad. The reason he
gives is that both the men and the judges are clothed. Those who
have criminal souls, for instance, may well be 'clothed with fair
bodies, nobility and wealth, and many witnesses appear with them
to testify that they have lived justly'. The judges, being alive, are
impressed by all this. 'Their eyes and ears and their whole body make
a veil in front of their soul.' So their judgments are not just, and men
are not rewarded or punished in accordance with their deserts.
He believes that if the judgment on a man's life is to be just, if the
judge is to have vision of the man's soul, he must not be impressed
by what the man's friends and relations say, nor by any of his
achievements. He must himself be completely detached from all this.

We should distinguish here between seeing into a man's soul, as
Sonia saw into Raskolnikov's and Socrates into Alcibiades', and
understanding what is *meant* by such expressions as 'seeing into a
man's soul'. Plato had much to say about the conditions that must
be satisfied for a man to have such vision. In the *Gorgias* Socrates
talks of the judge contemplating with his soul the soul itself of each
man. He believes that if the judge is to have spiritual discernment
he must have broken off all his ties with this world, his family,
friends, people who hold him in esteem, his possessions, achievements, even his virtues – everything, in short, which makes him a
'somebody'. But the conditions for the possession of spiritual discernment are not the same as the conditions for the possession of an
understanding of Plato's or Dostoyevsky's language, and those who
speak and understand that language do not necessarily possess the
wisdom which both Plato and Dostoyevsky sought in their own
lives. As a philosopher I am not concerned even to speak that
language, or to induce others to speak it, but only to clarify its
grammar. That is what I mean by understanding what it means to
speak of the soul. This involves elucidating such conceptual connections as exist here, for instance, between spiritual discernment and
the kind of compassion we find in Sonia or the kind of detachment
which Socrates aimed at in his own life. That is why it is important
to consider what Socrates says and how Dostoyevsky speaks and
many others who had something to say in this language.

When we do so we see that the soul is conceived as including

G

both what is bad and what is good in a man, his hatred, greed, envy and selfish ambitions, as well as his kindness, love and moral aspirations. Much of what is regarded as belonging to the soul, all the bad and a large part of the good, is thought of as being self-centred, self-regarding or at least personal, rooted in the life of the body. I say *personal* in the sense that the more active it is in a man's life, such as when he is genuinely in love, the more he becomes attached to life. Certainly not everything that is personal in a man's soul is self-centred or self-regarding and does not, therefore, call for moral condemnation. But it is only to the genuinely *impersonal* part of the soul that the vision which Socrates speaks of belongs. This is the part of the soul which responds to the affliction of another – Sonia's 'Oh, I don't think there is anyone in the world more unhappy than you are!' – or cries out against real injustice. It is the part of the soul which loves in self-effacement, forgives the unrepentant criminal, and feels humble gratitude for what it receives. In its pure form, it is not often that what is attributed to it finds expression in human life.

This distinction between what is personal and what is impersonal in human beings is logically involved in talking of the soul. Socrates says that to be able to contemplate with the soul itself, a man's soul must undergo purification. A man will have spiritual discernment to the extent to which he can rise above what is personal in him. People sometimes speak of this as coming to possess 'inwardness' – a notion I shall say something about a little later. In the *Phaedo* Socrates says that 'while we are alive we shall be closer to knowledge the less commerce and communion we have with the body, apart from strict necessity'. We must eat, of course, and we need to sleep. There is nothing specially personal in these things. But we must avoid gluttony, all forms of greed, and self-indulgence. It is when we become gluttons, for instance, that we are 'possessed by the nature of the body'. It is important to remember that this is the context in which Socrates opposes the body and the soul.

Socrates is concerned with the way we face life and death, with the possibility of being happy even in the most adverse of circumstances, and of facing death without fear. He would have said, if he used such language, that there is an internal relation between realising these possibilities and possessing the kind of knowledge he sought. A necessary condition of that knowledge is detachment from our bodies, not letting ourselves be possessed by passions and desires that are carnal in orientation and, therefore, self-seeking or at least self-sustaining. It is not the body as such that Socrates regards as an obstacle to spiritual life. Obviously we cannot but live 'in the flesh', but we need not live 'according to the flesh'[1] – we can live a *spiritual* life. In Kierkegaard's words, 'Time and eternity *can* rule in the same man *if* he is pure in heart'.[2] A happy domestic life, for instance, in no way excludes an active concern for spiritual values in that life.[3] When Socrates opposed the body and the soul he did not mean to deny that the soul is in part, and even largely, carnal in nature. But neither did he deny that physical life can be spiritual in orientation. What he meant to contrast were two different orientations of the soul: the temporal and the eternal. The former belongs to the personal part of the soul, the latter to the impersonal.

When we speak of 'the life of the soul' it is the latter orientation that is in question. But how does it differ from any other aspect of moral life? There are those who largely pay only lip service to moral values and there are those in whose life a genuine concern for moral values plays an active role. Whether or not a man of the latter kind possesses spirituality depends both on the man and on the kind of values for which he has regard. For surely if what the man gives of himself is important in this respect, so is the kind of demand which his values make on him. So there are two things that we need to understand here: (i) The contrast between a genuine moral outlook on life which is worldly in orientation and a *spiritual* outlook on the world – i.e. the possibility of distinguishing between worldly and spiritual values in the sphere of the ethical. (ii) The contrast between an *inward* relation to spiritual values and a merely *outward* relation to them.

(i) To see what the first distinction comes to, consider the values and ideals that Callicles looked up to and those for which Socrates was prepared to die. Callicles' attitude towards what Socrates called 'the philosophic life' is a moral one. He condemns that life and finds it shameful. He thinks that Socrates ought to 'learn the accomplishments of active life' and that he is morally deceived for not doing so. He finds Socrates' life disgraceful because in it Socrates fails to be a man. 'Man', as Callicles is using the word, is an evaluative term. He has contempt for the majority of people who lack the qualities of character he admires. Much in the way that Socrates would not call Archelaus happy, Callicles does not call 'cobblers and cooks' happy: 'How can a man be happy that is in subjection to anyone whatever?'

---

[1] Thomas Merton, *No Man is an Island* (Dell paperback) p. 108.

[2] *Purity of Heart*, trans. by Douglas Streere (Fontana paperback) p. 89.

[3] Can one say the same of a political life dedicated to serving the people of one's country? Here Plato disagreed with Socrates. I owe this point to Dr Hugh Price.

Callicles professes to live by certain ideals which he values more than just being alive and he does distinguish between appearance and reality in his own relation to those ideals, attaching importance only to the latter. He knows that courage is something that cannot be copied and his contempt for a man who cares for the appearance of bravery is twofold – first because he lacks true courage and secondly because he is servile to the opinion of others.

But his conception of courage is different from that of Socrates, even though they overlap. For Callicles courage is a form of vitality, a 'large and liberal sentiment'. Hence he does not see any courage in the kind of patient resignation which Socrates advocated and practised. Thus while Callicles did distinguish between appearance and reality, he could not have acted as 'a man' with the ring of Gyges on his finger. For once invisible there would be no scope for him to exercise the kind of bravery and resourcefulness he so much admired. In contrast, Socrates could continue to be virtuous even if invisible, even in the secret of his heart.

Secondly, Socrates and Callicles differ in their conception of the kind of difficulty or obstacle that lies in the path of virtue or manliness. For Socrates the obstacle is part of the very tissue of life and it can be surmounted, if at all, only by self-renunciation. Here the ideals for which the self is renounced are not commensurable with the self, and its fruits are regarded as gifts for which the recipient takes no credit. For Callicles the reason for overcoming one's weaknesses are commensurable with the very fears and desires that are judged to constitute those weaknesses, and the kind of discipline this requires relies on the energies of the self. What is achieved is something one can be proud of rather than thankful for.

Thirdly, if one is to be proud one has to have achieved the task – a task which calls for qualities that are regarded as superhuman. And failure is always shameful. Whereas for Socrates it is not the attainment of his ideals that is important, but the striving to relate one's life to them. What is blameworthy is not failing to measure up to these ideals, as with Callicles, but indifference towards them. Thus Callicles has only contempt for the majority of people whom he calls 'riff-raff', whereas Socrates' attitude towards those who do evil is one of pity. Contempt is a turning away from what one finds shameful; it emphasises one's distance from what one finds contemptible. Whereas pity is a turning towards what one finds pitiable. It is an attitude of love. One who feels sorry for someone who has done something bad does not feel himself separated from him by what he possesses himself. Thus at the heart of contempt is the worship of force; at the heart of pity is humility. Simone Weil said that humility is the only virtue that does not have a worldly counter-part.[1] She meant that a humility that is worldly would be false – whereas courage, as we have just seen, may be both worldly and genuine. The converse is true of force. It has no spiritual counter-part. Virtues that are spiritual are self-effacing.

Fourthly, though there is a place for shame in both Callicles' and Socrates' moral outlooks, in Callicles' case the pain at being found wanting in manliness is tinged with self-regard. This pain in the two cases may be said to belong to two different levels of the soul. The former belongs with all that is personal, while the other transcends it – or at least it is possible for it to do so. Correspondingly there is no room in Callicles' moral outlook for guilt or remorse, since concern for other people doesn't enter into it. There is respect for the kind of people Callicles would praise, but no unconditional respect for human beings as such. Consequently, though Callicles does use the word 'ought' in the absolute sense when he speaks of how a man *ought* to live, he never speaks of 'obligations towards other people'. Callicles would, I think, be prepared to die rather than be found wanting in manliness. But this is different from choosing to suffer wrong rather than doing wrong oneself. Only the latter involves a spiritual attitude to life, since in the former case one's reason for preferring death to life is pride – a pride, it is true, that cannot be understood without taking Callicles' moral beliefs into account, but one which nevertheless belongs with the kind of motive which makes a man resign his post because he is passed over in promotion or because he is not the best. This is the level of the soul at which our greeds and jealousies, our ambitions, loves and hates, our competitiveness as well as our sense of fair-play exist and thrive. In contrast, remorse belongs to a 'deeper' level of the soul and is one gateway to a life of the spirit. It goes without saying that the term 'deep' which I have just used is a value term and belongs to the language in which people speak of the soul.

(ii) Callicles' moral outlook, however, is not the only pole against which what it means to have a spiritual outlook on life is to be understood. Most of us do not share Callicles' values, but only few possess Socrates' spirituality. It is not so much *what* we believe in that is to blame for this as *how* we believe. The distinction I have in mind is to be found within those who profess to believe in Christian values. Such a person may be *outwardly* virtuous and true to the values in which he believes – and I do not mean 'only in appearance'.

---

[1] 'God in Plato', in *On Science, Necessity and the Love of God*, trans. and ed. Richard Rees (OUP) p. 101.

Tolstoy's Kitty Scherbatsky, for instance, had been a kind and decent girl before the incidents that led to her parents taking her abroad; but she lacked *inwardness*. Abroad she groped unsuccessfully for ideals which her life had so far not encompassed and then settled for something much more modest. Yet her experiences and the recognition of her failure changed her *inwardly*, in the sense that judging by her actions and her moral beliefs the change amounts to very little. She was a decent girl to begin with, she had always been morally scrupulous and naturally kind, and she continued to be so. Consider how little the change in her amounts to outwardly in contrast with the spectacular change in Tolstoy's Kasatsky when he resigns his commission, enters the monastery and three years later is ordained to the priesthood by the name of Sergius. It is not until the end of the story that Father Sergius succeeds in becoming truly indifferent to everything in the world which sustains his existence at the level of the personal – especially to human praise.

This was not the way for Kitty and yet when she returns to Russia her life has gained an inwardness which Father Sergius' life lacks most when he is at the height of his career – when he feels 'his own inner life wasting away and being replaced by external life'. What does this inwardness amount to in Kitty's case? Largely, I think, to the deepening of her regard for the values she was taught as a child – kindness, love, humility, honesty. Her sense of the difficulty in realising these values and remaining true to them is a measure of this depth. Now she will not, for instance, jump to do good deeds as lightly as before. She will be more self-critical in her actions. Her kindness will not be less spontaneous, but it will be more measured, more realistic, and more steadfast. She will be more aware of the possibility of doing harm while striving to do good and she will not let her eagerness blind her to this possibility. Similarly for her word which will not be given lightly in order to please. The change in Kitty is thus a spiritual reorientation. But since what she turns her back on is not a life of callous indifference and moral dissipation it belongs to her moral development.

A reorientation of the soul is necessarily a change in a person, though not all changes in character and behaviour are spiritual. A person's reorientation to life is spiritual only when it is a reorientation to the good, which may take the form of a change in his moral beliefs or a change in his relation to the moral beliefs which he continues to hold – as with Kitty. In either case the reorientation can only be seen in the light of the good and it cannot be assessed in morally neutral terms. That is, the changes in the person concerned can be seen in relation to his soul only from a certain moral perspective. Otherwise they will be on a par with any other change in character, life and behaviour.

It may be said that if the soul turns one way, in the direction of the good, away from the self, it lives; if it turns the other way its life diminishes. This is a grammatical remark; it sets out part of the grammar of the soul. Tolstoy speaks in this grammar when he says that the more Father Sergius gave himself to worldliness (e.g. received visitors and felt glad of the praise they heaped upon him) 'the more he felt that what was internal became external': 'it was as if he had been turned inside out'. Here inwardness, that is the kind of orientation in which the life of the soul is to be found, belongs to Father Sergius' relation to his moral and religious beliefs, to what they mean to him as an individual. His 'inner life' is that aspect of his life in which these beliefs are active. The more his soul is claimed by worldliness – and Tolstoy well illustrates what this means – the more his life becomes external, that is ceases to have any relation to his moral and religious beliefs and becomes senseless. This is what is meant by saying that his inner life is at an ebb. His religious duties, for instance, become a burden and the crowds of people who come to see him every day leave him indifferent. While his life continues to bear some relation to his beliefs he has moments of lucidity when he feels aghast at what is happening to him, and he even plans to cut his hair short, dress as a peasant, and go away. These thoughts, feelings and struggles belong to his 'inner life' not in the sense that they are covert. They bear a relation to his moral and religious beliefs. While they continue to exist his soul remains alive. It is in just this sense, I think, that remorse and hope are characterised as *states of soul* and are seen as belonging to the 'inner life'. Similarly for happiness, in the sense in which Socrates spoke of it.

In a paper entitled 'The Idea of Perfection'[1] Miss Iris Murdoch misunderstands what might be meant by an 'inner life' by those who speak of it in moral and religious contexts. She identifies it wrongly with something that Wittgenstein opposed, namely the Cartesian idea. Since she insists, rightly, that it makes sense to speak of the inner life in connection with certain moral and religious questions, she thinks, wrongly, that Wittgenstein's anti-Cartesian arguments can only have a limited application. She asks whether someone, perhaps a Catholic in confession, who sincerely utters the words 'I repent' may be said to have genuinely repented, in the way that someone who says 'I promise' is considered to have

---

[1] *The Sovereignty of the Good* (Routledge, 1970).

promised, whether or not later he breaks his word. I agree with her entirely that even if such a person were to amend his life, this would not necessarily mean that he had genuinely repented. But *not* because repentance is something that takes place within him while the change in his behaviour is something that takes place outside. A man, for instance, who gives up a life of dissipation and turns over a new leaf in order to avoid hell fire in an after-life is very different from one who is overcome with remorse. The latter person's life has gained a new dimension, one that is not commensurable with his earlier life. So he has changed inwardly, his life has gained inwardness, in the sense that his repentance has taken roots in his subsequent life. This is not simply a matter of what he does and does not do in the future, but of how he lives – a matter of the character or quality of his life. Whereas, in contrast, the former person's life has changed only outwardly in that in it there is no expression of any mourning for his earlier life. Perhaps now he avoids the harsh words that had been characteristic of that life, is attentive to his wife, and refrains from beating his children. But in his motives for doing so, and in the rest of his life, he continues to be as selfish and uncharitable as before. Miss Murdoch quotes Professor Hampshire's words that 'to copy a right action is to act rightly'. This is precisely a view which makes the relation between morality and conduct purely external and makes the question of where the agent stands as an individual of little concern to the character of his actions – and Miss Murdoch is right to criticise it.

We see that a person attains inwardness when he makes his own a moral outlook in which humility and charity are the prime virtues. One can act in servility to any kind of moral value, ape any form of moral virtue. But it is in identity with only one form of value that one finds inwardness – though this form of value has diverse manifestations in different cultures. I am thinking of the kind of value which one can make one's own only by becoming selfless. It is in this inwardness that the life of the soul is to be found. This is how I understand the expression 'within' in Christ's saying that the Kingdom of God is *within* you. He also spoke of it as 'outside' this world and in eternity. These come to the same thing, since inwardness is an orientation of the soul towards a good that lies outside the world and which can only be attained through detachment from everything that belongs to this world. It is by transcending worldliness that one finds inwardness.

3. For Wittgenstein in his *Notebooks 1914–16* this orientation is a matter of the will conceived as 'an attitude of the subject to the

world' (p. 87). He speaks of the will here in the sense in which Kierkegaard spoke of willing the good. He says, for instance, that ' "to love one's neighbour" means to will' (*NB*, p. 77). This is not a question of doing this rather than that and it cannot be confined to any particular course of actions. What I said about repentance is true here too. One cannot love one's neighbour *at will* and nothing that one can choose to do will amount to loving one's neighbour. Yet clearly one can work towards it and whether or not such love can grow in one's heart depends on what one does. There is a sense in which one can choose to give one's heart to some things and refuse to give it to others. It is this sense of 'will' that Wittgenstein distinguishes from the sense of 'will' which belongs with the things we can do at will.

The will in this latter sense cannot, of course, be irrelevant to morality. But any ethics that does not see beyond it will necessarily ignore an important dimension of moral life – the dimension of a person's relation to the values in which he believes. It is here that Wittgenstein speaks of the 'ethical will'. This finds expression not in what a person does in this or that situation considered separately, but in what he does and suffers considered as a whole or unity, one that characterises the person's own conception of his life and actions. Where there is no such unity the subject has no attitude to the world as a whole – though he may still be *trying* to relate himself to it.

Not strangely, Wittgenstein speaks of a life which has such unity as a 'happy' or 'harmonious' life – one in which one is 'in agreement with the world' (*NB*, p. 75). One must not forget that the kind of unity in question is possible only if one wills the good. If one wills anything else the means one will be prepared to adopt at a particular time will depend on the contingencies of one's situation, in which case the centre of what unity one's life has will not lie within one – it will not lie in one's regard for certain limits which one is unwilling to transgress. Wittgenstein asks whether it is possible to will the good without willing anything in particular – that is without exercising one's 'will as a phenomenon': 'Or is only he happy who does *not* will?' (*NB*, p. 77). Obviously, willing the good, loving one's neighbour, necessarily involves acting one way rather than another in particular situations. In that sense it seems impossible 'to will the good and not will'. Yet Wittgenstein wants to say that there is no 'objective mark' of the happy life (*NB*, p. 78), in other words that the kind of happiness with which he is concerned belongs to the 'inner life' in the sense we have considered. That is he does not consider the conformity of a life to certain moral standards to be sufficient for that life to be a happy one. Such conformity would be a merely 'outward' criterion, like the mere mending of one's ways in the case of repentance. What would be missing here, the 'inward' attitude, is a genuine love of the good, one manifestation of which is love of one's neighbour. While this love, if it is in a man's heart, is bound to find expression in what he does in particular situations, it cannot be confined to what he does in any one situation. It 'goes beyond' or 'transcends' all such situations or, as Rush Rhees puts it, it goes deep with him, the suffering of a human being is anything but a trivial matter for him.[1]

What is Wittgenstein thinking when he asks 'Is only he happy who does *not* will?' (*NB*, p. 77)? In that entry he has not yet distinguished between willing and wanting and it seems to him that so long as one wants anything one is vulnerable to the contingencies of the world, and so unhappiness remains an open possibility. But this does not mean that one cannot be happy, since all that one desires may be granted. And Wittgenstein would have said that even when a man has all he wants it does not follow that he is happy. He would have agreed with Socrates that Archelaus couldn't have been happy even if what Polus claimed were true. So when he said that 'not wanting is the only good' he could not have meant something like the following: The less you want the less likely you are to be frustrated and be made unhappy. Therefore if you want nothing you cannot be made unhappy. Puzzled, Wittgenstein asks: 'Is it good to want *nothing* for one's neighbour?' (*NB*, p. 77.) This is in obvious contradiction with most of what he says.

If a man were to succeed in avoiding pain and frustration by somehow reducing his desires and he then said that he was happy, Wittgenstein would probably say that this was a *low* conception of happiness. For he is not looking for a way of escaping or avoiding the miseries of the world, but of meeting them, and 'not willing' is just such a way. It is an attitude towards the world akin to what Kierkegaard meant by 'patience'. In that sense it is an expression of will. When Wittgenstein speaks of 'wanting nothing' he means 'wanting nothing *for oneself*'. Further down he asks whether a man can be happy if he cannot ward off the misery of this world (*NB*, p. 81). Wittgenstein answers that he can – 'through the life of knowledge'. What he means by 'knowledge' is very close to what Plato called 'knowledge' or 'wisdom'. A necessary condition for it is *detachment* – what Wittgenstein calls 'renouncing the amenities of the world' (*NB*, p. 81). This does not mean indifference to the pain

[1] 'Some Developments in Wittgenstein's View of Ethics', *Philosophical Review*, LXXIV, No. 1 (1965) p. 21.

of others. Quite the contrary. For a man who is immersed in a life of worldliness will be relatively deaf to other people's cries of pain. Detachment is a positive renunciation of such a life which allows the soul to turn to the good, to become sensitive to moral considerations. It should not be confused with what Nietzsche called 'objectivity'. The condition of such renunciation is love – the kind of love that is present in pity for the afflicted, forgiveness of those who wrong one, gratitude for those who help one, and remorse for the wrong one has done to others. It is this love which both Plato and Wittgenstein see as a form of knowledge[1] – this love which for Wittgenstein is an attitude of the will towards the world as a whole.

It may be called love of the good, and the kind of pity which Dostoyevsky portrays in Sonia is a concrete manifestation of it. In that form it is what usually goes under the name 'love of one's neighbour'. The relation between such selfless love and the kind of knowledge in question is internal. In her paper 'The Idea of Perfection' Miss Iris Murdoch tends to represent it as external – even though she knows better than to think so. She says that if one loves someone one will want to be fair to him, even in one's thoughts, and if one's desire is strong enough the chances are that one will succeed. Here the relation between the love one has and what it brings into focus, or enables one to know, is a contingent one, and the knowledge in question has little to do with what Plato and Wittgenstein in his *Notebooks* were concerned with. What they were interested in is the moral perspective of selfless love. One who possesses such love will, for instance, see all men as equal with respect to their claim to justice and compassion. He will think of the goods of this world as of no very great moment. He will see the good things and the bad things in life as 'so many graces of fate' (*NB*, p. 81), not reflecting the deserts of those whose fortune they form part of. This is the kind of knowledge or vision that belongs to selfless love. Knowledge here does not mean anything like 'justified true belief', though there is a sense of 'truth' that belongs with it and also a distinction between 'knowledge' and 'mere opinion'.[2]

When Wittgenstein said that 'the life of knowledge is the life that

---

[1] Not in the *Tractatus*, but certainly in the *Notebooks 1914–16*.

[2] I do not have the space to discuss what these come to, except to say that in this context 'true' characterises a *measure*. Socrates at the end of the *Gorgias*: 'What I am going to tell you, I tell you as the truth'. The reference is to the story of the judgment day and Socrates' claim is that he cannot fill anything else with personal content. As for the distinction between 'knowledge' and 'opinion', it refers to whether or not a person has made his own the values which he has learnt or accepted. Plato would have said that knowledge begins only where moral instruction ends.

is happy in spite of the misery of the world' (*NB*, p. 81) the happiness
he was thinking of is not one that is indifferent to the misery of the
world, though it is one which that misery need not and even, perhaps, cannot destroy. I do not know what Wittgenstein thought about
the relation between this kind of knowledge and personal affliction.
When at the beginning of Sophocles' play, Antigone tells her sister
that she will bury her brother, her words are reminiscent of Wittgenstein. For she tells her sister that nothing can harm or injure her
whatever happens: 'And if I die for it, what happiness! / Convicted
of reverence – I shall be content / To lie beside a brother whom I
love.' But in her last words there is despair – even as there was in
Christ's words on the cross: 'Never a bride, never a mother, un-
friended, / Condemned alive to solitary death. / What law of heaven
have I transgressed? What god / Can save me now? . . .' Simone
Weil has said that even in the pit of such affliction one can find a
happiness 'which leaves pain and suffering completely intact', a
happiness that is inseparable from 'the loss of personal existence'.
She does not say that a person who has found the love and knowledge which are one and the same thing is safe in the face of such
affliction. She only says that if the orientation of spirit which has so
far survived threat and danger can now survive the thought of
having been abandoned, the soul will receive what it has thirsted
for. All that she claims is that it is possible for a man's spiritual
orientation to survive such affliction.

I think that what a person's spiritual orientation can survive is a
measure of the depth of his spirituality or inwardness, and what he
receives in return is proportionate to this depth, since the gift
belongs to his inwardness. If one speaks of desire, longing or thirst
in this connection, one should remember that this desire belongs
to the impersonal part of the soul and that it is to be contrasted
with wanting something for oneself. Unlike desires that belong to
the personal part of the soul, there is no logical distinction between
having such a desire and finding fulfilment. What delays the fulfilment of a man's spiritual aspirations is their impurity. When in his
Notebooks Wittgenstein spoke of happiness he was speaking of a
state of soul which contains its own reward.

In the *Tractatus* he spoke of a kind of reward and punishment
which resides in what one does and in the way one lives (6.422).
He contrasts this with a reward or punishment that *follows* what one
has done and is external to it. He speaks of the latter as reward and
punishment 'in the usual sense of the terms' and he reserves the
term 'ethical' for the former case. But where a person's reward or
punishment lies in certain *consequences* of his actions it is possible,

and indeed normal, for him to think of these under an aspect that is internally related to the moral character of these actions – i.e. to see what he has done as something good or bad and, therefore, as *deserving* these consequences. The pleasure or pain which he finds in them is thus inseparable from his seeing them under the aspects of reward or punishment. A reprimanding look, for instance, may be unpleasant to a child and punishment enough just because it is a reprimanding look. The point is that when a person sees certain consequences of his actions as reward or punishment he is thinking of them in *moral* terms.[1]

More important still, where a man sees certain consequences of his actions as reward or punishment there are two different ways in which he could relate himself to them. He may make his own the world's judgment that he is guilty and suffer the condemnation of others conveyed to him in the punishment he receives without mourning the evil he has done. Here he sees the pain inflicted on him under the aspect of punishment, though his suffering lacks inwardness. Or he may repent his crime, feel remorse, and be ready to atone for it. His suffering then gains a spiritual dimension. Similarly for his attitude to someone else's crime. He may blame this person and feel indignant, or he may pity him in the way that Sonia pitied Raskolnikov. Only then does he, in Kierkegaard's words, 'hear the voice of eternity'.

Wittgenstein says that 'eternal life belongs to those who live in the present' (*TLP*, 6.4311). Part of what he means by 'living in the present' is indifference to the 'consequences' of one's good and bad deeds, that is to whether or not they bring one rewards, and whether or not they escape punishment in the 'usual' sense of this term. Thus for those who have heard 'the voice of eternity' and who 'live in the present' the only kind of reward and punishment that matters is the kind which 'resides in the action itself'.

Both Socrates and Wittgenstein claim that a man who lives an evil life is necessarily punished and unhappy, whether or not he repents his crimes and feels remorse. They also claim that a man who dedicates his life to justice is necessarily rewarded and happy, no matter how the world treats him. Both these cases present a difficulty, though not the same one. If we wish to understand the sense of Socrates' words that 'the greatest of all misfortunes is to do wrong' or Wittgenstein's claim that evil never goes unpunished, we should remember the kind of pity in Sonia's reaction to Raskolnikov: 'Oh, I don't think there is anyone in the world more unhappy

---

[1] I owe this point to Professor Peter Winch. See his paper 'Ethical Reward and Punishment', in his book *Ethics and Action* (Routledge, 1972).

than you are!' The kind of attitude we have here is one that goes against the grain with most people. It is intelligible only within the perspective of selfless love. But it is even more difficult to understand the sense in which Christ or Antigone could be said to have been 'happy' at the time they felt most abandoned – not by the world but by the very thing to which they had offered their life as a sacrifice. The despair of that moment must have been the greatest single test of their faith. If one said of such a person that he was happy one would be expressing one's own 'envy' of him for having been worthy of such a trial. Thus Simone Weil who said that one may wish to be a martyr but one can't desire the cross,[1] nevertheless wrote: 'Every time that I think of the crucifixion of Christ I commit the sin of envy'.[2] Unless one can understand such a desire, and that means understand what someone like Simone Weil sees in the crucifixion of Christ, one will not be able to go the whole way in understanding the claim that it is possible for someone who has devoted his life to justice and charity to be happy *come what may*.

We see that Wittgenstein was concerned with a distinction within the sphere of the ethical, i.e. between a worldly yet ethical attitude to reward and punishment and a spiritual one. I suggested that these two attitudes are possible within the framework of our 'earthly' institutions of reward and punishment. But when punishment in its 'usual' sense succeeds in awakening repentance in the criminal's soul, his punishment will shift its centre of gravity from the world's treatment of him to the crime he has committed. He will care less about the temporal *consequences* of his crime and more about its *significance* – about what he has done. In its 'usual' sense, then, punishment *can* and, some say, *ought* to be a breaking down of the barriers of the criminal's personality so that spiritual values can enter into his life.[3] In *Crime and Punishment* Dostoyevsky speaks of this as a 'rebirth'.

It should be clear that what Wittgenstein says in the *Tractatus* about reward and punishment goes together with what he says in

---

[1] 'On ne peut pas vouloir la croix': 'La Croix', in *La Pesanteur et la Grâce*, p. 93.

[2] 'Spiritual Autobiography', *Waiting on God*, trans. by Emma Craufurd (Fontana Books, 1959) p. 49.

[3] 'Punishment is solely [i.e. ought to be] a method of procuring pure good for men who do not desire it. The art of punishing is the art of awakening in a criminal, by pain or even death, the desire for pure good' – Simone Weil, 'Human Personality', *Selected Essays* 1934–43, trans. Richard Rees (OUP, 1962) p. 31. She adds that this requires 'the spirit of truth, justice and love' in those who administer it, as well as in everyone else who is connected with the working of the institution.

his *Notebooks* about happiness and the life of knowledge. In the *Tractatus* he writes: 'When an ethical law of the form "Thou shalt . . .", is laid down, one's first thought is, "And what if I do not do it?" ' (6.422). The answer may be: 'If you disobey it you will lose your soul, or God will punish you'. But these are *not* 'consequences' of your breaking the law or commandment. If they were, the question 'How can you be sure?' would make sense. Neither are they the reasons why you should obey the law. If you obeyed it for the good of your soul you would have already lost your soul a little. It would be the same if you obeyed it to avoid punishment, whether on earth or in heaven.

This is what Wittgenstein is thinking when he says: 'If I do so-and-so, someone will put me in fires in a thousand years. I wouldn't budge. The best scientific evidence is just nothing.'[1] If I did budge for that kind of reason, my actions would be intelligible in terms of fears and desires about which there would be nothing particularly religious. They would not be related to any spiritual concern. Wittgenstein says that 'if there were evidence, this would in fact destroy the whole business' (ibid.). For it would make what is in question into a future event, on a par with others, the significance of which is determined from the perspective of such desires and aversions. Whereas the story of the Judgment Day, for instance, in which Socrates puts his faith, gives him quite a different perspective – one which makes his own desires the object of judgment. He feels sorry for Callicles, to whom the story 'seems fiction', because of what he misses in his *present* life, not on account of some future event contingently connected with it.

Contrast with: 'It would be disastrous if we didn't believe that the enemy is preparing for an attack. For we would be caught unprepared.' Here evidence is crucial and it would be disastrous if we did not do our utmost to assess the likelihood of such an attack. What counts as a disaster in this connection is determined by our fears and desires, and these are independent of the belief in question: 'What if we don't believe that the enemy will attack? When I tell you what will happen if you don't, you see what I mean.' Whereas if Callicles were to ask Socrates, 'What will happen to me if I don't believe in your story of a heavenly tribunal?' what Socrates describes would not be seen by him as a disaster. Or if Socrates answered him, as he does, in terms of the language of the story, that is in terms borrowed from contexts where we speak of unpleasant things happening to us, what he says will meet with incredulity. For it would

[1] *Lectures and Conversations on Aesthetics, Psychology and Religious Belief*, ed. Cyril Barrett (Blackwell, 1966) p. 56.

seem that Socrates' belief is of the kind whose truth must wait on evidence.

The truth of a belief in a Judgment Day, then, need not rest or wait on evidence. When it does, the way it guides the believer's actions is quite different from when it does not do so. When it waits on evidence, it is a belief in a contingent truth and not an absolute in terms of which the believer measures his life and actions. It is only where a man can see sense in measuring his life in this way that it becomes possible for him to want to raise himself above the level at which his greeds and jealousies, his ambitions, loves and hates exist. Without such a possibility no spiritual concern can enter into a man's life. That is why, I think, Wittgenstein says that 'if there were evidence, this would destroy the whole business'.

Similarly for an ethical law of the form 'Thou shalt . . .'. If it were possible to justify obedience to it this would make what the law expresses into what Wittgenstein calls a judgment of relative value. Here one would be taking the question 'What if I don't?' as somebody might ask it of a doctor who says 'You ought to stay in bed for a few days'. The answer, of course, would be in terms of *consequences* which would follow if one disregarded the doctor's advice. The advice takes for granted that the patient wants to get well and avoid these consequences, and it points out the way to do so. The patient has reason to follow the doctor's advice, as anyone in his position would, on account of these consequences and their relation to what he wants. In his 'Lecture on Ethics' Wittgenstein argues that in moral contexts the word 'ought' is not used in this way.

So a man who never steals, cheats or does anyone an injustice because he believes that justice and honesty are the best policy, and one who has regard for justice as an absolute value, do not believe in the same thing. Given the ring of Gyges the former would see no reason why he should not steal, cheat and wrong his neighbour, and he would think of anyone who acted otherwise in those conditions 'a miserable fool'. How such a man lives normally is commensurable with what he would do were he to wear the ring. Whereas the kind of life the latter man lives and the kind of life he condemns are not in this way commensurable. The former, Socrates would say, is a 'way of life in which the prize outweighs all the prizes of this world'. It is these two prizes that are incommensurable. In the one case it is one's desires, fears and ambitions that determine what one lives for; in the other case it is one's moral beliefs that do so. One hopes one will be able to live by those beliefs *whatever the circumstances*. If one wants to be able to do so, if one is afraid of failing (Dmitry: 'It's something else I am afraid of now: that that new man may leave me') then this desire and this fear are themselves determined by one's moral beliefs.

Wittgenstein's distinction between absolute and relative value, however, does not coincide with the distinction I made earlier between worldly and spiritual values. For, as we have seen, when Callicles says 'Socrates, you are neglecting what *ought* to engage your attention', he is not using 'ought' in a relative sense. Yet the values in which he believes are worldly and not spiritual. Still I think that Wittgenstein was primarily interested in spiritual values when he spoke of ethics. If we don't bear this in mind we shall miss part of what he means when he speaks of ethics as transcendental and says that absolute values must lie outside the world.

In the 'Lecture on Ethics' he argues that while 'all judgments of relative value can be shown to be mere statements of fact, no statement of fact can ever be, or imply, a judgment of absolute value'.[1] If some of his arguments for this conclusion are bad we must not allow this to blind us to what is important in what he wants to say. He imagines a book which contains descriptions of 'all the movements of all the bodies in the world dead or alive' and also 'all the states of mind of all human beings that ever lived'. This 'world-book', as he calls it, might include 'the description of a murder with all its details physical and psychological'. But it will not contain anything 'which we could call an *ethical* proposition. The murder will be on exactly the same level as any other event, for instance the falling of a stone.' We find the same idea in Hume: 'A young tree which overtops and destroys its parents, from whose seed it sprung, stands in all the same relations with Nero when he murdered Agrippina'.[2]

Wittgenstein would have denied this later. He would have said that parenthood involves much more than the biological relation Hume had in mind. It involves the institution of the family which is itself a nucleus of moral attitudes in most human communities. These attitudes belong to our notion of the family and to our understanding of parenthood.[3] The same goes for the ideas of destruction, killing and murder. In the case of the young tree the surroundings that are presupposed when we talk of an action such as killing and attribute intentions to the agent are totally absent – I mean the

---

[1] *Philosophical Review*, LXXIV (1965) p. 6.

[2] *An Inquiry Concerning the Principles of Morals* (The Liberal Arts Press, 1957) p. 111.

[3] Just as much as the attitude I naturally take to human beings is part of my concept of a human being – see pp. 164–5 above.

surroundings of human life.[1] In so far as these are left out and what is parallel in the two cases is made the centre of attention it is impossible that anything that may be called a crime should come into focus.

The facts which Wittgenstein's world-book mentions cannot have any ethical import because of the way they have been selected. It is his whole philosophy of language that is to blame for this in a way which I cannot now discuss. He would have denied later that all facts are 'on exactly the same level'. He would have no objection to characterising someone's having lied to his wife, for instance, or his having betrayed her trust as a *fact*, provided that this is true, and he would have agreed that facts such as these are not devoid of ethical significance. Still he would have wanted to retain something of his earlier distinction between fact and value and continue to regard ethics as incapable of being made into a science.

This does not mean that there can never be any intelligible transition from statements of fact to judgments of value – e.g. He beat her cruelly and in doing so committed a terrible injustice. The fact stated already possesses ethical significance and the transition in question is a familiar move within the kind of language-game. We do justify such judgments of value by statements of fact. We have here an example of what we *call* moral justification.[2] But such justification is made possible by certain values which people have regard for; it takes these values for granted. They belong to the framework within which one may derive an 'ought' from an 'is' and cannot *themselves* be derived from any facts. It is these that Wittgenstein compares with logical principles (*TLP*, 6.13, 6.421) and he is thinking of the way they set limits to our conception of the situations in which we act and determine what are intelligible alternatives for us in specific cases. But there are important differences which Wittgenstein does not discuss – the one exception being the extra dimension in the case of ethics of a person's relation to his values.

So when Wittgenstein characterises ethics as 'transcendental' he is thinking of the way ethical norms or absolute values limit our conception of the world in which we live: they are among our measures or forms of description, not among what we measure and describe. (Compare with *TLP*, 6.211.) But there is more to his claim that ethics is transcendental. For what is transcendental is

---

[1] See Part 1 above.

[2] What Wittgenstein says about 'grounds' and 'justification' in the *Investigations*, I, 480 with regard to Hume's doubt about whether past experience can be a ground for a prediction can be suitably adapted to meet Hume's query about whether a statement of fact can ever justify a judgment of value.

contrasted not only with what we can use language to talk about, but also with what is worldly. '*How* things are in the world is a matter of complete indifference for what is higher [or spiritual]. God does not reveal himself *in* the world' (*TLP*, 6.432). Here God's transcendence is contrasted with the devil's worldliness. The latter belongs to this world; he speaks to the 'natural' part of our souls – appeals to our greeds, lusts and ambitions. His promises have no counterpart among the promises made by prophets on God's behalf. In *that* sense God makes no promises: 'The heavenly father lives only in secret'.[1] If he did not live in secret and made promises, and if we renounced the world for the goods promised, this would be false renunciation. As Simone Weil puts it: 'He who gives bread to the famished sufferer for the love of God will not be thanked by Christ. He has already had his reward in this thought itself. Christ thanks those who do not know to whom they are giving food.'[2] There are two points here – one, that this thanking is not something that *follows* the act of charity,[3] and two, that it is not something that we can have *in view* when acting: 'There are times when thinking of God separates us from him' (p. 107). She writes:

> If all realities were transparent it would not be God but simply the sensation of light that we would be loving. It is when we do not see God that we have to become really detached from the self in order to love him. That is what it is to love God.[4]

In other words, unless God 'lives in secret' there can be no 'supernatural' love. Unless there is a good that lies *outside* the world, one we can only will by 'renouncing the amenities of the world', there can be no life of the spirit. When Russell said that were he to find himself confronted by his Maker he would ask him why he made the evidence of his existence so insufficient he showed a complete incomprehension of spiritual matters.

This question of the asymmetry between spiritual value and evil needs much more discussion. Wittgenstein is not always clear about it in the *Notebooks* and the *Tractatus*. But it could not have been far from his thoughts when he spoke of 'living in eternity' and contrasted 'seeing objects from the midst of them' and viewing them 'from outside'. The examples he gives in his 'Lecture on Ethics' also bear this out. I am especially thinking of his example of

---

[1] Simone Weil, *La Connaissance Surnaturelle* (Gallimard, 1950).
[2] *Waiting on God*, p. 68.
[3] See pp. 182–5 above.
[4] 'Some Reflections on the Love of God', *On Science, Necessity and the Love of God*, p. 154.

wondering at the existence of the world, which he describes as 'the experience of seeing the world as a miracle'.

This kind of *reverence* belongs with the other attitudes I spoke of earlier – compassion, gratitude, forgiveness, hope (not any kind), remorse, terror (not any kind). In his 'Remarks on Frazer' Wittgenstein speaks of it as a 'form of the awakening spirit'.[1] What it means to speak about the soul, the sense of the various expressions that belong to this area of language ('inwardness', 'inner life', 'transcendence', 'purity of heart', 'eternity', 'self-renunciation', etc.) is to be found in the complicated forms of life which permit these feelings and attitudes to flourish. I took my examples mainly from early Greek society at the height of its culture and from Christian literature. But we find these forms of life also among the so-called primitive people. In *The Golden Bough* (Wittgenstein tells us) Frazer misunderstands both the practices he writes about and the notions which belong to these practices – presenting them as errors. Wittgenstein speaks of this as the 'narrowness of spiritual life we find in Frazer'. He writes:

> Frazer is much more savage than most of his savages. For the latter will not be so far removed from an understanding of a spiritual matter as an Englishman of the twentieth century. His explanations of primitive practices are much cruder than the meaning of these practices themselves.

Wittgenstein's attitude to such practices was one of respect. He recognised that what found expression in them is far from trivial and meaningless, and the last thing he wanted to do was to belittle these practices. He concluded his 'Lecture on Ethics' with the following words:

> Ethics as far as it springs from the desire to say something about the ultimate meaning of life, the absolute good, . . . is a document of a tendency in the human mind which I personally cannot help respecting deeply and I would not for my life ridicule it.

Philosophically, he confined his attention to criticising all those attempts at explanation which distort and trivialise the significance of this tendency and the practices in which it finds expression. I do not know whether there is very much more that one can do here, except find examples which speak for themselves, help to bring out what is in them by comparison and comment – like a literary or art critic. Perhaps this is what made Wittgenstein say that 'ethics cannot

[1] *The Human World*, No. 3 (May, 1971).

be put into words'. It may be that a philosopher can do something more here – something which Plato, Kierkegaard and Simone Weil did, but not Wittgenstein – namely, use and deepen the very language whose sense is under discussion. But this is a dangerous exercise, and only the most talented, those who have something to say in that language, should permit themselves this liberty. For if one is not careful one will commit philosophy where it must remain on the level of differences. Wittgenstein stuck to 'criticism' and beyond that preferred to remain silent – out of philosophical integrity and also religious humility. I think that the last sentence of the *Tractatus* has a significance that goes beyond the confines of the philosophy of language which he later criticised and abandoned: 'What we cannot speak about we must consign to silence' (7).

4. *Summary* I have tried to say something about what it means to talk of the soul and to sketch out part of the grammar in which we talk about spiritual matters.

I began by elucidating Wittgenstein's remark to the effect that it is not an hypothesis that human beings have souls and that a human being's soul is not something he possesses – in the way he may possess a liver. It belongs to our conception of a human being: 'My attitude towards him is an attitude towards a soul. I am not of the *opinion* that he has a soul.'

To speak about a man's soul is to speak about him in a certain way: But in what way? A spiritual life is one dimension of human life: But what does it amount to? These are questions I turned to in the second part of the paper. I argued that talk of the soul makes sense only in the framework of certain moral values and that a spiritual life is one that bears a relation to these values. But what sort of values? I tried to illustrate the kind of values in question by contrasting the values in which Socrates believed with those for which Callicles speaks in the *Gorgias*. This led me to distinguish spiritual values from those that are 'of this world'. I then tried to say something about a sense of 'inwardness' and 'inner life' that belongs to the soul and considered what the contrast between 'inner' and 'outer' comes to in this context.

In the third part of the paper I turned to Wittgenstein's contribution to these questions. My main contention was that when he spoke about ethics he spoke about what I called 'spiritual' values and that he had interesting and important things to say. I tried to elucidate some of these, though they need a fuller discussion, and I pointed out how what he said belongs in a tradition of thought which runs from Plato through Kierkegaard to Simone Weil.

Wittgenstein is silent about these questions in his later writings. I do not think that this is because he lost interest in them or because he thought that they come from confusion. Perhaps if he had lived longer he would have returned to them. I do not know.

12

THE 'PREJUDICE IN FAVOUR OF PSYCHOPHYSICAL PARALLELISM'

Les Holborow

WITTGENSTEIN refers to psychophysical parallelism in this apparently prejudiced way in paragraph 611 of *Zettel*, in the course of a rather remarkable passage. It begins at 605 with the claim that 'One of the most dangerous ideas for a philosopher is, oddly enough, that we think with our heads or in our heads'. Subsequent sections develop this remark in a way that demonstrates Wittgenstein's rejection of the view that thinking is any sort of process in the head, whether a physiological process or a matter of the operations of 'a nebulous mental entity'.[1] Indeed he appears to consider that these ontologically opposed alternatives have a common source, in that they both derive from the mistaken view that there must be a mediating process between psychological phenomena such as my present remembering and my experience of the remembered event (cf. *Z*, 610). If we find no suitable mediating physiological process, we are easily led to assume that there must be a process of a rather different sort, and hence we are led to believe in a 'nebulous mental entity'. But this whole line of thought in fact depends on a 'primitive interpretation of our concepts', an interpretation which we uncritically made at the stage at which we assumed that there must be a process of some sort mediating between the phenomena. We are reminded of Wittgenstein's earlier remarks in *Philosophical Investigations*, I, 308:

> How does the philosophical problem about mental processes and states and about behaviourism arise? – The first step is the one

[1] I am informed that 'nebulous' is a more literal translation of Wittgenstein's German than the word 'gaseous', which Anscombe employs in the standard edition. 'Nebulous' also seems to me to convey an appropriate suggestion of vagueness and mystery.

that altogether escapes notice. We talk of processes and states and leave their nature undecided. Sometime perhaps we shall know more about them – we think. But that is just what commits us to a particular way of looking at the matter. For we have a definite concept of what it means to learn to know a process better. (The decisive movement in the conjuring trick has been made, and it was the very one that we thought quite innocent.)

In *Zettel*, 611 the prejudice in favour of psychophysical parallelism is said to be 'a fruit of primitive interpretations of our concepts', which clearly implies that if only we can expose and consequently reject these primitive interpretations the problems to which the doctrine of psychophysical parallelism provides an answer will no longer arise. If Wittgenstein is right about this a great deal of previous philosophical theorising will be jettisoned, for it seems clear that several other widely discussed doctrines, of which the central state theory is the most conspicuous, must also suffer.

David Armstrong's version of the central state theory, as developed in his *A Materialist Theory of the Mind* (London: Routledge and Kegan Paul, 1968; hereafter *MTM*), would appear to present a fascinatingly close paradigm of the line of thought that Wittgenstein wishes to attack. For Armstrong explicitly presents a two-stage argument, first seeking to show that 'the concept of a mental state is the concept of that, whatever it may turn out to be, which is brought about in a man by certain stimuli and which in turn brings about certain responses', and then maintaining that 'modern science declares that this mediator between stimulus and response is in fact the central nervous system, or more crudely . . . the brain' (*MTM*, p. 79). Here we seem to have first the assumption that there must be a mediating process, and only subsequently a decision as to its nature.

But it is hardly fair to describe Armstrong's belief that there must be a mediating process of some sort as an 'assumption', for this is a thesis for which he argues at some length. He claims to show by a detailed examination of the specific concepts of the many different mental states that they are all to be analysed on this common pattern, and that the generic concept of a mental state is therefore to be characterised in terms of the pattern. It emerges that the causal role of the central states or processes in bringing about responses is normally more important than the fact that they are the effect of stimuli, and Armstrong therefore concludes that 'the concept of a mental state is primarily the concept of *a state of the person apt for bringing about a certain sort of behaviour*' (*MTM*, p. 82).

We must then turn to science for further information about the nature of these states. We find that there is sufficient empirical evidence to support the view that they are in fact physico-chemical states of the central nervous system.

How, then, does Wittgenstein seek to undermine such an account? It is interesting that the argument in *Zettel* begins by claiming that it is natural to assume that there is no process in the brain correlated with associating or thinking. As Wittgenstein writes in the first half of *Z*, 608:

> No supposition seems to me more natural than that there is no process in the brain correlated with associating or with thinking; so that it would be impossible to read off thought-processes from brain-processes. I mean this: if I talk or write there is, I assume, a system of impulses going out from my brain and correlated with my spoken or written thoughts. But why should the *system* continue further in the direction of the centre? Why should this order not proceed, so to speak, out of chaos?

This argument might seem to begin with the second stage of Armstrong's account, that concerned with the question of whether the contingent identification is plausible. Armstrong's view is that the matter is to be decided by assessing the scientific evidence, and he makes no claim that the identification is compelling apart from such evidence. Given then that Wittgenstein was writing between 1945–8, since when there have been enormous advances in brain research, it might seem that his case against the central-state theory merely reflects the comparative lack of scientific evidence at that time.

But even if such factors have some weight, it is quite clear that this is not the basic consideration for Wittgenstein. For he wishes to deny that there need be any internal process at all, whether physiological or, as he expresses it in *Z*, 611, involving a 'nebulous mental entity'. Thus Wittgenstein is committed to denying the view that the analysis of mental concepts such as thinking must incorporate a reference to an inner state with causal powers. It is a philosophical mistake, in his view, to feel that there is any conceptual pressure to postulate an immaterial state when we fail to find a suitable physiological one.

It is worth noting at this point that the discussion in *Z*, 608 proceeds in terms of the case of spoken or written thoughts. Wittgenstein is prepared to allow that the system of impulses going out from the brain is probably correlated with the spoken or written thoughts, and he therefore clearly does not wish to deny that the information-content of the thoughts which are expressed can be present in a coded form in the nervous impulses, and can thus in principle be inferred from them. He does after all write in Z, 256:

> Philosophers who think that one can as it were use thought to make an extension of experience, should think about the fact that one can transmit talk, but not measles, by telephone.

His objection is rather to the assumption that the system should 'continue further in the direction of the centre'. If the cases envisaged are those where the writing or speaking is spontaneous and not preceded by conscious reflection, then it does seem that the grounds for expecting to find brain processes correlated with the thoughts would have to be of a causal nature. These are not the cases which tempt us to adopt a psychophysical parallelism, for there is no temptation in these cases to speak of an inner mental process of direct awareness of the thoughts which might then be correlated with a brain process. If we are to speak of an awareness here, it is an awareness of what we are doing and producing by our actions in the world. The central-state theorist invokes brain processes in these cases not to identify conscious mental processes with them, but in order to account for such differences as that between purposive and non-purposive utterances, thoughtful and thoughtless remarks, informed and uninformed comment. In his view the difference in each case is one of mental, which turns out to be physiological, causation. In the case of silent 'internal' thought where psychophysical parallelism seems initially to be on stronger ground, a different account is given by the central-state theorist, and a different account would seem to be required of Wittgenstein. But he seems to imply in Z, 608 that the conclusion that there need be no central process applies to thought-processes in general, and not just in those cases where the thoughts are spoken or written. We have already seen that the section begins by referring in quite general terms to the supposition that 'there is no process in the brain correlated with associating or thinking'. The second half of Z, 608 develops Wittgenstein's alternative to this view in the following terms:

> The case would be like the following – certain kinds of plants multiply by seed, so that a seed always produces a plant of the same kind as that from which it was produced – but *nothing* in the seed corresponds to the plant which comes from it; so that it is impossible to infer the properties or structure of the plant which

comes out of it from those of the seed[1] – this can only be done from the *history* of the seed. So an organism might come into being even out of something quite amorphous, as it were causelessly; and there is no reason why this should not really hold for our thoughts, and hence for our talking and writing.

The final sentence here seems to confirm that the doctrine that there need be no central cause is meant to be entirely general. But how can Wittgenstein so ignore the obvious difference between the cases of wholly extroverted thought and private soliloquy? Surely conclusions drawn from a consideration of the former cannot be applied without further argument to the latter?

I think that the answer to these questions lies in earlier sections of *Zettel*, where Wittgenstein explicitly attacks the view that unexpressed thinking is a private process. He does not deny that something goes on when we think, but he remarks 'It is very noteworthy that *what goes on* in thinking practically never interests us' (*Z*, 88). If we could hear what went on in a calculating prodigy who gets the right answer 'it would perhaps seem like a queer caricature of calculation' (*Z*, 89). Then in *Z*, 96 he writes:

Sure, if we are to speak of an *experience* of thinking, the experience of speaking is as good as any. But the concept 'thinking' is not a concept of an experience. For we don't compare thoughts in the same way as we compare experiences.

This of course connects with the remarks in *Z*, 256, quoted above, to the effect that thinking is not an extension of experience. To say that someone had a thought of a certain sort is not to say that he had an experience of a given type, or that he engaged in an activity of a certain type. For various experiences and various activities are compatible with one's having the same thought. Thus the thought that a man had can correctly be reported in words even though he neither spoke nor imagined the words at the time in question. Wittgenstein describes a case of this type at some length in *Z*, 100.

But it might still be urged that what is reported here is nevertheless a mental activity of thinking which occurred at the time in question. Wittgenstein does not wish to deny that something might have gone on, or that we could have words in our language for the various

---

[1] Anscombe translates this clause '. . . it is impossible to infer the properties or structure of the plant from those of the seed that comes out of it', which is clearly an error.

sorts of things that do go on when we think. As he says in
Z, 122:

> Remember that our language might possess a variety of different
> words: one for 'thinking out loud'; one for thinking as one talks
> to oneself in the imagination; one for a pause during which
> something or other floats before the mind, after which, however,
> we are able to give a confident answer . . .

His point is that the word 'thinking' in *our* language is not a word
such as any of these, for all of these activities count as thinking.
Neither is thinking an additional activity over and above these
others, for someone who in 'thinking over' a problem talks to
himself, or to someone else, does not carry out two activities (Z,
123). But because talking to oneself or another can sometimes be a
case of thinking and sometimes not, we are tempted into imagining
thinking as something that accompanies or underlies these other
activities: we think of it as 'the stream which must be flowing under
the surface of these expedients, if they are not after all to be mere
mechanical procedures' (Z, 107). This is no doubt a 'primitive
interpretation' of the concept.

But if the thinking is neither the talking nor some other underlying activity, what is it? Wittgenstein answers that it is no one
thing, process, or activity. Thinking is a 'widely ramified concept'
(Z, 110) best illustrated by giving a range of examples, illustrating
when we say that a man thinks: for example, when 'in a definite kind
of way, he perfects a method that he has' of doing things (Z, 104);
when he *learns* in a particular way (Z, 105); when he intersperses his
work with 'auxiliary activities' of the sort illustrated above (Z,
106).

It is not our present task to decide whether an adequate account
of thinking can be developed along these lines, but I hope that it is
now clear why Wittgenstein wishes to claim that even silent soliloquy
is not a process of thought, any more than talking is. Both can
express thoughts, and we *are thinking* when we engage in either of
them in the appropriate way, but neither of them is or is accompanied
by the thinking.

If talking and silent soliloquy have, in Wittgenstein's view, an
analogous relation to thinking, then we can explain why he assumes,
in the passage from Z, 610 that we were considering earlier, that the
conclusions drawn about there being no need for a central process
in the case of spoken thoughts also apply to silent thinking. If there
need be no central process correlated with intelligent speaking, he
reasons that there need consequently be no central process corres-

ponding to whatever it is that goes on in the case when the thought is unspoken. One might wish to object here that whatever goes on must be caused physiologically, but Wittgenstein could then reply that any such physiological causation would be on a par with the way in which he has allowed that a system of nervous impulses causes my speaking. In the former, as in the latter, case there is no reason why the *system* must 'continue further in the direction of the centre'. I say that Wittgenstein 'could' reply in these terms because I am conscious that he might have wished further to qualify such a comparison by adding some cautionary remarks about the dangers of treating whatever goes on when we think silently as a happening on the same level as speaking or talking. But as long as it is allowed that we can speak of mental activities and happenings occurring at definite times and bearing the same sort of relation to thinking as speaking and writing do – and the previous argument to the conclusion that thinking is not a mental activity seems to take this for granted – then we need go no further into this thorny problem. Our main concern should be the doctrine that there need be no central process, and we are now in a position to give it our undivided attention.

The central question is whether there is any good reason to believe that our thoughts must be caused by a brain process from which they could be 'read off'. Armstrong attempts to demonstrate the necessity of referring to an inner causal state by considering the case of a man who fails to pass on information required by a friend whom he meets because he *fails to think* of it at the time. Armstrong makes it clear that he regards this case as elucidating the fundamental notion of thinking. He claims that when I fail to think of p in such circumstances what failed to happen 'is simply that the knowledge-that-p, although a state of my mind, failed to be causally active in my mind at that time. In particular, it failed to act upon my will so that I imparted the information' (*MTM*, p. 344). At the second stage of the analysis, this mental causation turns out to be physiological. To think of p in the more specific sense that implies that p comes consciously before my mind involves an occurrent introspective awareness of the fact that I know p, an awareness also caused by the state of knowing-p.

I do not find this very compelling as a general account of the concept of 'failing to think of'. Our ordinary prescientific understanding of the notion of failing to think appears to regard this as a matter of failure to exercise a capacity that we possess with respect to the potential object of thought, rather than a failure of that potential object to act on our will. And how is the account to be applied to cases where what we fail to think of is not previously acquired information, but, for example, an eventuality that we fail to foresee, as when I fail to think of the possibility that the disreputable friend whom I am now inviting to stay with me may be impossible to dislodge before my parents-in-law arrive? Presumably Armstrong's account of such cases would have to be in terms of a failure of certain items of tacit knowledge to cause me to draw the appropriate conclusion.

But leaving these more difficult cases aside, it is interesting to notice that in the simpler case of the uninformed friend the doctrine that there must be a central cause can draw strong support from the doctrine that memory requires such a cause. For it emerged in that case that failing to think of was a matter of failing to remember, and it seems that this will often be so. Now it has often been held that our concept of memory contains a causal requirement. Martha Kneale makes the point succinctly in her Presidential Address to the Aristotelian Society:

> It is involved in the ordinary notion of memory or recollection that the memory event should have as a part-cause the occurrence of the event recollected. This is what makes it so easy for us to accept the story of brain traces as a physiological condition of remembering. They fill in the gaps in the causal chain which is felt to be necessary to explain recollection.[1]

It might consequently be thought that, at least where my thinking of something is a matter of remembering it, there must be a successful causing of a present recollection by a past event.

But we must be cautious here. First, it will not do to assume without argument that what goes for memory of events also goes for memory of facts. Mrs Kneale's requirement is concerned only with the former. But secondly, it does not in Wittgenstein's view follow from the fact that there is a regularity between two temporally remote states of affairs that there must be an intervening causal process. That is surely the point of the fable of the seed and the plant, and in *Zettel*, 610 Wittgenstein himself applies this doctrine to memory:

> I saw this man years ago: now I have seen him again, I recognize him, I remember his name. And why does there have to be a cause of this remembering in my nervous system? Why must something or other, whatever it may be, be stored up there *in any form*? Why *must* a trace have been left behind? Why should there not

[1] *Proc. Arist. Soc.* LXXII (1971–2) p. 2.

be a psychological regularity to which *no* physiological regularity corresponds? If this upsets our conceptions of causality then it is high time they were upset.

Anscombe translates this last sentence 'If this upsets our *concept* of causality then it is high time *it was* upset' (my italics); but I think that this is too strong given that Wittgenstein uses the plural *Begriffe* reinforced by a *sie* in the final clause. The point is of some importance in determining how strong Wittgenstein thinks the conceptual pressure in favour of belief in an inner process to be. But even if we accept my suggested weaker version, this sentence still appears to concede that it is natural for us, given our present concept of causality, to assume that there must be an intervening process. But the claim is that there is something improper, something bogus, about this conceptual pressure.

What, then, are the sources of the conceptual pressure that we feel? The simplest consideration, reflected in Mrs Kneale's remarks, is that if cause and effect are remote in time they must be connected by a causal chain. In the case of memory the most obvious place to look for such a causal chain is in the central nervous system, for our experience indicates that beings who remember all possess a central nervous system, and there is much evidence that interference with this system disrupts the functioning of memory. But it has been argued with considerable cogency by Roger Squires[1] that the connection between the remembered event and the memory should not be regarded as a causal process. Memory is rather a matter of the *retention* of the relevant knowledge by the person who remembers, and such retention does not require a persisting causal process, but merely that the person should retain certain capacities over the period of time that is in question.

One can accept Squires' contention that the retention of such capacities should not be described as a causal process while still insisting that their persistence must be due to some continuing state of the nervous system. But Squires argues against any such attempt to retain the notion of a memory trace. 'It is misleading because skills, abilities and capacities are not inside us like cells, nerves, and muscles. But it is doubly misleading because, even if we accepted the metaphor of memory as a storehouse containing abilities, it would not follow that in order to retain an ability there needs to be a successive set of states each producing the next' (p. 196). We have already accepted the point that the successive states need not be regarded as successive causes. But why is it unreasonable to believe

[1] 'Memory Unchained', *Philosophical Review* LXXVIII (April, 1969) pp. 179–96.

that the persistence of an ability is to be explained in terms of the persistence of a state? This does not require us to believe that the ability itself is 'inside us, like cells, nerves, and muscles', for to speak of the ability itself is not to speak of the states that explain its retention. The ability is exercised in remembering, but no physiological state can be so exercised.

But if physiological states are to explain the exercise of the ability, it would seem that they must be regarded as causally efficacious when we do remember. Squires presents an interesting argument against an earlier attempt by Martin and Deutscher[1] to explain how this could be so. The argument centres around the difficulty of distinguishing, on any such account, between a memory trace and a prompt. Martin and Deutscher agree that such a distinction is required if the account is to accord with 'the common-sense thought that someone who remembers something does not have to see it again, or something like it, or hear a full description of it, in order to tell about it' (p. 183). If the memory trace is thought of as a stored representation which facilitates reports of the past by becoming available, or causing some other representation to be available for inspection at the relevant time, then the process appears to be one of prompting rather than remembering. We have not explained remembering, but only a type of prompting which might then lead the person to remember. The central point here is succinctly made by Wittgenstein in *Zettel*, 662–4:

662. Remembering: a seeing into the past. *Dreaming* might be called that, when it presents the past to us. But not remembering; for, even if it showed scenes with hallucinatory clarity, still it takes remembering to tell us that this is past.

663. But if memory shows us the past, how does it show us that it is the past? It does *not* show us the past. Any more than our senses show us the present.

664. Nor can it be said to communicate the past to us. For even supposing that memory were an audible voice that spoke to us – how could we understand it? If it tells us e.g. 'Yesterday the weather was fine', how can I learn what 'yesterday' means?

These sections help us to understand what is involved in memory, over and above prompting. We can be prompted to remember, but the prompting is in that event a cause of the remembering. There is nothing inconsistent in the proponent of memory traces holding that

---

[1] 'Remembering', *Philosophical Review* LXXV (April, 1966) pp. 161–96.

the traces can cause mental images which prompt us to remember, as long as he does not claim that this is sufficient to explain remembering. Indeed there is a case for claiming that the mere occurrence of mental images so caused is a type, though clearly not the central type, of remembering. For we do sometimes ask, when images occur, 'Am I remembering or imagining?'. And it makes sense to say in retrospect 'I must have in fact been remembering my schooldays when I indulged in that reverie about the smell of fresh cut turf and the tense excitement before a race at an athletics meeting'.

But such cases cannot be central. How then can a brain trace be operative in bringing about the condition in which I 'just remember', without prompting, what happened? The proponent of brain traces must at the very least maintain that the brain trace accounts for the content of the memory: for the fact that *this* is remembered, rather than for the fact that it is *remembered*. To speak metaphorically, the trace is what is stored in the storehouse, and cannot on its own explain how it is brought out of store when we remember, or how it is identified as coming from *that* store, the *memory* store, when it is brought out. To translate out of the metaphor again, it would have to be added that when I 'just remember' without prompting the trace is causally efficacious in that the information it contains produces a response directly, without giving rise to an image or any other representation. Squires implies on pp. 195–6 that any such account as this makes the distinction between relearning and remembering an arbitrary one, for remembering now looks like a species of relearning. There are two differences between the causal account that we have developed, and that of Martin and Deutscher, which enable us to avoid the force of this objection. First, we have said nothing that commits us to the view that our *concept of memory* must be analysed in terms of the notion of a memory trace; our position has rather been that given our concept of cause, and Squires' analysis of memory in terms of retention of knowledge, it is still reasonable to invoke the notion of a memory trace in explaining memory. Secondly, we have explicitly acknowledged that there is a crucial feature of memory, namely the awareness that what is remembered *happened in the past*, which the explanation does not cover. It can plausibly be maintained that the presence or absence of this factor is what distinguishes the central cases of remembering from relearning.

But in defending such a view against Squires we seem to have been led into employing that very concept of causality which Wittgenstein was prepared to challenge. As applied to memory, the question was

H

whether the information which was retained needed to be stored in any form at all. We have now suggested that it is reasonable to expect that this is so. We might now reasonably ask Wittgenstein what role he thinks that the intervening physiological processes do serve, for we noted above that it is only beings who have brains, etc., who can remember.

I think that Wittgenstein intended in *Zettel*, 612 to indicate his answer to this question, though it is not perhaps immediately clear that this is its function. Wittgenstein describes a situation in which someone takes notes while a text is recited to him, and is later able by consulting these notes to reproduce the text. The notes are not writing, not connected by rules with the words of the text, but they are nevertheless essential to the performance:

> . . . without these jottings he is unable to reproduce the text; and if anything in it is altered, if part of it is destroyed, he sticks in his 'reading' or recites the text uncertainly or carelessly, or cannot find the words at all. – This *can* be imagined! – What I called jottings would not be a *rendering* of the text, not so to speak a translation with another symbolism. The text would not be *stored up* in the jottings. And why should it be stored up in our nervous system?

This is a most interesting example, for while we can agree with Wittgenstein's insistence that such a situation can (in a sense) be imagined, I am equally sure that it is just the sort of case where we should feel that some further explanation is called for. Why should a series of apparently meaningless jottings be necessary to the performance? Why, indeed, should we speak of the seed as 'producing' the tree as Wittgenstein does in *Z*, 608 if there is nothing about the seed which helps to account for the fact that it is a tree which is produced? Our concept of cause is such that we expect there to be an explanation for such correlations.

But is it in order to apply our concept of cause in these cases? In *Z*, 613 Wittgenstein asks why there should not be a natural law connecting a starting and a finishing state of a system, and not covering the intermediary state. Then he adds: 'Only one must not think of *causal efficacy*.' But the jottings in *Z*, 612 do seem to be causally efficacious in producing the response. One might feel a certain hesitation, certainly, in saying that the seed was causally efficacious in producing the subsequent tree, for it is only when acted on by the right sorts of environmental agents such as heat, light and moisture that it will grow. The fact that the seed grows into the tree also makes it inappropriate to identify the seed as the cause of the tree: it grows into and thus in a sense *becomes* the tree. But in this process we do expect to be able to trace an ordered development: we expect to find chemical mechanisms such that given the composition of the seed and the nature of the material and energy impinging upon it the development can be explained in terms of laws. Why should we not expect to find a similar explanation for psychological regularities? Such a similar explanation would not necessarily be in terms of a remembered text being stored up, intact, in our nervous system, for it may be that what is stored produces a memory of the text only when it reacts with other factors, just as a seed produces a tree only given the right environmental conditions. Similarly in Wittgenstein's story about the jottings, it would be reasonable to believe that the speaker's notes were a series of partial prompts, such that the text can be recovered from them only in the light of a detailed knowledge of the speaker's idiosyncratic associative habits. But it remains true in this case that the jottings are causally efficacious. To interpret the example in this way gives no support to the view that a causal explanation is not to be expected, and consequently does nothing to support the more general thesis that we should not seek physiological explanations of psychological phenomena. Wittgenstein's examples are not convincing as they stand: they need to be supported by some further argument.

Donald Davidson[1] has recently argued for the view that there cannot be strict psychophysical laws in a way that promises to illuminate our problem, for the argument is produced as part of a defence of the identity theory. Davidson's main point is that psychophysical laws are impossible because of an uneliminable difference between physical and mental concepts: they just do not go with each other. Physical concepts promise to provide a comprehensive closed theory, mental concepts do not, and 'a law can hope to be precise, explicit and as exceptionless as possible only if it draws its concepts from a comprehensive closed theory' (*ME*, p. 94). The attribution of any propositional attitude to an agent is possible only 'within the framework of a viable theory of his beliefs, desires, intentions and decisions' (*ME*, p. 96), but this framework is unlike the physical system in that it is subject to adjustment in the light of overall considerations of rationality: 'if we are intelligibly to attribute attitudes and beliefs, or usefully to describe motions as behaviour, then we are committed to finding in the pattern of

[1] See his 'Mental Events' in *Experience and Theory* ed. Lawrence Foster and J. W. Swanson (Massachusetts, 1970) (hereafter *ME*); and also 'Psychology as Philosophy', in *Philosophy of Psychology*, ed. Stuart C. Brown (London: Macmillan; New York: Barnes & Noble, 1974) (hereafter *PP*).

behaviour, belief and desire a large degree of rationality and consistency' (*PP*, p. 50). These conditions have no echo in physical theory. But mental events cause, and are caused by, physical events which *qua* physical are predictable and explicable in terms of the laws of the closed physical system. Thus there is no argument from the anomalous nature of mental concepts to the conclusion that there are events that are in themselves undetermined or unpredictable: 'it is only events as described in the vocabulary of thought and action that resist incorporation into a closed deterministic system. These same events, described in appropriate physical terms, may be as amenable to prediction and explanation as any' (*PP*, pp. 42–3). Davidson concludes that as events which are causally connected must under some description instantiate a strict law, such mental events as are either causes or effects of physical events must have a physical description under which they instantiate a strict law: hence all such mental events are physical events.

Wittgenstein would clearly reject this conclusion, but much of Davidson's exposition of the anomalous character of the mental could fairly readily be restated in Wittgensteinian terms: it incorporates and illustrates the principle that a man's utterances have to be understood as moves in a language-game which embodies a form of life. This account of the mental also has the consequence that, for example, thoughts cannot be inferred with scientific reliability from brain processes, for the occurrence of a thought is clearly a psychological event of a type which raises questions of rationality and consistency. But Wittgenstein and Davidson part company at the point at which the latter argues that the causal relationships between the mental and the physical imply that the mental events in question have a physical description under which they are explicable in terms of strict laws. It is just this concept of causality that Wittgenstein refuses to apply to psychological events, where by 'psychological events' is meant not 'incorporeal inner processes', but occurrences such as intelligent speaking and writing, remembering and perceiving. Wittgenstein is committed to a denial of Davidson's assumption that such events can be explained in the context of a closed comprehensive system covering all physical events. That Wittgenstein wishes to exempt the actions of human beings from this form of explanation becomes apparent in *Zettel*, 614, where he discusses the fact that we see a tree standing up straight even if we incline our heads to one side so that the retinal image is that of an obliquely standing tree. After dismissing the explanation that we supply a correction in the way that we take our visual impression as 'gratuitous', Wittgenstein writes:

Well – but now that the structure of the eye is known – *how does it come about* that we act, react, in this way? But must there be a physiological explanation here? Why don't we just leave explaining alone? – But you would never talk like that, if you were examining the behaviour of a machine – Well, who says that a living creature, an animal body, is a machine in this sense? –

One is tempted to comment that this is the point where Wittgenstein's own prejudices become most explicit, for he seems to recommend that we give up trying to explain such phenomena scientifically without even having made an attempt – which is of course very different from expressing a reasoned scepticism about the results of any such attempt. Now it may be that physiology is not the most promising direction in which to look for an explanation of the perceptual constancy in question. It seems likely that a psychological explanation citing such facts as that we have learnt to base our beliefs about up and down on the perception of standardly vertical objects like trees will be more illuminating. Let us assume that this explanation is confirmed, for such hypotheses can be tested by experiments in perceptual psychology. It is surely not unreasonable then to proceed to investigate the physiological basis of this learning. Perhaps there are reasons to doubt that we shall ever be able to read off beliefs from brain states, and therefore to be sceptical about the chances of explaining the psychological phenomena. Indeed if Davidson's account of the general character of physiological explanation is correct, then it seems to me to show that the success of such an explanation would show that psychological concepts were in a clear sense epiphenomenal: a complete, exact and strict explanation can be given of all that happens without using them. If we wish to defend the autonomy of any part of human thought and action, then we appear to be committed to denying that reasons for thinking or acting have such an epiphenomenal character. Davidson seeks to avoid this conclusion by maintaining that such reasons *are* efficacious causes because they are also describable in physical terms: but this is not to show that they are efficacious *qua* reasons, which is what any doctrine of autonomy worth the name needs to show. If we are to establish that psychological phenomena cannot be explained physiologically, we must first elucidate the allegedly anomalous features of the mental, and then actually come to terms with whatever scientific explanations are proposed. Wittgenstein clearly made a distinguished contribution to the first of these tasks, but fails in his attempt to show that the second is unnecessary.

13

SILENT SOLILOQUY

Roger Squires

1. SPEAKING is so closely associated with making noises that such descriptions as 'silent soliloquy' and 'soundless monologue' have an air of paradox. Yet people frequently say things to themselves in such a way that not even a close observer has any reason to think they have done so. It is therefore tempting to suppose that on such occasions a sequence of surrogate speech sounds is produced in the person's head which he alone hears or introaudits, as if what distinguishes silent inner speech from normal speech is that the word substitutes are conveniently hidden from all save their producer.

But the vehicles of inner speech are not sounds. For no decibels are recorded on even the most sensitive meter and it would be a turn up for the anatomy books if our heads contained a soundproof studio. Moreover, there is no competition between internal monologues and the purring of the cat or the din on the radio. They are never drowned out by aeroplane noise. ('I can't hear myself think' was a joke.) It is absurd to wonder how loud or how quiet silent speech is.

If inner speech is not in sound presumably it needs to be in code, just as writing, morse and semaphore use words coded into a different medium. Yet no one is able to say whether he engages in internal inscribing, flag waving or flower arranging, let alone to reveal details of his code in the head. People are sometimes prepared to reveal in what tone of voice, with what emphasis and in which dialect they said something to themselves. Could this survive coding? And why does the time taken by internal utterances correspond so well to the time taken by 'external' utterances, when there is no such correspondence between morse, semaphore and smoke signals? Finally, if the media are different, why can't we internally flagwave what we are at that moment saying? The idea of a private speech code is readily cracked.

When someone speaks subvocally things sometimes go on inside him which he is able to distinguish. There may be hums or whispers, snortling sinuses or twitches of the tongue, sinews stretching or muscles tensing. These things are apparently too crude to be speech sound substitutes. When someone says to himself, carefully and deliberately, 'Plato and Aristotle were not machines', surely he is not (mis)hearing or decoding these occurrences, even if he can detect some?

Suppose we find that silent speech can be scientifically monitored by observing minute movements of the voice box. Or we find that there are characteristic electrical patterns in the brain which appear to correspond to appropriate words. This would not vindicate the hypothesis about private speech vehicles. Someone who learns to read off what another is saying from his lip movements has not discovered the medium of speech. We don't speak by making lip movements; we are usually quite oblivious to them. We are similarly unaware of the movements of our larynx or the electrical patterns in our brain when we speak silently. We may make movements or patterns as we say thing subvocally but we do not say things subvocally by making movements or patterns. A correspondence between internal occurrences and ordinary speech sounds does not in itself demonstrate the existence of an inner medium.

It might be desperately suggested that the inner movements or patterns are 'heard as noise'. Why don't they compete with other noises? So long as nothing can be detected with ear-trumpets or whatever, the favoured suggestion must surely be that the person is imagining that he is hearing things, rather than that he is hearing things audible only to him. No startling physiological discoveries prompt these popular ideas about what the silent speaker must be doing. So let us not worry about inner speech sounds or private codes. We can dispense with the unhappy medium. This is not surprising. For we need sounds, flags or flowers to communicate and there is no call to communicate with ourselves.

2. It strikes many as mad to deny that silent speech is or involves inner processes monitored by the speaker, even if it is conceded that the inner landscape does not exactly contain vehicles of speech. To doubt this landscape or flow of experience seems to them an unseemly Behaviourism, pretending to be anaesthetised. Such a self-denying ordinance apparently clashes with the plain evidence of

introspection. In *A Materialist Theory of the Mind*[1] D. M. Armstrong considers the example of someone who has performed a calculation in his head. He challenges Wittgenstein thus:

> But is this all there is to it? Is 'calculation in the head' little more than a period of silence followed by an intelligent answer? At least sometimes when we 'calculate in our heads' are we not aware of a *current event*: something that goes on in us at the time of the calculation? . . . it is not a piece of overt behaviour. It may be replied that during the 'calculation' we were disposed to say and do certain things, and that we are afterwards able to report the existence of these dispositions. But, granting this, was there not something *actual* going on, of which we were aware at the time?' (p. 69)

He says later that the same argument will apply to all other sorts of thinking to oneself or of mental activity.

Certainly silent speech and calculation in the head are not merely periods of quiet followed by recitals or dispositions to give answers. You have to learn how to do them and engage in them more or less at will. When a person does mental arithmetic he does not wait until the yeast leavens the lump; he may have to strain at it and what he does may be done carefully or carelessly, with or without proper attention. Furthermore, no doubt the cortical activity and muscular movements (or whatever) are interesting enough for the physiologist to jib at the idea that working something out in the head is merely a bit of silence. But is there good reason to suppose that in working things out a person is aware of these inner processes or events – or, indeed, of anything else which can properly be described as 'going on inside him'?

If we ask someone who has been calculating in his head whether he was aware of something actual going on inside him at the time, he may reply, 'Yes, I added 17 and 18 to make 35, then took away 7 . . .', or, 'I said silently to myself "17 and 18 makes 35. Take away 7 . . ."'. These replies are possible because we do things in our heads by saying things to ourselves or visualising numbers. But this does not settle the matter in favour of the view that these are monitored internal processes, any more than the original idiom, 'He did it in his head', shows that he was an inner workman. That you can 'see things in your mind's eye' does not show that you have a faculty for perceiving inner landscapes. Similarly, the fact that silent speech may be described as 'hidden', even 'going on inside',

[1] Routledge & Kegan Paul, 1968.

coupled with the further fact that people sometimes calculate by speaking silently, does not prove that such calculation involves internal processes. The question is whether this talk of 'things going on inside' is an unidiomatic description or a picturesque rephrasing of such facts as that people often don't know what a subvocal speaker is doing unless he tells them. To look and see whether inner processes occur or to conduct a poll are futile decision procedures.

In other parts of his book Armstrong gives an argument for the necessity of introspection. He takes for comparison the example of going out for a drink through busy streets.

> . . . if I am to bring off this feat, things like the shut door, the obstructing persons, the traffic, must all be things that I become aware of, and this awareness must have the effect of adjusting my behaviour so that, despite the obstacles, I still get to the bar. (p. 139)

Similarly, he maintains,

> An intention to work out a certain long-division sum purely in one's head is a mental cause that initiates and sustains mental activity. We are informed of the results reached at each stage of the activity by introspection (just as in the case of physical action we are informed by perception). (p. 162)

On the next page he concludes that

> There must be some method whereby information about the current state of affairs can be fed back to the driving force behind the teleological sequence. But if the teleological sequence in question is a sequence of events in the mind, this means that the agent must become informed of what is currently going on in his mind . . . so we have given a 'teleological deduction' of the existence of introspection.

It is not clear what the calculator is supposed to introspect. Not that $37 + 48 = 85$ or that $85 \div 5 = 17$, for these are not mental states (whatever they are). Armstrong says we 'become aware of the current stage in the mental calculation' or, again, 'become apprised of our current mental state.' But are stages and states 'proper objects of perception'? It is true that the teacher can see the stage a scribbling pupil has reached in a proof, onlookers can see the stage a race has reached and the housewife sees the state of the house when she returns from holiday. But although the teacher can tell you what his pupil's figures looked like, the onlookers can tell you what the racing cars looked like and the housewife can tell you what the chairs and carpets looked like, they would be mystified to be asked what the stage in the proof, the state of the race or the state of the house, looked like. Nor would an oculist draw direct conclusions about a person's vision if he was poor at seeing the state of a chess game or a second-hand car, as he certainly would if he was unable to see the chess pieces or the car wheels and number plate.

A person becomes aware of stages and states by seeing such things as chairs, cars and chess pieces. What he sees serves to explain, from one point of puzzlement, how he has or acquires the information. There is no better reason to think that 'mental' stages and states are proper objects of introspection. By analogy with perception, introspection would be what partially explained knowledge of mental stages and states. So what would its objects be? It is apparently assumed that in performing 'mental acts', such as dividing or saying numbers to ourselves, we bring about changes in some mental landscape and that we must somehow scan these inner activities, at least to the extent that we look to see how things stand from time to time in order that we know where we are in our calculations. We should certainly not accept such an account merely because it seems to explain how we keep our place in mental calculations or internal monologues.

Consider an analogy from another field, the football field. In a recent film on How to Dribble, George Best said: 'Don't look at the ball. You'll find with practice that you don't have to look to know where it is. You can just feel it there. All good dribblers develop this sixth sense.' One can easily imagine some soccer Socrates doubting the existence of such an extra sense and being met by an appeal to plain evidence; 'That's how George does it. And look at the Brazilians . . . etc.' The disputants would be at cross purposes. When he talks about a sixth sense, about sensing the position of the ball, Best is not advancing an explanation of how the dribbler knows where the ball is without looking at it. He is redescribing that fact in picturesque terms. If there 'really' were a sixth sense similar to sight he would no doubt advise footballers to learn to shift without using it.

To deny the sixth sense explanation is not, of course, to resort to magic. If the question is how you learn to dribble without looking at the ball the answer is probably, 'by practising hard in this way and that', and if the question is how the whole thing is possible, no doubt there is a physiological 'mechanism', the cogs and levers of which are unobserved and undirected. What causes confusion is that a primitive bogus explanation of a phenomenon is used as a picturesque redescription of it. Someone who denies the explanation is then taken to be denying the phenomenon and held to be refuted by a plain appeal to the evidence. Such an appeal is of no value until the describer-explainer makes clear which game he is playing. Then we can see well enough whether he has fielded the ball or given away a penalty.

Compare what a schoolteacher might say in a lesson on How to do Mental Arithmetic: 'Don't write the running total down or say it out loud. You'll find with practice that you don't have to see it written down or say it in order to remember what it is. You just hold it before your mind. All good calculators develop this inner sense.' If this is intended as a primitive explanation there is absolutely no reason to believe it. We might find that someone did long calculations apparently in his head by scribbling running totals on his cuff and glancing at them later. But it is superstition to suppose that we can never learn to manage without such aids, so that when we calculate in our heads we must have inner mental cuffs on which we unobservably scribble and to which we can introspectively refer. When the schoolteacher talks of holding the number in or before your mind, this is, or should be, only a graphic redescription of an acquired ability. We have to learn to let the cuff drop.

Let us return to our philosopher who, blinking into the light, finally goes for a drink. He may, especially on the way back, lose his way, forget where he is. Perhaps he looks at the street name board or some familiar building and discovers how to continue his journey. His perception partly explains how he knows where he is. When he returns to his study he is equally likely to get lost in his calculations and he may find his place again. Could there be something analogous to perception which explains how he knows once again what stage he has reached in his calculations? The short answer is that there could be, but there isn't. There is no independent reason to believe in inner scribbling on mental cuffs and the mere fact that it features in a possible explanation is no excuse for fairy-tale physiology.

But there is a further moral in the case. When he gets lost after his drink the philosopher is in fact at, say, Russell Square, even though he doesn't know that he is. But where is he when he gets lost in a calculation? It is implausible to say that he has just added 37 and 48 and is about to divide by 5, even though he doesn't know that he is. Maybe he *was* there and about to do that, but the moment he loses his way in the calculation he no longer seems to be at that place at all. He won't say, 'Heck, where am I? I'll introspect around for landmarks'. No. He has *forgotten* where he got to and needs to remember what steps he has taken. Phrases such as 'losing his place', 'knows where he is', 'looks to see how things stand', need to be looked at with extreme circumspection when used of things done in the head. The geographical analogy is not close.

3. It is a recognised howler to suppose that a speaker needs to listen to his own internal or external utterances in order to know what he is saying, though this used to be a common mistake. For example, William James in his *Principles of Psychology* quotes approvingly from M. V. Egger: 'Before speaking, one barely knows what one intends to say, but afterwards one is filled with admiration and surprise at having said and thought it so well'.[1] His admiration should have been tempered in this instance by the reflection that although the description may fit an inspired orator before and after an impromptu speech it is a travesty of ordinary conversation. If you were constantly surprised at what you said it would be as if some ventriloquist had thrown words into your mouth or as if you had swallowed a parrot. It would be doubtful if *you* had said anything at all.

When a person acts we need not suppose that he observes either the changes which he brings about or the changes which occur in him when he acts. Suppose he twiddles his thumbs and waggles his fingers behind his back. He does not normally witness the changes he brings about. Nor is he aware of the physiological changes in his fingers, arms and brain which are necessary if he is to do such things. He may feel slight muscular tensions, but these will be far too vague for him to infer from them what his hands are doing. Indeed, it is quite possible that if his hands had in fact been paralysed without his knowledge he would still believe he was moving his fingers about. If he has to observe the relevant changes in order to know he has succeeded why doesn't the lack of such observations reveal his failure to him? No, we can do things without observing any happenings. We know what is going to happen before it does and only need to look, if at all, to check that it happens.

How are we to account for the agent's 'knowledge of his own intentions and actions' and the speaker's 'knowledge of what he is saying'? Ryle claims in *Concept of Mind*[2] that someone calculating in his head or saying things silently to himself is engaging in an

[1] William James, *The Principles of Psychology* (London: Macmillan, 1890), volume I, p. 280.
[2] Hutchinson, 1949.

imaginary or fancied 'production-cum-audition' – he imagines himself making and hearing sounds. But he later says incautiously that a person may 'eavesdrop on' (p. 184) or 'listen to' (p. 169) his own silent monologues. It is a fair protest that *fancied* speeches can no more be listened to or overheard than they can be drowned out by the radio or half-deafen the hearer (points Ryle rightly insists on).

In 'An Honest Ghost?'[1] A. J. Ayer fastens on Ryle's remarks about internal monologues, cinematograph shows of visual imagery and so forth, commenting that 'the existence of inner processes appears . . . to be conceded' (p. 56). Silent soliloquies head his list of 'mental residues' which allegedly furnish an inner life robust enough to haunt even Ryle. He thinks Ryle has not refuted the view that we have 'privileged access' to such 'inner processes', that 'we obtain our knowledge of them, when we have it, in a way that is not available to anybody else' (p. 64). Similarly, H. D. Lewis, in holy-unholy alliance, grumbles about Ryle's account, or lack of account, of our knowledge of our own silent monologues. He claims that we know 'what they are like in the very process of conducting them. This is not "eavesdropping" on ourselves. It is much more immediate and has no parallel in any way we monitor or eavesdrop on the utterances of other persons.'[2]

What exactly is the silent speaker held to know which 'can only be known in the first instance' to himself (Lewis) 'in a way that is not available to anybody else' (Ayer)? I think the answer is taken to be perfectly obvious. We don't know what he is saying to himself unless he tells us. He does know this. Similarly, when the ambassador hides his amusement by keeping a straight face it is assumed that *he* knows that he is amused even if no one else does. 'How do I know what I think unless I say it?' is the joke of the chatterbox. 'How do I know what I feel unless I make a fist, laugh or tremble?' is the corresponding joke of the extrovert. And the tempting, indeed the standard, rejoinder is: 'Don't be silly. You don't have to speak to know what you think. You know what you think and feel without expressing it.' Such knowledge as this, 'non-perceptual knowledge', 'knowledge without observation', is seen as peculiarly 'direct', 'immediate', even 'infallible', 'incorrigible'. Its objects, such as thoughts and intentions, are treated as inner processes or states to which their 'owner' has 'privileged access' and about which he is a 'unique authority'. The whole of these elements composes the person's mental life, his stream of consciousness.

[1] *Ryle*, ed. Wood and Pitcher (Macmillan, 1971).
[2] *The Elusive Mind* (George Allen and Unwin, 1969), p. 83.

It is an enormous merit of Wittgenstein's *Philosophical Investigations* that it begins to emancipate us from this traditional view and to forge alternative answers to the question whether such items of knowledge about a person as that he thinks such-and-such are also items of knowledge for that person. There is now a large question mark over such sentences as 'He knows what he is saying (to himself or out loud)', 'He knows what he is doing or, at least, intends to do', 'He knows what he thinks, believes, wants, is waiting for', even, 'He knows he is angry, astonished, terrified, amused or in agony'. Whereas there is no doubt that you may or may not know what someone else is saying, intends, is waiting for and so on, there is a doubt whether it makes sense to say that, of course, you know this is your own case. If it does not make sense, there would be no immediate, infallible knowledge, no unique authorities; no need to postulate inner processes and states to which a person has privileged access. The stream of consciousness would be an illusion.

4. It is quite common to meet such linguistic constructions as 'He jumped a jump, danced a dance, drank a drink or sang a song'. Suppose someone asks you if you can teach him to sing songs and dance dances. You say, 'Can't you sing? Can't you dance? Oh, well, that's easy these days . . .' But he corrects you, 'Of course, I can sing and dance, but I want to know how to sing a song and dance a dance'. Ever helpful, you reply, 'Which song and dance do you mean? Maybe I'll know it.' But now he replies, 'Oh, no particular song and dance. I just want to learn how to sing songs and dance dances and not merely to sing and dance as I do now!' Now is the time to give him, not a singing and dancing lesson, but a language lesson. You need to explain about cognate accusatives, that it is a mistake to suppose that there is something you can sing other than songs, that you can't dance a dance as opposed to something else, that in the statement 'he sang a song', as he understood it, the accusative is redundant, so that the statement amounts to no more than 'he sang'.

All very correct. But what interests me is the following cul-de-sac. Suppose the teacher did not take the linguistic path, but tried to offer a singing and dancing lesson, thus: 'Come on, then. Just sing this. Now that. Well done! You sang a song every time. In fact it's so very easy you can hardly fail once you can sing. It is one of a wide range of infallible achievements open to human beings. What a mystery that we should be so unerringly successful.' In an attempt to show that the teacher was as confused as the student we might protest, 'There are no such infallible achievements', and he would no doubt reply, 'It is a plain fact that people drink drinks, sing songs and dance dances. How can you deny it?' What we deny is his interpretation of such statements as expressing infallible achievements when the accusatives are grammatical redundancies. I think this song and dance has its parallel in the dispute about privileged access and infallible knowledge. These notions are philosophers' nonsense that arises when the opportunity to correct linguistic confusion has been missed.

It is assumed that the statement, 'He knows what he is saying (to himself or out loud)', means that he knows what others know when they know what he is saying. Then there is a mystery both about the acquisition of this knowledge and its unerring success. The reason is that there is no such knowledge and the statement cannot mean what it has been assumed to mean. That it has perfectly respectable uses is an obstacle on the way of seeing the imposter of a use. For example, 'He knows what he is saying' may indicate that the speaker knows the significance or consequences of what he is saying. That this is not the controversial use is shown by the fact that he may well not know what he is saying. He is no unique authority on its importance or its implications.

'But surely the person silently soliloquising knows what he is doing and others don't unless he tells them or otherwise gives it away?' The description, 'He knows what he is doing', has many innocent employments, but its use here is every bit as dangerous as 'He knows what he is saying'. For example, it may refer to knowledge of consequences: 'You may think he does not realise this chemical will poison the inhabitants, but I'm afraid he knows very well what he is doing'. Or it may indicate expertise: 'You are all in knots. Make way for someone who knows what he is doing.' It may denote decisiveness and purpose, as opposed to hesitation and lack of planning: 'The Liberal thought he was there to persuade the delegates or perhaps merely state the case: the Communist knew what he was doing'. It may also signify an ability to name or label an action: 'I'm not sure whether Mummy is poaching, scrambling or addling it. Ask her – she probably knows what she is doing.' There is no quarrel with the uses in these examples and no privilege or mystery about the knowledge involved. It is just as easy to suppose the agent does not know what he is doing.

The use which traps us seems to be a kind of redundancy. Suppose we are sitting around on deck-chairs trying to guess what the gardener is doing as he walks round and round, stamps on the handle of a spade and whistles carefully. Failing, we may say,

'Well, at least the gardener knows what he is doing'. I think this is a jokey equivalent of 'He's doing *something*, all the same'. That is why, if he does not know what he is doing, in this sense, there is no rhyme nor reason in it and he is not doing anything. So we can say: 'If he is doing something, he must know what he is doing'. But this is a remark about how we use the phrase, 'knows what he is doing', and not a report of direct and infallible knowledge.

Similarly, 'He knows what he is saying', in one rarefied employment, is a way of stressing what is involved in saying something. You can't say something accidentally or by mistake or without realising what you are saying (save in the sense that you can be ignorant of importance and implications). But this is again a 'grammatical' remark and not a report of infallible knowing or unerring achievement. Once again, someone who does not know what he is saying is not someone who is saying something and does not know it – he is not saying anything. Similar stories can probably be told about, 'He does not know what he intends, thinks, wants, is expecting, whether he is surprised, amused, terrified' and many more.

In the case of speech, there is a qualification which does not interfere with the general argument. Suppose the minister makes a silly remark and some Polonius on the diplomatic staff mutters, 'Damn fool!' He may not realise that he spoke, fully believing that he only said it to himself. In this sense, a person can know that he is speaking, speak accidentally or by mistake. Conversely, a person in a football crowd may think he is shouting, 'Goal!' or 'Don't look at the ball' when he has in fact lost his voice through previous shouting and his present failure to speak is disguised by the general noise level. No such possibilities of failure exist for his alleged 'knowing that he is saying something and what it is'.

Theorists have conjured metaphysics out of such statements as 'a person must know what he is up to and what he is saying to himself', but this only seems compelling because the statements can express linguistic maxims or reminders. The traditional difficulties that beset positive accounts of direct and infallible knowledge should alert us to this, as should the inconceivability of someone saying something and not knowing it, being up to something and not being aware of it. Another consideration is the apparent lack of any difference between someone who merely says or believes or is surprised by something and someone who, it is alleged, also knows that he is. For instance, we expect things of someone who knows there is a tiger in the building which we don't expect of someone who does not. But what should we expect of someone who 'knows he believes' there is a tiger there which we would not expect of someone who 'merely' believes it? Neither will linger over coffee! In the case of many 'psychological' descriptions the alleged distinction between their merely being true of someone and his knowing they are true of him is without a difference, like the alleged distinction between punching a punch and merely punching.

5. When a person speaks silently to himself what does he know that others normally don't know unless he tells them? I have rejected the standard answer that he knows directly and infallibly that he is saying something and what it is, which inner saying allegedly constitutes a mental process, part of his stream of consciousness. But the question seems legitimate. When a person ties a knot or twiddles his thumbs it may be odd to describe him as 'knowing that he is tying a knot or twiddling his thumbs', but he does know that certain things are happening – the string is changing its formation, his thumbs are twiddling – and it is these happenings that he brings about. What happenings does the subvocal speaker bring about and how does he know about them?

It is easy to acquiesce in the following reasoning at this point. 'Although people need not observe the changes they bring about when they act (wave flags, open doors and so on), they usually observe them when learning to act in these ways and the changes are usually clear for all to see. We describe their act by reference to the difference it makes. Now a person who talks under his breath or arithmetises under his ink brings about no external, open changes. But since he is certainly doing something he must bring about internal, hidden changes. And he presumably learns to do this by at least sometimes in some way observing what he brings about.' After rejecting some unsuccessful rejoinders, I hope to show that you can get no hidden change out of this argument.

The changes made obviously don't have to be movements against a stationary background, though preoccupation with arm waving, pushing, pulling, walking and running encourages such an assumption. It is equally an action to keep still, refrain from laughing or hold your tongue. When the vicar slips on the banana at the Harvest Festival probably the congregation would laugh unless they inhibited their natural reaction. Although they may take special steps to achieve this, such as thinking of the day the canary died or gritting their teeth, they may have no more inkling of how they keep straight faces than of how they bend their knees. It is tempting to suppose that, just as the congregation hides its amusement so the subvocal speaker hides his thoughts. Perhaps he would have said out loud 'Help, everyone is asleep!' if he hadn't stopped himself from doing so. The gate is then open to escape from the hidden change argument by pointing out that the difference made in what would have happened is not 'internal'. Silent speech is no more the production of internal changes than keeping your eyes open when you are tired.

But this won't do. It is artificial to say of a subvocal speaker that he would have said it out loud unless he had stopped himself. You might as well say, when he speaks out loud, that he would have said it to himself if he hadn't produced certain sounds! Moreover, the parallel with amusement does not run true. For, at least sometimes, when people laugh at funny situations, when their eyes droop with tiredness, these are rather things that happen to them than things they do. By their efforts they can change what would have happened to them. But saying things inwardly is itself something they do, not something that would have happened to them. Whether what they say is uttered or kept back is a detail. What is it that is done in either case?

Here is another inviting escape. When a person adds 57 and 28 in his head a change is certainly brought about. Before, he didn't know, couldn't tell you, that they made 85. Now, he does know, can tell you. Similarly, when someone solves an anagram without re-arranging the jumbled letters, when he 'sees' the solution, he has brought about a change in what he can do. Now he could rearrange the letters with no delay, for example. It may be held that when a person conducts internal monologues this is a series of usually minor achievements. But changes in his skill are not changes in his skull. They are changes in what he can do and, as such, not objects of observation.

In a helpful article in *Mind* (1956), 'Why we cannot witness or observe what goes on "in our heads" ', H. Hudson points out that someone who does something in his head often gets answers without giving them, makes decisions without stating them or forms plans without revealing them. As he fully realises, silent speaking is not an achievement of this kind. For you get the answers or form the plans by saying or picturing things to yourself. Silent saying can be interrupted and goes on for a certain time, whereas these results are either attained or not. Wittgenstein asks in the *Investigations* (*PI*, I, 236): 'Calculating prodigies who get the right answers but cannot say how. Are we to say they do not calculate?' If the answer just comes to them in a flash, without working out, as it seems to, then they no more calculate in their heads than we do when we add 2 and 3. When a person does have to work something out he often does it by saying things subvocally or picturing numbers. It appears that these activities have to be distinguished from what is achieved by engaging in them.

There is certainly a close relation between silent speech and certain accomplishments. Consider the verb 'to ask oneself' as a synonym of 'to wonder'. Non-native speakers say such things as, 'I asked myself what the date was'. Let us suppose he did say to himself under his breath, 'What is the date?' If he finds out the date, he may still say to himself, 'What is the date?', but it would be improper to describe him as *asking* himself the date, for he cannot wonder what it is when he already knows it. Similarly, reflexive verbs such as 'to tell oneself', 'to exhort oneself', 'to remind oneself' and 'to blame oneself' need to be separated from 'to say subvocally'. When you tell or remind yourself of something this may involve silent speech. But it may not. And silent speaking can occur when no verbs of this type are appropriate. Comparably, you can utter words or pronounce sentences without thereby asking, stating, warning, recalling or exhorting.

Other attainments may well be involved in silent speech. Keeping silent could be described as such. The remainder of the paper is an attempt to show what else is involved without sliding back into the river of consciousness.

6. The cook bustles into the kitchen, puts on his rubber gloves, turns on the oven and empties potatoes into the bowl. Any kitchen visitor can see that he is preparing dinner. Even if an avalanche or a chef's stroke prevents him from doing anything else, even if he immediately decides to give up and have a cook's holiday, he still was making the meal for a certain time. Yet to say he was making dinner refers beyond the things that were happening at that time. A layman might come in, don the gloves, switch on the oven, empty the potatoes and yet not be preparing dinner. For he may have been quite unable to continue. When the avalanche comes it doesn't stop him making dinner, for the meal wasn't going to get made anyway. The description, 'Cook is making the dinner', looks forward to what is going to happen in the absence of avalanches or changes of mind.

It is tempting to hold that whereas a kitchen visitor may not know whether the person is beginning to cook a meal or merely switching switches, the person himself knows this infallibly in a way all his own. But I do not see what would be meant by saying that he was beginning to cook dinner and didn't know it and 'he knows he is preparing dinner' seems to add nothing to 'he is preparing dinner'.

Nevertheless, the person, if he is cooking dinner, no doubt knows quite a bit that the observer may not know. For instance, he knows the potatoes will get peeled and put into the saucepan, that in a few minutes the meat will be roasting in the oven . . . and, barring accidents or change of plan, that a meal will be ready to serve. If he does not know such things, if they take him completely by surprise when they happen, then he is not making the dinner. Nor, when he switched on the oven, was he beginning to make it, preparing it. This kind of knowledge is built into the description of the action.

The observer may know these things also. But if he does not, the cook can still be making the dinner. If the cook doesn't know them, the description fails. But there is surely no infallibility in the cook's knowledge. He may not know how to make dinner, so that his expectations are utterly disappointed. Suppose an unexpected avalanche occurs just after the cook has started. What is his knowledge in such a case, for he did not know what would happen? It is odd to say that he knows what will happen if there is no avalanche, for thoughts of avalanches have not occurred to him. But we can say afterwards that if there had been no avalanche, the meal would have been cooked and the cook's expectations would have been fulfilled; he would have known there would be a meal on the table. Only if this is so can we describe him as preparing a meal, beginning to make dinner, before the avalanche struck. Similarly, if he changes his mind it is still true of him earlier that if he had not brought about a change in what happened his expectations as to what would happen would have been correct. Notice that there is nothing infallible about such expectations. What is indubitable is that, if the cook does not have them, he cannot be described as making dinner or even beginning to make it. The linguistic truth that if a person is doing something he must know what is going to happen gets transmuted into the metaphysical claim that he must know what he is doing.

Let us try out the idea that someone who says something silently to himself begins to say it, prepares to utter it, but prevents himself from making a sound. He sets in train events whose terminus would not be news to him in the way that it probably would to anyone else. Then he blocks the natural sequence, so that others don't find out either that the sequence started or what its terminus would have been.

We can point to things which constitute the cook's beginning to make dinner, such as his switching on the oven. What corresponds to this when the person begins to say something? As a result of scientific investigation we may find there are various internal happenings. Our physiology Ph.Ds may be able to say which are the beginnings of speech and which events block that outcome. The key question is whether the person needs to be aware of these internal happenings. 'If not, how does he know that he would say such-and-such unless he stopped himself?' He knows how to speak. When he speaks, his expectations about the utterance are correct, without benefit of inner scanning. If the utterance has been blocked, we do not need to postulate inner scanning to explain how he knows what would have happened. The addition that he blocks it himself does not change the case.

Unfortunately, the analogy with the cook breaks down in other ways. If the cook did not at some stage intend to make the dinner then even if he went through the early motions correctly he was only going through the motions, not beginning to make dinner at all. By the same token, we could not attribute to him the expectation that the dinner would get cooked. But it is clear that usually when we say things to ourselves we have absolutely no intention of making full-dress speeches. The whole point is to avoid this. Therefore, we should probably not be described as beginning to speak. Moreover, it seems that there is more to the performance than making the opening moves. In silent saying, a person also may follow through as if speaking, though sound production and lip movements are inhibited.

Here is a better parallel. When a boxer pulls a punch he could have hit harder. But it is not merely a weaker blow than usual. The boxer sets out as he would to deliver a heavy blow, somehow checks its force, but carries on with it as if it really were a heavy blow. In silent speech we set out as if to utter a word, somehow check the utterance, and yet follow through in certain ways as if we had uttered it. Silent soliloquies are the pulled utterances of a shadow speaker. We need not credit silent speaker or sparring boxer with the intention to give full-dress performances at any stage, but they must know how to and they do exercise this knowledge. Similarly, when someone plays a Beethoven sonata on his desk with his fingers it would be nonsense to maintain that he could not play it on the piano. He exercises his piano-playing skill in the absence of the instrument.

The finger pianist may show you at the piano what he was drumming on his desk, though he may forget. He could not have shown you at the time, of course, or he would not have been merely drumming. Similarly, Hamlet may tell you later what he was saying to himself, if he doesn't forget. But he could not have told you at the time, for that would have been saying it out loud. Where the parallels unhelpfully end is that we can see the pulled punch thrown by the sparring boxer and the finger movements of the shadow pianist, whereas we cannot hear Hamlet's silent soliloquies. But nothing forces us to suppose that Hamlet himself must eavesdrop or be aware at all of internal movements or processes.

Suppose we paralyse a person's arm without his knowledge and then order him to move it. We find that a dial moves. We get the dial to move in different ways by making him try to move in different ways. We teach him how to do this at will. Next, we teach him to do it without benefit of artificial paralysis by keeping his arm stiff himself. Now we ask him to do it when the dial has been removed. How should we describe what he does? How does he move the dial? An account of the weird mechanism is not what is needed here. It is quite possible that what he does is to flex certain muscles, that he moves the dial by doing this. But it also seems possible that he should be quite ignorant of anything that goes on in his arm or anywhere else. Yet he does something all right. We cannot just describe it in relation to what it sometimes brings about, namely, dial-movements, since these can be brought about in other ways. We need to refer back to the skills he exercises in moving the dial in this way, his long-standing ability to make ordinary arm movements. We might be tempted towards apparently contradictory descriptions such as 'making stationary or shadow movements'.

Silent speech is like this. By exercising the ability to speak (but not producing utterances or lip movements) you can rehearse your lines, get the answers to sums, remind yourself of what you have to buy and so on. But you can speak subvocally without moving any of these dials and the activity has to be described in initially paradoxical ways, such as internal speech, soundless monologue and so forth. When people refer to it as an 'inner process' or 'hidden phenomenon' they may only be reminding us that the 'external' phenomena of noise-making and lip-moving are not present and that, as a result, it is very difficult for people to find out when a person engages in internal monologue and what he says to himself. As such, it is a description of what everyone admits.

But we hanker to know how the trick is possible and what is going on. Wisely, we get or imagine the physiological story of laryngeal movements, cerebral processes and what not. Unwisely we suppose that to speak subvocally is precisely to produce such inner changes, that it is literally an inner process or activity revealed only to the speaker. This dubious explanation gains acceptance in the eyes of the unwary by confusion with the un-controversial description. The identification won't do. Silent speech cannot be the truncated movements and short-circuitings investi-gated by the physiologist, for unless the person can be described as 'making as if to speak' and 'holding his tongue', such goings on would not make him a subvocal speaker, even if he had done, what he normally doesn't do, namely, produced these goings on delibe-rately. Nor is there any guarantee that the physiology is the same on all occasions or in all silent speakers. Moreover, if the identity is maintained, we shall need heady physiology to explain how the speaker knows what is going on inside him.

Perhaps the mentalists who resist identification with physical goings on in favour of spiritual goings on show some awareness of these difficulties. But we need not be haunted by their ghosts. Talk of the inner and the hidden should be taken as describing the inscrutability of subvocal speakers and in-the-head calculators not as explanations of this in terms of secret passageways. Wittgenstein and Ryle disputed the explanation, but were surely happy to 'concede' the description. Which is why a Canute-like insistence on such things as silent speech and mental arithmetic in no way stems the tide of their revolution in our thinking about human beings.

14

WITTGENSTEIN ON CERTAINTY

A. J. Ayer

WITTGENSTEIN's book *On Certainty* which was first published in 1969, eighteen years after his death, is a collection of notes which he composed during the last eighteen months of his life. As his editors explain in their preface, these notes, which were written at four different periods, are all in the form of a first draft. They are more repetitive than they no doubt would have been if Wittgenstein had been able to revise them. Even so, they are characteristically succinct and penetrating, and the argument which they develop is easier to follow than that of the general run of Wittgenstein's later work.

The peg on which the argument is hung is that of G. E. Moore's defence of common sense. Moore had attempted to safeguard what he called the common-sense view of the world against the arguments of philosophers who doubted or denied it simply by claiming that he knew it to be true. For instance, he took it to be part of this common-sense view 'that there are in the Universe enormous numbers of material objects',[1] which exist in space and time, and he construed this proposition in such a way that it followed from a set of particular propositions, such as that he had a body which had existed for some time and during that time had been 'in contact with or not far from the surface of the earth', that there had at the same time existed many other things, 'also having shape and size in three dimensions', from which his body had been at various distances, that these things included other human bodies, and that many things of these different kinds, including the earth itself, had existed for many years before he was born.[2] These were all propositions which he claimed to know for certain to be true, and he

[1] G. E. Moore, *Some Main Problems of Philosophy*, p. 2.
[2] G. E. Moore, 'A Defence of Common Sense', *Philosophical Papers*, pp. 32–5.

also claimed that the truth of propositions corresponding to these was known for certain to many other people. In the same way, he attempted on one occasion to prove the existence of external objects simply by holding up his two hands, and saying that the propositions 'Here is one hand' and 'Here is another' were known by him to be true. And a little later, by recalling that he had held up his hands some time before, he proved that external objects had also existed in the past.[1]

The point of this procedure is that if Moore really did know what he claimed to know, it would follow that any philosopher who denied the truth of any such propositions, or even held it to be doubtful whether any of them were true, must be wrong. For what is known to be true cannot fail to be so, whatever arguments may be mustered on the other side. It might then appear that the question to be answered was whether Moore's claims were justified.

In a way, Wittgenstein does address himself to this question, but not straightforwardly. He is concerned rather to show that it does not seriously arise. He does not deny the truth, or even the certainty, of propositions of the sorts that Moore took for his examples. On the contrary, he maintains that to express any doubt of their truth, in normal circumstances, would be nonsensical. At the same time, he argues that if it were significant to doubt them, it would not be sufficient to allay the doubt for anyone just to say that he knew them to be true. Not only that, but Moore was, in his view, actually at fault in saying this. The reason why he held him to be at fault was not that the propositions themselves were any less certain than Moore took them to be, but that to say, in the circumstances in which Moore did say them, such things as 'I know that this is a hand' or 'I know that the earth has existed for many years past' was a misuse of the expression 'I know'.

Let us begin with the point that merely to say that one knows a proposition to be true is not an acceptable method of proving it. If one is asked for a proof of some proposition which one believes, something more is required than the bare statement that one is convinced of its truth. But what difference is there between saying that one is certain that something is so and saying that one knows that it is so? There is no important difference, says Wittgenstein, 'except where "I know" is meant to mean: I *can't* be wrong.'[2] But then this claim has to be justified. As Wittgenstein puts it, 'It needs to be *shown* that no mistake was possible.'[3] Some objective reason has to be given for concluding that I must be right.

[1] G. E. Moore, 'Proof of an External World', *Philosophical Papers*, pp. 146–8.
[2] *OC*, 8.   [3] *OC*, 15.

Philosophers get the idea that if they know something they cannot be mistaken about it, because the use of the word 'know' carries the implication that what is known is true. If some proposition which I thought I knew turns out not to be true, it will follow logically that I did not know it. This is not, however, to say that my state of mind was other than what I took it to be, as if I had confused the mental attitude of knowledge with that of mere belief. My feeling of certainty might be exactly the same, whether I knew the proposition to be true or whether I only thought I knew it. It might be said that the feeling was justified in the one case and not in the other, but the difference then would lie not in the quality of the feeling but in the status of the proposition in question and the grounds that there might be for accepting it.

It follows that if one is seeking to be assured of the truth of some proposition, the fact of someone's saying that he knows it to be true will not meet the purpose unless one has some good reason for believing what he says. Even if his honesty is not in doubt, we have to be satisfied that he is in a position to have acquired this piece of knowledge, and we have also to be satisfied that the proposition which he claims to know is one for which there are sufficient grounds. If we are not satisfied on either of these counts, we shall be prompted to ask him how he knows, or what makes him think he knows, whatever it may be. In the more common case, in which we are less concerned with his standing as an informant than with the value of the information that he professes to be giving us, we shall in effect be asking him for evidence that what he says he knows is really so.

There are two conditions that have to be fulfilled, if this demand is to be met. The evidence which he supplies must give adequate support to the proposition in question; and it must itself consist of one or more propositions which we have a sufficient ground for taking to be true. But then, if this means that these propositions have to be supported in their turn by further propositions for which we have to furnish sufficient grounds, we are in danger of embarking on an infinite regress. To put a stop to the regress, we must at some point come to propositions which are acceptable in their own right. Such propositions will owe their security, not to the support of other propositions, but to their own content or to the conditions under which they are expressed.

Wittgenstein does not deny that this is so. Indeed, he treats Moore's examples as propositions of this sort. What he does deny is that we can legitimately speak of such propositions as being known to be true. Reviewing Moore's procedure, he remarks, quite correctly, that the point of Moore's examples is not that they furnish information which others might not have. They are, and are intended to be, typical of propositions which, in the appropriate circumstances, we all accept without question. And this suggests to him that in saying, in the way that Moore does, 'I *know*, I am not just surmising, that here is my hand' one is expressing not an ordinary empirical proposition but 'a proposition of grammar'. To prove in this way that there are physical objects is like proving that there are colours by saying 'I know, I am not just surmising, that I am seeing red'.[1] The implication is, I suppose, that these propositions embody rules of meaning. To deny, in these circumstances, that that was a hand or that I was seeing red would be to show oneself ignorant of what the words 'hand' and 'red' were used to mean.

But then, Wittgenstein argues, 'If "I know etc." is conceived as a grammatical proposition . . . it properly means "There is no such thing as a doubt in this case" or "The expression 'I do not know' makes no sense in this case." And of course it follows from this that "I *know*" makes no sense either.'[2]

Is this so? Let us set aside for the moment the more interesting question whether the proposition 'Here is a hand' has, in these circumstances, the same title to certainty as the proposition 'I am seeing red', and consider only the proposition that I am seeing red, where this is taken to imply no more than that the colour red is exemplified in my present visual field. If this proposition is true, does it make no sense to say that I do not know that it is true? And if it were senseless for me to say that I did not know it to be true, would it automatically follow that it was also senseless for me to say that I did know this?

I am not convinced that Wittgenstein gives the right answer to either of these questions. It is surely possible for someone to be seeing a colour which he fails to identify correctly, and in that case the statement that he did not know what colour he was seeing, so far from being senseless, would be true. But would this, in the present case, prove anything more than that he had not learned how to use the English word 'red'? On the assumption that he does understand what this word means, would it not be senseless for him to say that he did not know whether he was seeing red or not? Even this seems to me doubtful. It is true that if someone were always at a loss to say whether or not a given colour-term applied to what he saw, we should infer that he had not learned the meaning of the term, but

[1] *OC*, 57.   [2] *OC*, 58.

this does not oblige us to conclude that he is ignorant of its meaning, if there are any occasions on which he hesitates. For instance, I think that I know perfectly well what the words 'blue' and 'green' mean; yet there are times when I am not sure which of them to use. There are also times when, having used one of them, I am asked to look again and then decide that I ought to have used the other.

It could still be argued that these were cases of verbal and not factual uncertainty. I do not find this convincing, but I do not want to make an issue of it. For let it be granted, for the sake of argument, that the truth of a man's descriptions of the colours which he sees is always a test of his understanding what the colour-words in question mean. The consequence of this will be that the proposition that he both understands what the word 'red' means and does not know whether what he sees is red becomes self-contradictory. It can be characterised as senseless only if one takes what seems the unwarranted step of denying any sense to contradictions. But then it certainly will not follow that the proposition that he knows that what he sees is red is also senseless. On the contrary, the premisses which exclude its negation must entail that it is true.

The same conclusion can be reached in another way. For someone to know that a proposition is true, it is sufficient that it be true, that he be confident of its truth, and that he have the right sort of grounds for this confidence. In the present instance, there is no doubt that the first two conditions are satisfied. All that can be in question is the third. But what better ground can he have for believing that he sees such-and-such a colour than the actual appearance of what he takes to be that colour in his present visual field? It is true that he may not be able to say how he knows that he is seeing this colour, if this is taken as requiring him to adduce some other proposition which supports his claim. He may have no other course than to repeat that this is what he sees. But if in order to know the truth of any proposition, we had always to know the truth of some other proposition which supported it, then, as I have already remarked, we should be committed to an infinite regress. At some stage our claims to knowledge must be founded directly on experience. This does not require us to hold that our accounts of what we are experiencing can never be mistaken. Even if I am the final authority with regard to my own sensations, I can sometimes find cause to revise my judgments of their qualities. The point at issue is that these are judgments for which one is not required to give any further reasons, beyond the actual occurrence of the data which they monitor. This is not, however, a ground for saying that we cannot know them to be true. The anomaly would rather lie in representing our knowledge as sustained by propositions which could not themselves significantly be said to be known.

What may have led Wittgenstein astray here is the fact that statements like 'I know that this looks red to me' or even 'I know that this is a hand' would only exceptionally serve any purpose. There are no common occasions for their use. In the ordinary way, the point of saying 'I know that so and so' is either to show that one has acquired some information which one may have been thought not to possess, or else to insist on the truth of some proposition, which has been or might be seriously challenged. In either case saying 'I know' gives an assurance which is assumed to be needed. But when the proposition in question is that I am seeing some familiar colour, or that these are my hands, there is normally no need for any such assurance. It is taken for granted that I can recognise ordinary colours: the proposition that these are my hands is not, in this context, one that anybody is seriously inclined to doubt. If someone were learning English and were engaged in mastering the use of English colour-words, there would be some point in his saying that he knew that what he saw was red. A man who had suffered a brain lesion which rendered him incapable of recognising ordinary objects might say to his doctor that he knew at least that these were his hands, as a way of marking the progress of his recovery. But these are exceptional circumstances. In the cases which Wittgenstein envisages, the objection to saying 'I know that . . .' is that it suggests that the circumstances are exceptional, when they are not.

From this we can conclude not only that the use of the expression 'I know that' may serve no purpose, but that it may be actually misleading. It does not, however, follow that its use in such cases is senseless, or even that it is not used to state what is true. This may be illustrated by another example. Although people most commonly believe what they assert, the conventional effect of prefacing an assertion with the words 'I believe that' is to weaken its force. It suggests that one is not entirely sure of what follows. If I say, for instance, 'I believe that Smith has been elected' I commit myself less than if I had said outright: 'Smith has been elected'. Nevertheless, it certainly does not follow that when I do assert something outright, I do not believe it. In exactly the same way, the fact that it may be pointless or even misleading for me to say such things as 'I know that this looks red to me' or 'I know that these are my hands' in no way entails that what I am saying is not true.

If statements of these sorts are very often true, does it follow that what one knows is certain? The difficulty with this question is to understand what certainty means. There is, as Wittgenstein said, a sense of the word 'certain' in which to ask whether a proposition is certain is just a way of asking whether it is known to be true, and in that sense, evidently, every proposition which is known to be true is certain. In Wittgenstein's special sense, which is perhaps only philosophical, a proposition, as we have seen, can be said to be certain only if it is inconceivable that one should be mistaken in thinking it true, and in that sense it is doubtful if the word has any application, at any rate to empirical propositions. It is, indeed, very unlikely that a man will be mistaken in his description of the way things look and feel to him, but I think, as I have said, that it has to be admitted as a possibility. Another mainly philosophical sense is that in which a proposition is said to be certain only if it is necessarily true. This is a condition which empirical propositions do not satisfy, though we shall see later on that where Wittgenstein attributes certainty to empirical propositions, he assimilates them to propositions of logic.

When philosophers talk about certainty, they also often treat it as a matter of degree. Thus, a philosopher who does not deny the truth of such a proposition as that there are trees in his garden, or even deny that there is a perfectly proper sense in which he can be said to know that it is true, may still wish to say that it is less certain than some proposition which records his current visual or tactual sensations. His reason for this will be just that by claiming more it runs the greater risk of being false. My descriptions of the colours which are exemplified in my present visual field may still be true even though I am dreaming or hallucinated. They may still be true even though the interpretations which I put upon my visual data are not corroborated by the tactual data which they would lead me to expect, or by the reports which I receive from other observers. This does not apply, however, to such a proposition as that there are trees in my garden. It is true that I accept it, on the basis of what I think I see, or remember, without looking for any further evidence. I take it for granted that the necessary corroboration would be forthcoming. Even so my present experience does not guarantee that it would be forthcoming, and if it were discovered not to be I should have reason to conclude that I had been mistaken. It is on this ground that philosophers like Russell have concluded that no proposition which implied the existence of a physical object was altogether certain. What they meant was that no such proposition ever logically followed from any set of propositions which merely recorded the content of one's current sense-experiences.

The logical point is sound, but it might have been better to make it more straightforwardly. The trouble is that one tends to forget that the word 'uncertain' is being used here in a technical sense, in which to say that all propositions which imply the existence of physical objects are uncertain is to say no more than that they do not follow from some limited set of propositions which refer only to sense-qualia. One tends to make it carry the further implication that these propositions about physical objects cannot be known to be true, that they are all of them seriously open to doubt. And indeed it would seem that Russell himself did think this to be so, at least during the periods when he held that physical objects were external causes of our percepts. Though he thought that the character of our percepts gave us some good reason to believe in these external causes, he also thought it to be a genuine possibility that they did not exist.

Rather than accept this conclusion, we should most of us nowadays either try to argue that it did not follow from the causal theory of perception, or else, if we believed that it did follow, regard this as a decisive argument against the theory. But are we right? What is there about our belief in the physical world that makes it sacrosanct?

Wittgenstein's answer to this is that it is not an ordinary factual belief, but rather part of the frame of reference within which the truth or falsehood of our factual beliefs is assessed. As he puts it, 'All testing, all confirmation and disconfirmation of a hypothesis takes place already within a system. And this system is not a more or less arbitrary and doubtful point of departure for all our arguments: no, it belongs to the essence of what we call an argument. The system is not so much the point of departure, as the element in which arguments have their life.'[1] The system is not, indeed, entirely sacrosanct, since it is susceptible of change, but its propositions can be said to be immune from doubt, in the sense that, so long as they hold their place in the system, it does not occur to us to doubt them. 'What prevents me,' asks Wittgenstein, 'from supposing that this table either vanishes or alters its shape and colour when no one is observing it, and then, when someone looks at it again, changes back to its old condition? – "But who is going to suppose such a thing?" – one would feel like saying.'[2] And then he continues: 'Here we see that the idea of "agreement with reality" does not have any clear application'.[3] I take it that what he means by this is that it is only in the light of certain assumptions that the notion of agreement with reality comes into play. The assumptions

[1] *OC*, 105.   [2] *OC*, 214.   [3] *OC*, 215.

themselves neither agree nor disagree with reality. They determine
the nature of the reality with which agreement is sought.

How far do these assumptions extend? This is not an easy question
to answer because the system is not clearly defined. Wittgenstein
speaks of it as an inherited world-picture and of its propositions as
being 'part of a kind of mythology'.[1] 'It might be imagined,' he says,
'that some propositions, of the form of empirical propositions,
were hardened and functioned as channels for such empirical
propositions as were not hardened but fluid; and that this relation
altered with time, in that fluid propositions hardened and hard
ones became fluid. The mythology may change back into a state of
flux, the river-bed of thoughts may shift. But I distinguish between
the movement of the waters on the river-bed and the shift of the
bed itself; though there is not a sharp division of the one from the
other. But if someone were to say "So logic too is an empirical
science" he would be wrong. Yet this is right: the same proposition
may get treated at one time as something to test by experience, at
another as a rule of testing.'[2]

The suggestion is that there is no clear-cut boundary either
between the *a priori* propositions of logic and mathematics and some
propositions that would ordinarily be counted as empirical, or
between these propositions and those of which the empirical
character is not in doubt. If it is the mark of a necessary proposition
that it is not exposed to empirical refutation, then the propositions of
logic and mathematics are indeed necessary, but the fact that it is
possible to make mistakes in mathematics and logic has the consequence that we cannot always be sure of the conclusions to which
they seem to lead us. All the same, there is nothing else for us to
rely on than our impression that we are following the rules. When
we have checked and re-checked a simple calculation, the suggestion
that we may still be in error is not taken seriously. If someone were
seriously to regard all our calculations as uncertain, we might
think he was mad, or perhaps only that he was very different from
ourselves. 'We rely on calculations, he doesn't; we are sure, he
isn't.'[3] In the same way, if we come upon a fundamentalist who
genuinely believes that the world came into existence in the year
4004 B.C., with delusive appearances of much greater antiquity,
we have no way of proving that he is wrong. Any evidence which
we take as showing that the world really has existed for many
millions of years can be taken by him as showing that the world
presents the appearance of having existed for many millions of years

[1] *OC*, 95.   [2] *OC*, 96–8.   [3] *OC*, 217.

before it really did exist. In the end, if we don't consider him mad, we have again to fall back on saying that he is simply different from us; he does not accept our canons of evidence.

It is the same with the sceptic, who argues that since our memories sometimes deceive us, they may do so always. As Russell once said: 'There is no logical impossibility in the hypothesis that the world sprang into being five minutes ago, exactly as it then was, with a population that "remembered" a wholly unreal past'.[1] This is a proposition which no sane man believes, but it cannot be disproved. We can check one memory-belief against another, but there is no way, free from circularity, of justifying memory in general, any more than there is a non-circular way of justifying induction. In the case of induction, indeed, it is not so much a matter of our adopting a set of general assumptions, as of acquiring certain habits of inference. 'Do we not,' says Wittgenstein, 'simply follow the principle that what has always happened will happen again (or something like it)? What does it mean to follow this principle? Do we really introduce it into our reasoning? Or is it merely the *natural law* which our inferring apparently follows? This latter it may be. It is not an item in our considerations.'[2]

To say that this inductive principle is not introduced into our reasoning is not to say that our reasoning does not presuppose it. The fact is, however, that the principle that what has always happened will happen again is too general and, indeed, too vague to sustain the inferences that we actually make. Not only is not every observed uniformity thought to be projectible, but by a suitable choice of predicates we can create as much uniformity as we please. We rely, therefore, not on a general assumption about the uniformity of nature, but on a set of hypotheses about the special ways in which it repeats itself. Such hypotheses are indeed already incorporated in our idea of 'what has always happened'. The predicates which we use to describe events themselves embody assumptions to the effect that such properties invariably go together.

In this matter, there is no clear distinction between the hypotheses which enter into the common-sense view of the world and those that we obtain from science. There is at most a difference of degree. Thus, one of Wittgenstein's examples of a proposition which might be said to be certain is the proposition that water boils at about 100°C. It would, as he says, be accepted unconditionally in a court of law.[3] Even so, the place which such a proposition occupies in

[1] *The Analysis of Mind*, p. 151.
[2] *OC*, 135.   [3] *OC*, 604.

I

our scheme of thought is not entirely secure. If it did come to grief we should not feel that the order of nature had been overturned. Indeed, Wittgenstein himself goes some way towards acknowledging this. 'If,' he says, 'I now say "I know that the water in the kettle on the gas-flame will not freeze but boil", I seem to be as justified in this "I know" as I am in *any*. "If I know anything I know *this*." – Or do I know with still *greater* certainty that the person opposite me is my old friend so-and-so? And how does that compare with the proposition that I am seeing with two *eyes* and shall see them if I look in the glass? – I don't know confidently what I am to answer here. – But still there is a difference between the cases. If the water over the gas freezes, of course I shall be as astonished as can be, but I shall assume some factor I don't know of, and perhaps leave the matter to physicists to judge. But what could make me doubt whether this person here is N. N., whom I have known for years? Here a doubt would seem to drag everything with it and plunge it into chaos.'[1]

It would, indeed, be astonishing if the water froze, but science itself prepares us for surprises. Events which were thought to be impossible are found to occur, arouse a passing wonderment, and are then accepted as a matter of course. How quickly we have assimilated the idea of the moon's being accessible to us! The later journeys of the American astronauts barely make the headlines. Yet this was one of the things that Wittgenstein, writing only a little more than twenty years ago, felt confident in excluding. 'If,' he said, 'we are thinking within our system, then it is certain that no one has ever been on the moon. Not merely is nothing of the sort ever seriously reported to us by reasonable people, but our whole system of physics forbids us to believe it. For this demands answers to the questions "How did he overcome the force of gravity?" "How could he live without an atmosphere?" and a thousand others which could not be answered. But suppose that instead of all these answers we met the reply: "We don't know *how* man gets to the moon, but those who get there know at once that they are there; and even you can't explain everything." We should feel ourselves intellectually very distant from someone who said this.'[2]

The example is unfortunate, but perhaps it needs only to be changed a little. Should we not feel ourselves intellectually very distant from someone who said the same things about Mars? It very much depends on who 'we' are. In 1938, before there was any serious thought of men's going to the moon, a realistic broadcast of

[1] *OC*, 613.   [2] *OC*, 108.

Wells's *The Shape of Things to Come* persuaded millions of Americans that men from Mars had invaded the United States. Thousands of Catholics, including at least one Pope, have believed in the 'miracle of Fatima', according to which sometime earlier in this century the sun left the sky, advanced towards the earth, opened to disclose the Virgin Mary, and then returned to its position, all without doing any violence to the solar system. The results of scientific technology are taken for granted, but the theories which lie behind them are not very widely understood, nor is their influence strong enough to prevent many people from holding beliefs which are inconsistent with them. Science is regarded as magic, with the result both that no limit is set in the popular imagination to the possibilities of travelling in space or even in time, and that occult theories and practices, however full of gibberish, are treated as serious rivals to it. If the measure of certainty is thoroughgoing acceptance, in a way which requires not only that one assents to a theory but that one holds fast to its consequences, then scientific theories are not so very certain.

What of Wittgenstein's other examples? Should I really feel that everything was being plunged into chaos if I found myself doubting whether the person sitting beside me was my old friend Professor W? The idea, presumably, is not just that I forget his name, which happens easily enough as one gets older, even in the case of people one knows very well, but that I am not sure whether the descriptions which I believe my friend to satisfy really are satisfied by the man beside me. Well, it is not hard to imagine circumstances in which I might be deceived. My friend might have a twin brother of whom I had never heard; he might have hired an actor to impersonate him. It is unlikely that the impersonation would be so good as to deceive me for very long, but it is not inconceivable. This is, however, only an isolated case. I cannot seriously envisage my being mistaken in this way about the identities of all my friends, of my own wife and children. But suppose that the persons whom I so identified were all to assure me that I was mistaken, I should suspect that they were playing a cruel practical joke on me, or that I had lost my sanity, or perhaps that I was having a bad dream.

But might not this be a dream? Might I not be dreaming that these are my friends: might I not wake up to find that my whole environment was really quite different from what it now seems to me to be? Wittgenstein deals very summarily with this sort of doubt. 'The argument "I may be dreaming",' he says, 'is senseless for this reason: if I am dreaming, this remark is being dreamed as well – and indeed it is also being dreamed that these words have

I*

any meaning.'[1] Again, later on, after claiming that he cannot be mistaken about his own name, he says 'But suppose someone produced the scruple: what if I suddenly as it were woke up, and said "Just think, I've been imagining I was called L. W.!" – well, who says that I don't wake up once again and call *this* an extraordinary fancy, and so on.'[2] And finally, having said that 'If someone believes that he has flown from America to England in the last few days, then, I believe, he cannot be making a *mistake*. And just the same if someone says that he is at this moment sitting at a table and writing,"[3] he goes on ' "But even if in such cases I can't be mistaken, isn't it possible that I am drugged?" If I am and the drug has taken away my consciousness, then I am not now really talking and thinking. I cannot seriously suppose that I am at this moment dreaming. Someone who, dreaming, says "I am dreaming", even if he speaks audibly in doing so, is no more right than if he said in his dream "it is raining", while it was in fact raining. Even if his dream were actually connected with the noise of the rain.'[4]

How good are these arguments? Let us examine them. For the proposition 'I truly believe that p' to be true, it is necessary and sufficient that 'p' be true and that I also believe it. Suppose that 'p' is the proposition 'I am dreaming'. In the cases that Wittgenstein envisages, this is true *ex hypothesi*. Consequently, if he refuses to allow that I can truly believe that I am dreaming, it must be because he assumes that the fact that I am dreaming makes it impossible for me to believe that I am. Indeed, he seems to go further. The implication of his example of the rain appears to be that so long as one is dreaming one cannot be credited with any occurrent belief. But why should this be so? Why should the fact that I am in the physical state of sleep, and that I show no signs of being conscious of what is going on around me, be taken to entail that I am not having any thoughts which can properly be characterised as either true or false? I can see no good reason for this view. If my memories of my waking reveries are taken at their face value, I see no reason why the same should not apply to my memories of my dreams. And if these memories are taken at their face value, then it will follow that I did have such and such thoughts while I was asleep and that I attached the same meaning to the words in which I formulated those thoughts as I attach to the words in which I express my recollections of them. I shall, indeed, have dreamed that these words were meaningful, but this does not

[1] *OC*, 383.   [2] *OC*, 642.
[3] *OC*, 675.   [4] *OC*, 676.

exclude their really having been so. It would exclude it only on the assumption that everything that is dreamed is false. But this surely is itself a false assumption, and one that the sceptic does not require. It is sufficient for his purpose that the stories which we tell ourselves in dreams be false in the main, not that they be false in every detail. An analogy may be drawn here with works of fiction, which are not debarred from containing some true statements. A work of fiction of which the action is set in London does not cease to be such because the topography of London is accurately represented in it. In dreams, such accuracy is seldom maintained, but there is no logical reason why it should not be. Indeed, it does not appear to be logically necessary that a dream should be false in any particular. For example, it is related of one of the Dukes of Devonshire that he dreamed that he was speaking in the House of Lords and awoke to find that he really was speaking in the House of Lords. Even if this story is untrue, it does not appear to be self-contradictory.

If the story is not self-contradictory, it is because to say that the Duke was dreaming that he was making a speech can be construed as saying no more than that the impression that he was making a speech was one that came to him while he was asleep. He was mistaken only in believing himself to be awake or at least in his failure to realise that he was not awake. This is, however, by all odds an exceptional case. The hold of dreams upon reality, in any straightforward sense, is sufficiently weak for the expression 'I must be dreaming' to mean much the same as 'This cannot really be happening'. It is, indeed, on this that the sceptic trades. But now we come to Wittgenstein's remaining argument. If the possibility that I am dreaming is to be one that I take seriously enough for it to make me uncertain whether my present experiences really are veridical, I must envisage myself waking to find that this has been only a dream. But then why should I take the experience of waking to be veridical? Why should not *that* be part of a dream and *this* the reality?

The answer to this is that if I seriously believe that I am now dreaming I must look forward to an experience of waking which I shall in fact take to be veridical. I shall, indeed, have no proof that it is veridical except that it coheres with the experiences that follow it and with what I take to be my memories of previous waking experiences, and that it is not itself followed by an experience of waking, which leads me to take it and its successors as being themselves the content of a dream. And then the same risk will be run by *this* experience. Thus my assessment of my current experience,

whether I judge that it is or that it is not veridical, is never conclusive. It is open to revision in the light of further experience;
and this further experience will be open to revision in its turn.

But this practically concedes Wittgenstein's point. We can,
indeed, protest that the argument 'I may be dreaming' is not
senseless, not only on the merely formal ground that it could logically
be the case that I am dreaming, but also because the expectation
which does occur in dreams, of waking up to find that one has been
dreaming, has sometimes been fulfilled. The fact remains, however,
that I do not now have this expectation, neither is there anything in
the character of my present experience to give me any reason
to have it. It is logically possible that in a few minutes time it will
seem to me that I am waking from a dream, but I have no present
ground for believing that this experience, even if it occurs, will
have more authority as an indication of what is really taking place
than those that I am having now. In short, the words 'I may be
dreaming' are not under these conditions the expression of a serious
doubt. It is as if I were to say 'All this may be an illusion' without
having any better answer to the question 'What makes you think
so?' than the formal point that since my interpretation of my present
experiences makes some demands upon the future it is logically
possible that it will not be substantiated.

Except that he at times appears unwilling to make even this logical admission, the nerve of Wittgenstein's argument is the requirement that doubt be serious; and the condition of its being serious
is that it be capable of being resolved. Returning to the example of
seeing colour, he maintains that to the question 'Can you be
mistaken about this colour's being called "green" in English?',
his answer can only be 'No'. 'If I were to say "Yes, for there is
always the possibility of a delusion", that would mean nothing at
all.'[1] 'But does that mean,' he continues 'that it is unthinkable
that the word "green" should have been produced here by a slip
of the tongue or a momentary confusion? Don't we know of such
cases? – One can also say to someone "Mightn't you perhaps have
made a slip?" That amounts to: "Think about it again". – But
these rules of caution only make sense if they come to an end
somewhere. A doubt without an end is not even a doubt.'[2] Similarly,
he remarks that 'Only in certain cases is it possible to make an
investigation "Is that really a hand?" (or "my hand"). For "I
doubt whether this is really my (or a) hand" makes no sense
without some more precise determination. One cannot tell from these

---

[1] *OC*, 624.   [2] *OC*, 625.

words alone whether any doubt at all is meant – nor what kind of doubt.'[1] This follows a passage in which he has argued that our customary use of words like 'hand' without any doubt as to their meaning 'shows that absence of doubt belongs to the essence of the language-game, that the question "How do I know?" drags out the language-game, or else does away with it'.[2]

From this point of view, it does not much matter whether we accept propositions like 'This is a hand' without further ado or whether we allow the question 'How do you know?' to divert us from propositions of this sort to propositions about sense-qualia. There is a philosophical interest in elaborating a 'language of appearances', because it helps us to realise how large an element of theory is already contained in our references to physical objects, and also makes it easier to exhibit the features of our sense-experiences on which the theory principally trades. So long, however, as we are operating within the theory, the margin which is allowed for error, though always present, is vanishingly small. There are standard tests for deciding whether or not we have identified an object correctly, or whether we are suffering some more radical illusion. When these tests have been carried out, the question is settled one way or the other: no provision is made for any further uncertainty. To go on to doubt the results of the tests, or indeed even to apply them when there is no special reason for thinking that anything is amiss, is to violate the principles on which the theory operates; in Wittgenstein's idiom, it is not to play the game. There is, indeed, always the logical possibility that future experiences will lead us to revise our beliefs in ways that we cannot now foresee, but it is part of our procedure not to take this possibility seriously, in any given instance, so long as it is merely formal: that is to say, so long as we have no positive reason for expecting it to be realised.

This might be thought to be a sufficient answer to the philosophical sceptic if his doubts were directed upon particular matters of fact. The truth is, however, that they are of quite a different character. They are not intended to make us more cautious in assuming that we know our own names or that we are using colour-words correctly, or that we were not born yesterday, or that we see with our eyes, or that we can identify our hands. A follower of Berkeley, who denies that there are physical objects, is not suggesting that the criteria which we use for determining the existence of such things as trees, or stars, or tables, or human bodies will not continue to be satisfied. He does not suppose that his own experiences

---

[1] *OC*, 372.   [2] *OC*, 370.

are generically unlike those of other people, or that they will be very different in the future from what they have been in the past. His peculiarity is that he wishes to interpret the evidence in a different fashion. He refuses to make the assumption that anything other than a spiritual substance is capable of existing unperceived.

But then is he not simply wrong on a question of empirical fact? If propositions of the sorts that Moore lists in his defence of common sense are in very many cases true, it follows automatically that a great many things which are not spiritual substances can exist unperceived; the trees in my garden, for example, the furniture in this room, and countless other physical objects of these and other kinds. It is true that Berkeley thought it possible to maintain both that there were trees and stars and tables and human bodies and whatever, and that there were no such things as physical objects, but here he was surely mistaken. If the words 'tree' and 'table' and all the rest of them are given their ordinary meanings, his position is self-contradictory.

The answer to this is that Berkeley would indeed be simply wrong if his denial of the existence of physical objects were put forward under the covering of the common-sense theory, which provides for their existence. But to treat his position in this way entirely fails to do it justice. So far from accepting the common-sense theory, he sought to overthrow it. His contention was not that the existence of things at times when they were not perceived was a possibility which happened not to be realised but that it ought not to be admitted as a possibility. He opted for a radically different way of interpreting experiences, in which this realistic assumption had no place. Consequently, Moore's and Wittgenstein's certainties do not touch him. For the doubts which they counter bear only upon the question whether the criteria which we use for determining the presence of physical objects are ever sufficiently satisfied: they have nothing to do with the question of modifying or replacing the criteria themselves. This is not to say that Berkeley or any other philosopher who has rejected the common-sense view has been successful in showing that the principles which furnish its theoretical background are logically defective, though even this needs to be proved by a rebuttal of these philosophers' arguments, rather than by a simple declaration of fidelity to common sense. The fact remains that whether or not there is anything wrong with our ordinary method of interpreting experience, the possibility of there being other workable methods is not excluded, as Wittgenstein indeed implicitly admits.

It is not even clear, without argument, that a view like Berkeley's cannot be taken of the theory with which we actually operate. Berkeley himself maintained that he was upholding the outlook of common sense against the false sophistication of a materialist philosophy, and although I believe that he was mistaken on this point, it is a question that is not settled by allowing Moore's claims to knowledge. The reason why it is not settled is that while Moore was wholly certain of the truth of the propositions which he enumerated he was not at all certain of their correct analysis. He did not know, and did not believe that anybody else knew, whether his seeing his hand consisted in the fact that some sense-datum was identical with part of the surface of his hand, or in the fact that the sense-datum stood in a causal or some other relation to a set of physical particles which were not themselves directly perceptible, or in the fact that the sense-datum was related in such and such ways to other actual and possible sense-data. The one thing he was sure of was that in expressing a proposition like 'This is a hand' one was saying something about a sense-datum, although other philosophers who have been equally certain of the truth of his examples have denied that sense-data come into it at all. But if there is so much uncertainty about what we know when we know such propositions to be true, the assurance that they are true does not amount to much.

This might be taken as support for Wittgenstein's argument that nothing useful is achieved merely by making claims to the possession of knowledge. But Wittgenstein's own attributions of certainty are open to the same objection. He gives many examples of propositions which he takes to be unquestionably true, but he does not say how any of them should be analysed. He may, indeed, have held that none of them stood in any need of analysis, but this at least is open to question. For instance, there is a long-standing problem with regard to the relation of common-sense propositions about physical objects to the propositions which figure in scientific theory. Are electrons and neutrons literally parts of the objects which we see? Are they logical fictions, which we introduce as explanatory tools? Or do they physically exist in a way that the objects in which common sense believes do not? Thus, Russell has argued that 'the coloured surface that I see when I look at a table has a spatial position in the space of my visual field; it exists only where eyes and nerves and brain exist to cause the energy of photons to undergo certain transformations. . . . The table as a physical object, consisting of electrons, positrons and neutrons, lies outside my experience, and if there is a space which contains both it and my perceptual space, then in that space the table must be wholly external to my perceptual space.'[1] If this were correct, the certainty of there being a table in front of me would come to no more than the certainty of the present occurrence of such and such percepts: all the rest would be a more or less hazardous conjecture. I do not say that it is correct. On the contrary, I think that there are insuperable objections to any theory which puts the constituents of physical space beyond the reach of our observation. But it is at least a serious attempt to dispose of a genuine problem. If we limit ourselves to saying that my acceptance of the proposition that there is a table in front of me is, in these circumstances, an obligatory move in the language-game that we ordinarily play then not only do we invite questions about the relation of this game to others that might be playable; we also leave room for differences of opinion as to what the game that we do play actually is.

I have spoken of our playing a language-game because this is an analogy that Wittgenstein frequently uses, but we need to consider how far it can be made to go. We do indeed modify our concepts on occasion in something like the way that we alter the rules of games, but we do not antecedently to any use of language decide what the rules are going to be. If we adhere to the analogy, we have to say that the language-game is one that is played before its rules are codified. This may be the point of Wittgenstein's remarking that 'the language-game is so to say unpredictable. I mean: it is not based on grounds. It is not reasonable (or unreasonable). It is there – like our life.'[2] He maintains also that it has its roots in action. 'Children,' he says, 'do not learn that books exist, that armchairs exist, etc. etc. – they learn to fetch books, sit in armchairs, etc. etc.'[3] And in another passage, having argued that 'justifying the evidence comes to an end', he goes on to say that 'the end is not certain propositions' striking us immediately as true, i.e. it is not a kind of *seeing* on our part; it is our *acting*, which lies at the bottom of the language-game'.[4]

But our actions are conditioned by our beliefs, whether or not these beliefs are consciously formulated, and our beliefs, when we do formulate them, are evinced by sentences which are intended to express what is true. When they fulfil this intention, it is for the most part not only because of the meaning of the words which they contain but also because things are as they describe them. So is not our use of language dependent not only on the rules of the game, but also, and indeed primarily, on the nature of things? Undoubtedly it is, but we have to remember also that what we count as the nature

---

[1] *Human Knowledge: Its Scope and Limits* (Allen & Unwin) p. 236.
[2] *OC*, 559.   [3] *OC*, 476.   [4] *OC*, 204.

of things is itself not independent of the fashion in which we describe them. This is the point, or part of the point, of Quine's ontological relativity. Our judgments about what there is are always embedded in some theory. We can substitute one theory for another, but we cannot detach ourselves from theory altogether and see the world unclouded by any preconception of it. I do not know that Wittgenstein would have cared for this way of putting it, but the impossibility of there being any cognitive process which would require the prising of the world off language seems central to his position. It has now been discovered that Wittgenstein was influenced by Kant, and whatever objections there may be to Kant's idealism, his dictum that 'intuitions without concepts are blind' appears unassailable.

15

WITTGENSTEIN'S THEORY OF KNOWLEDGE

Christopher Coope

I SHALL start by considering the apparently paradoxical doctrines that Wittgenstein put forward about knowledge: they show how the concept of knowledge is, as he says, 'specialized'. This is not, as I shall show, a very important issue in itself, but it leads on to other points, of more interest: how it comes about, for example, that 'not all corrections of our beliefs are on the same level'. I shall then discuss the idea that we inherit a certain picture of the world that forms the background of our experiments and researches. This idea, which is not of course unique to Wittgenstein, is, however, developed with many fresh insights. I end with some discussion of Wittgenstein's reported views on religious belief, which should not, in my opinion, be regarded as part of his contribution to philosophy, the interest of them being, perhaps, more biographical than philosophical.

From Wittgenstein's writings we can put together certain propositions about knowledge that at first sight seem obviously wrong, not to say perverse; so I shall call them paradoxes. The first is rather familiar:

(1) I cannot be said to know that I have a pain, even if I have one. But there are other doctrines less familiar. For example:

(2) Situated as I now am, I cannot be said to know that I am standing here in front of you who are listening to me.

(3) I still cannot *say* that I know that I am standing here in front of you, even if it is true that I know it.

These remarks sound sceptical, but that of course would be quite the wrong way to see them. In fact, Wittgenstein would say of someone who claimed to have all sorts of peculiar doubts about the existence of the past and so on, that despite the curious things he might *say*, his daily life showed that he knew all sorts of things he claimed to doubt: there is a connection between belief and behaviour, however difficult it is to describe, a difficulty we shall meet again in the final section of this paper. The ancient Sceptic, Carneades is reported to have needed to be led about, lest he walked into a fire or over a cliff, and the example is used by Professor Price[1] to show how sceptical beliefs may really make a difference to a man's life. However, Diogenes says that Carneades lived to a great age and went blind.

I shall make another general point. These three paradoxes cannot be put down to some eccentric account of knowledge on Wittgenstein's part. His views on the matter are fairly orthodox: in general he follows the analysis that has been with us since Plato – that knowledge is true belief plus an account. He has nothing to do, for example, with a new doctrine that has sprung up in recent years, the doctrine that if you know something you cannot also be said to believe it, although he is reported as saying that a man who says he believes something will commonly be understood to mean that he does not also know it – i.e. that he 'only believes' it.

I shall deal with the first of these paradoxes quite briefly. Let us consider this point: we may have the ability to say what is true, without its being a mere guess, without its turning out to be true as a matter of luck, and *yet* this ability does not show that we know what we say. What we say might be useful information to someone else and *he* may come to know about us as a result of being informed, but it is still not a case of our passing on our knowledge to someone else. So I can say that I am in pain, it is a true description of my state, and I do not say what is true by luck or accident, but it still does not follow that I know that I am in pain, and this not because I have set some unusually exacting standard which something has to reach in order to be knowledge. (I say, interpreting Wittgenstein, that it is a description, and not just an *expression* of pain in view of the later remarks in Part II of the *Investigations*.) Saying 'I have a pain' is a performance, but there is no additional performance that we could call 'getting it right', not even a performance which causes us no difficulty. This is hidden from us perhaps, because we can of course *say what is untrue*, by lying or in absence of mind. But it is quite wrong to say for example 'It is the easiest thing in the world to be right about such things'. That would be like claiming to have given a whole lecture without a single spelling

---

[1] *Belief* (London: Allen and Unwin, 1969) p. 266.

mistake. As there is no such thing as a spelling mistake in speech, so there is no such performance as avoiding making such mistakes in speech.

Now knowledge is a matter of getting something right. We don't only have: A-knows-that-$p \supset p$, but the stronger thesis: A-knows-that-$p \supset A$-gets-it-right-that-p. Thus we can say truly that we have a pain, but cannot, in the sense explained, 'get it right'; there is, that is to say, no such thing as getting it right in these cases. Consequently there is neither knowledge nor ignorance in this matter. (There is an inconsistency between Z, 483 and *OC*, 41 about the *place of pain*.)

It is useful to compare this case with others where we can say with truth how things are without having grounds. Examples which Wittgenstein gives include (1) one's knowledge of what one had for breakfast, (2) one's knowledge of elapsed time, (3) one's knowledge of the position of one's limbs. One can of course have grounds in these cases, but one need not, and often has not: one can just *say* what is the case without grounds. An interesting intermediate case: one can tell from, say, a facial expression, what a person is thinking. Here there *is* something that one 'goes by' – the facial expression. However, if one is asked what it was *about* the face that enabled one to judge, one may be quite unable to say, and this would not be because one lacks the vocabulary. (One might naturally call this ability, if unusually well developed, a case of 'intuition'.) A somewhat similar example: hearing the direction of a sound. We don't usually have to say: that is the direction of the kitchen, that is the sound of the kettle, so the sound must be coming from over there.

But in all these cases, and this is the point to note now, we can go wrong. Hence we reasonably talk about being right, however matter of course it is to *be* right. ('Getting it right' is a wider notion than 'saying something true', e.g. solving an anagram and so on.)

Let us now turn to the second of my two paradoxes. I said that, in Wittgenstein's view, it would be nonsense for me, situated as I am, to say that I know that I am standing here in front of you. Now this is just the sort of claim that G. E. Moore made in his lectures, and Wittgenstein quite rightly thought that Moore had something important to say. But it was, Wittgenstein thought, a mistake to claim to *know* the sort of items that featured in these litanies of Common Sense that Moore liked to recite.

His point can be put like this: if I know something, I will often have grounds (and in some situations grounds will be necessary, *OC*, 91). But this, as we have seen, is not the fundamental thing. What *is* necessary is that (i) I can check the matter (ii) where mistake is likely, then I have checked it. Thus I can tell that my arm is bent, to return to one of our earlier examples, without looking, and in fact without grounds. Here, there is, we said, such a thing as 'getting it right', and now we add; it is also a matter that can be *checked* – I can look and see. Mistake, though possible, is quite unusual. Hence we can say that we *know* that it is bent *without* performing a check which would of course be easy.

But now it is instructive to notice that the chain of checks quickly comes to an end. I cannot in turn, in ordinary circumstances, check that my arm is bent after I have looked at it. A check is some precaution against a mistake, and there is no such thing as taking precautions in this situation.[1]

I can 'go through the motions' of taking a precaution. And if 'proof' means 'valid argument with true premisses' I can provide myself with a proof. But this would not be a proof that does any work, for as Wittgenstein remarks, the premisses would be no more certain than the conclusion they were brought in to support. (On all this, see Wittgenstein's clear statement at *OC*, 243.)[2]

We can repeat checks we have already made over and over again, and it may readily appear that each time we merely reduce the possibility of error. A practical man, we might suppose, will soon be satisfied, but there is always a residual uncertainty that further checks could have diminished. This is however a questionable picture, as an example will show. Suppose I am counting a pile of banknotes. It is rather important not to make a mistake, so I recount as a check, and might even recount two or three times. Now let us perform the 'experiment' of counting over and over again, checking each time to see whether the notes are sticking together, etc. Consider these three results.

26	26	26	26	26	26	27	26	26	26	26
26	26	26	26	26	26	27	27	27	27	27
26	26	26	26	26	26	31	42	18	26	22

---

[1] We must distinguish the cases where I have *made* sure, from those where it just *is* sure without my having made it so. In both cases, there is no such thing as a further check, but only in the first is there knowledge. This point is necessary if we are to avoid the absurd consequence that one can cease to know something by making sure of it.

[2] In this connection Wittgenstein (*OC*, 1) refers to 'a curious remark of J. H. Newman': I have no idea what he had in mind, but it is interesting to note that Newman, describing how, in his opinion, Protestants of his time came about their belief that the Catholic Church was a 'simple monster of iniquity', says that they would, for the most part, not produce grounds, but would say such things as: 'It is too notorious for proof; everyone knows it; every book says it . . .' *The Present Position of Catholics in England*, 1892 ed., p. 50.

I think we should not have said in any of these cases that there were other than 26 banknotes – before the deviant results came in. But what should we say afterwards? In the first case we should say that we had miscounted on the occasion that we got 27, in the second case we should say that the number of notes had increased by one, and in the third case that we were no longer in any position to count banknotes. And of course there would be other cases and circumstances where we might not know what to say. The important point, however, is that 're-testing' soon becomes a formality, a 'going through the motions' as I put it, and cannot increase the likelihood that there were 26 notes in the pile, not even 'theoretically' or 'minimally' by such procedures. In this sense, this sort of testing comes to an end, in Wittgenstein's phrase.

However, this is not in my view a matter of the *certainty* of there being 26 banknotes in the pile, only that its certainty cannot be impugned on *this* ground: that any number of recounts are both possible and yet unmade, and who can be certain what the future will bring? But anyone can think of a number of tall stories of whose truth we might become convinced, and reasonably so in some circumstances, stories that cast a doubt on the adequacy of our grounds for our belief about the banknotes. Now we may, here and now, say that we know that these stories are false, and be reasonable in so saying. The mere invention of such stories does not justify a doubt. But something that could happen could reasonably make us doubt, nevertheless.

Now though I do not think that Wittgenstein would have agreed with all that, there is a remark which might show a point of contact. There seems, in Wittgenstein's view, a certain drawback to confident assertion in the Moore manner. A man might be ever so sure that there was bread before him, having, we might suppose, never so much as heard of 'transubstantiation' and its doctrinal background. To him, transubstantiation and all that would be as tall a story as one is likely to hear. Yet for someone who believed it, an option that Wittgenstein thinks possible for intelligent men (see *OC*, 239), there might be quite new grounds for doubting that it was bread that he was looking at. And might not the future convince us of the truth of this kind of Christianity, or indeed of other extraordinary doctrines which might shake the confidence we *now* rightly have in certain judgments? But it is apparent that such radical changes of outlook could not, for Wittgenstein, have much rationality about them, and *this*, an aspect of his thought for which I have rather limited sympathy, I discuss later on.

Do we always have a *choice* whether to say 'There were 26 banknotes and now there are 27' or to say 'We must have miscounted'? Quine seems to suggest that this is always so, when he writes 'Any statement can be held true come what may, if we make drastic enough adjustments elsewhere . . .'.[1] But does not this somewhat blunt the admirable distinction he makes elsewhere between the desire to be right, which is the love of truth, and the desire to have been right, which is the pride which goeth before a fall? Keeping consistent may involve 'making adjustments', but being rational which is the test of our love of truth involves more than this, however difficult this 'more' is to describe.

Do we *ever* have a choice what to say, when 'evidence is facing evidence' as Wittgenstein says in *OC*, 641? Well we have a choice, we have to make a decision, in this sense: that we are here not under orders what to think (as we so often are, as rational men). But we do *not* have a choice in this sense: that we can take our pick what to believe, and no questions asked. For if there is nothing to choose, we must believe neither.

I wrote above 'something that could happen could reasonably make us doubt', and I think that further discussion of this point is needed. Norman Malcolm, in his essay 'Knowledge and Belief' which, as he says, is influenced by Wittgenstein, writes: 'In order for it to be possible that any statements about physical things should *turn out to be false* it is necessary that some statements about physical things *cannot* turn out to be false'.[3] This seems to me altogether too strong. Everyone will admit that we can find out that something is the case which is incompatible with some belief or hypothesis, without our having to make the rather tough claim that nothing that could happen would rationally count against our having found out. And I do not think that Wittgenstein would have supported this strong doctrine; it is enough that there are things we *do* not doubt. His considered view best comes out at *OC*, 519: 'In order for you to be able to carry out an order there must be some empirical fact about which you *are not* in doubt' (my italics). (See also *OC*, 344.) Wittgenstein says further: 'But since a language-game is something that consists in the recurrent procedures of the game in time, it seems impossible to say in any *individual* case that such and such must be beyond doubt if there is to be a language-game – though it is right enough to say that *as a rule*

[1] 'Two Dogmas of Empiricism', sec. 6, in *From a Logical Point of View* (Cambridge, Mass.: Harvard U.P., 1953).

[2] W. V. Quine and J. S. Ullian, *The Web of Belief* (New York: Random House, 1970) p. 90.

[3] In *Knowledge and Certainty* (New Jersey: Prentice Hall, 1963) p. 69.

some empirical judgment or other must be beyond doubt'. (Italics in text.) That is, with regard to Malcolm's inkwell, it would be quite wrong, in Wittgenstein's opinion, and surely in fact, to say that 'certain concepts *require* him to take up the attitude that nothing that could happen could count against its existence'.

There are two points that Wittgenstein makes that should not be allowed to blur this picture. One is that the usual signs of doubt in unusual circumstances could not be regarded as signs of *doubt* at all. But we are of course not here interested in what a person could intelligibly claim to doubt, but with the question whether in some cases nothing that could happen could render some matter *doubtful*, that is uncertain. I may indeed not intelligibly claim to doubt that there is this inkwell before me, things being as they are. But the matter might yet be *made* doubtful if some things happened, which in point of fact I, perhaps, know are not going to happen.

A second point, which I shall discuss at greater length, is the distinction that Wittgenstein makes between *being mistaken* and other cases of false belief. This is not some fine point of usage; it is of no interest at all whether 'mistake' is quite the word that is needed. There is an interesting difference, however we choose to describe it. We should look at Wittgenstein's examples: A false belief of mine that I am sitting at a table writing would not be a mistake, nor would a belief that I have flown from America to England in the last two days (*OC*, 675). One could only be mistaken about such a thing if one was for example packed in a box for the journey. If my belief that I have never been to the moon was false, it would not count as a mistake (*OC*, 661). I cannot make a mistake about $12 \times 12 = 144$ (*OC*, 654). I can't be mistaken about my name (*OC*, 629). I can't be mistaken that the name of this colour is 'green'. (The usual contexts must be assumed, of course.)

We can get some idea of the distinction that Wittgenstein is making from these examples, but it is not an easy thing to describe. He suggests (*OC*, 74) that a mistake doesn't have a cause – it also has a ground. This does not seem to be true of, say, mistakes of absence of mind. If I think it is Wednesday when it is in fact Tuesday, this may be due to misinformation or mere unthinking-ness. Clearly both cases would often be what Wittgenstein is calling a *mistake*, but the latter example, where I merely find myself thinking that it is Tuesday, may have causes but does not have grounds. Mistakes are therefore not always a consequence of grounds that prove inadequate. However, it seems a *sufficient*, if not necessary, condition of being mistaken that one has grounds for one's error.

Wittgenstein goes on to say: 'roughly: when somebody makes a mistake, this can be fitted into what he knows aright' (*OC*, 74). Does this mean: that I can understand how I come to hold this false belief? That seems too vague. Do I really understand how I come to think it is half-past five when it is really only five? I may not have the least idea. Of course I can 'understand someone having such a false belief' if I just mean that I know that this sort of thing does happen sometimes, but this does not serve to delimit mistakes among other false beliefs. I know, for example, that we may unfortunately come to believe that we are kings and queens; it happens not infrequently, but for all that it will not be a mere mistake.

But there is another account which may prove more satisfactory and seems to fit in with the sort of thing Wittgenstein says. Let us try the following. A man who makes a mistake, we shall say, could have taken precautions which would have shown him the falsity of what he believed. This, it seems to me, is the important thing. It might have been quite irrational or obsessional to take these precautions – 'not worth the trouble'. But it is necessarily true that a mistake, to *be* a mistake, could have been *avoided*. And this does not mean that 'if circumstances had been different the mistake would not have been made'. That could be said of *any* false belief. Rather we should say: he could have had grounds for putting things right. The tense of the verb is here important; past mistakes, in belief as in other matters, may now be past putting right.

In this connection let us turn to what Moore said at Ann Arbor. Moore was giving a lecture on certainty, and as usual, started out with a list of items which he said that he knew for certain. Now one of the items on the list read: 'There are some windows with daylight coming through them.' Unfortunately, they were merely artificial windows, with electric lights behind them. This was therefore a mistake: Moore could easily have made a check. We should compare this with other items from Moore's list: e.g. that he had never been far from the surface of the Earth.

The example of transubstantiation is worth returning to at this point. Let us consider the possibility that a man is examining what he thinks is bread, but which is really the body of Christ. He is sure that it *is* bread. Could he have had grounds for judging differently? The matter seems not clear. We may agree that he is not careless in what he believes. If the matter had been put to him that perhaps things were not as they seemed, there may have been tests he could have performed and they would have told him that it was bread. And such tests, as we saw, would quickly 'come to an end': further looking, and tasting, chemical analysis and so on, would be no tests at all, merely the appearance of such. But now – with a different

background of belief he *could* have performed tests, quite different
tests, in fact the tests that a Catholic might perform: 'were certain
words said, by a certain person, in a certain context . . .' and so on.
Chemical analysis would now be held irrelevant.

Now since it is unclear, both in Wittgenstein's opinion and no
doubt in fact, whether the difference in background belief is
susceptible to rational discussion, and to what extent 'grounds' are
relevant, it is equally unclear whether the belief that this is bread,
if false, is the sort of false belief which counts as a mistake. The
example is of interest in showing the importance of background
belief in our present discussion. If a change of such a system of belief is necessary in order to come to see that we were wrong, and
such a change cannot be rational, then one's former beliefs, even
granted that one is changing for the better, cannot be *mistakes*.
Mental illness is only one sort of explanation how one came to have
such background beliefs. Indoctrination is another; one thinks of
the king who was taught that the world began with *him* (*OC*, 92).

Mistakes are thus a special sort of false belief. But we still have to
put that distinction to work, and here there seems to be a difficulty;
for Wittgenstein goes on to say that where a mistake, in the sense
we have discussed, is no longer possible, then a proposition is certain
(*OC*, 194). Now it would seem that '*p* is certain' just like '*p* is known'
entails *p*. So if 'a mistake with regard to *p* is no longer possible'
entails '*p* is certain' it would also entail *p*, by transitivity. But
mistakes may be impossible about propositions which are false,
if our account has been right. Furthermore, one might be incapable
of mistake about each one of a set of beliefs which might yet be
inconsistent.

On the other hand, '*p* is certain' does not only entail *p*, but also
'a mistake with regard to *p* is no longer possible'. And it may be
right to say that '*p* is certain' even when it is not (because for example,
p is false). And in this light we should see the notion of 'what was
appropriate to say' in the three cases of the counting of the banknotes. Wittgenstein makes this point clearly: 'It would be wrong
to say that I can only say "I know that there is a chair there"
when there is a chair there. Of course it isn't *true* unless there is, but
I have a right to say this if I'm sure there is a chair there, even if
I'm wrong '(*OC*, 549). And similarly, it may be right to say 'I can't
be mistaken' even when, as things turn out, I not only can be, but
am mistaken (see *OC*, 633).

Is this just an application of the point that it may be rational, or
truth-caring, to think what happens not to be true? And how, for
Wittgenstein, is it decided what it is rational to think? Sometimes he

just gives a list of what a rational man *does* think: a rational man just *is* the sort of man who thinks these things, at least in our time, for he rightly observes that what is rational to think varies from one historical period to another. But if I say 'It was once rational to believe that men could dance to make rain, and now it is not' what am I saying? It is not explanatory to say: People used to *call* such a belief rational, and now no longer. For we want to know what they mean when they call themselves rational, and why anyone should care about being so. Furthermore any account of rationality will have to allow that it could be rational to believe what everyone says is not so; and that what everyone says is rational to think could in the event be most irrational. Wittgenstein's thoughts on these matters are disappointing. At *OC*, 336, in reply to the question whether there is any objective character in what it is rational to think, he says, without further comment: '*Very* intelligent and well-educated people believe in the story of creation in the Bible, while others hold it as proven false, and the grounds of the latter are well known to the former'. It is, however, not clear what this is supposed to show. It might follow that there was no objective standard of rationality in this case, or that the matter was too difficult for there to be just one judgment compatible with rationality. Or of course, that very intelligent and well-educated people are quite able to be irrational. For it might seem that rationality is a sort of virtue, and as with other virtues, good learning might not be sufficient for the acquiring of it.

If it is rational to believe that one cannot be mistaken, if, that is, one is not just bluffing, for example (*OC*, 669), then one will not be worried that the belief might yet be false. Here, one can say, as Wittgenstein does in *RFM* about Descartes' Demon, ready to deceive us no matter what care we take: *Was ich nicht weiß macht mich nicht heiß.*[1]

It is now time to pass to the third of my paradoxes. This, you may remember, read as follows: Even if it is true that I know that you are sitting in front of me, I still cannot say that I know it. We perhaps should note that nothing hangs on the use of the first personal pronoun. It would be equally impossible for me to say: 'C. C. knows that you are . . .' What we have to consider is something very hard to take: that you can say something that I understand, and that I can (apparently) say the same thing, in this case using the very same words, and fail to say anything at all.

Wittgenstein considers the example of a forester who goes into a

[1] *RFM*, II, 78.

wood to decide which trees are to be chopped down. Suppose after pointing to various trees, he were to add: 'I know that that is a tree'. Wittgenstein holds that what the forester says is senseless, although it would be all right for us, watching him, to conclude 'He knows that that is a tree – he doesn't examine it, or order his men to examine it' (*OC*, 353).

Let us remember a point made by Wittgenstein: 'My life shows that I know or am certain that there is a chair over there, or a door, and so on. I tell a friend, e.g. "Take that chair over there", "Shut the door", etc., etc.' (*OC*, 7). This is, as we saw, a point to make to a man who claims not to know, *really* know, anything. But now, Wittgenstein goes on (*OC*, 6), we cannot give samples of this knowledge in the manner of Moore, saying 'I am standing up' and so on. I cannot even ask myself, 'Don't I know then that I am standing here?' We have a curious echo of the Tractarian thesis that what is shown cannot be said (*TLP*, 4.1212). The words have to be said in a proper context if they are to add up to a proposition. This can be clearly seen from *OC*, 464: 'My difficulty can also be shown like this: I am sitting talking to a friend. Suddenly I say: "I knew all along that you were so-and-so". Is that really just a superfluous, though true, remark? I feel as if these words were like "Good Morning" said in the middle of a conversation.' (The whole page of *On Certainty* is relevant.)

The example of the forester *is* very paradoxical. We need only consider that the forester may *overhear* someone saying 'N. N. knows that it is a tree', and I think we can assume that he understands what is said, but still . . . he cannot say the very thing he understands. He cannot understand it in his mouth, *qua* uttered by him. He cannot consider whether it is true. If this is right, Moore should have had an assistant at his lectures to read out 'Moore knows that he has never been far from the surface of the earth, Moore knows that he has two hands . . . etc.' A release from this extravagance would be welcome.

We need first to mark the distinction that Professor Anscombe makes when she contrasts the unintelligibility of certain forms of words, which are 'excluded from the language', and the unintelligibility of a *man* who uses words which are not at all excluded. In certain circumstances the reply 'For no particular reason' to the question 'Why are you doing that?' would be unintelligible, in the second sense.[1] Now it seems that we understand what certain forms of words mean without reference to context: they have a life of their own. There are certain inscriptions that are interpretable as English

---

[1] *Intention* (Oxford: Blackwell, 1969), Sec. 18.

words coherently combined, without our having any idea of the inscriber's plans or purposes, or indeed whether they were meant to be English at all. Nor, to understand them, do we have to imagine a use for them, which may not even enter our thoughts. The inscriber may have meant something quite hidden from us. The words: 'It is very fine today' may have meant 'Slip the microfilm into my pocket'; but that does not entitle us to say that the first sentence, although in the overwhelming majority of cases about the weather, is on the rare occasion about microfilm and pockets.

We not only know, in many cases, what certain words mean, but we also know that they are true, outside any context. Thus certain sentences, with demonstratives in them, or hidden demonstratives, e.g. those beginning 'Long, long, ago . . .' need a context if they are to have a truth-value. Again, names must have bearers. But there may be certain sentences with truth-values that do not depend on context: we can consider whether they are true without knowing who said them, or when they were said. But we still might not understand someone who said such things out of context, we might have no idea what he was up to. We might even doubt that he understands what he is saying: if he says such things, patent falsehoods, or truths-out-of-the-blue, must he not be deranged in some way, or making a slip of the tongue, and so on? Wittgenstein makes this point at *OC*, 468: 'Shouldn't I be at liberty to assume that he doesn't know what he is saying, if he is insane enough to want to give me this information?' (See *OC*, 80.)

It is perhaps worth mentioning here that nothing hangs on Frege's point about assertion, that unasserted propositions have truth-values. I wish to say that certain English sentences have truth-values independently of being asserted *or*, say, considered. I want to call in question the natural interpretation of Wittgenstein's remark: That only in use has a proposition its sense (*OC*, 10). (I think we can take it that Wittgenstein did not mean that a proposition has a sense only when it is being asserted.) Is it not obvious that there are many true propositions that will never even be considered? e.g. propositions of the form 'There are more than *n* stars'; that propositions do not become true or false *on* being considered. If I discover that a proposition is false by finding a false consequence, then it *had* that false consequence before I or anybody else thought of it. We must distinguish between what a man says, what he means to say, and what is his point in saying it. If a man makes a slip of the tongue, there is another sentence which expresses what he meant to say. What he meant to *do* by saying it, to inform, to surprise, to annoy, to remind, to put forward for consideration and so on, is something different again. If we can't make anything of the man's point in saying something, it perhaps becomes unclear that he means to say what his words are naturally taken to mean. In this way we can perhaps understand how a man can say what is true: 'I know that that is a tree', without our being able to make out whether he means what he says, or what he could be at by saying such a thing.

Wittgenstein would not allow, it seems, that sentences which are not in use (being considered or asserted in appropriate circumstances) could have truth-values. Now we may agree that the marks or sounds don't have truth-values except *qua* sentences *of some language* – English, for example. (See *OC*, 10.) But propositions, unlike tools, do not have to have a use. The idea of a society with certain tools in its toolbox which are never used seems absurd, for what would make such objects tools? But a society with sentences in its language which are never used is possible, because actual.

Any conjunction of English sentences is an English sentence. The longer and more inconsequential the conjunction, the more difficult it would be to imagine a use, or an appropriate context; but the truth conditions would remain perfectly easy to state. Propositions seem thus quite unlike such stereotyped expressions as 'Good Morning' which only have life in a suitable medium.

I have now discussed our three paradoxes, and before I go on to other topics I want to consider whether the points made by means of them are of much importance. So we will turn again briefly to the first: that the concept of knowledge only comes in where there is such a thing as being wrong. I can imagine someone agreeing with this and yet feeling that there was very little of interest in the matter; that it would be unhelpful to say that it was something *true*, for there are many truths which are recherché but dull. Moreover, he might feel that the concept of knowledge could be naturally extended to cover cases where one can say what is true without accident or luck playing a part, without there being such a thing as 'going wrong', that there is some striking analogy which makes such an extension natural. This sort of objection has to be answered if what we are doing is to deserve the name of philosophy. Wittgenstein himself said that his 'reminders' were 'for a particular purpose', and that we draw boundaries, as we are doing in this case with the concept of knowledge, with some end in view. And if we look at the context, in *Philosophical Investigations*, we can see what such an end might be. What I have called a paradox is part of his solution of the problem of *Other Minds*. When we get involved with this problem we start by taking as an example of knowledge *par excellence* in these matters, the knowledge we have of our own thoughts and feelings, and it is a stage in Wittgenstein's solution of this problem, to see that strictly speaking, this is not knowledge at all. Thus Wittgenstein writes 'It is correct to say "I know what you are thinking" and wrong to say "I know what I am thinking" ' and he adds 'A whole cloud of philosophy condensed into a drop of grammar'. The context of the other passage about 'I know that I'm in pain' is quite similar. If you wish, once you have seen the point, to proceed to call it quasi-knowledge, well then, that is all right (I should say).[1]

The second paradox turned on Wittgenstein's idea that knowledge can only be of what it is also possible (intelligible) to doubt (*OC*, 10) or where it either has been or is possible to check what one knows. Hence Moore was wrong to say that he knew. Here again, it seems to me that as long as we are clear about the peculiar features of Moore's examples, it is perfectly harmless to go on using the word 'know' in connection with them. It *was* harmful, in Wittgenstein's view, to say *I know* in these cases, for he held, I think rightly, that it suggested that Moore was *defending* common sense by saying what he did, where no defence was needed. It was like trying to give grounds where no grounds were needed, and then, finding the defence none too strong, just asserting one's way out of it. One might almost say: no one doubted the existence of the External World till the British Academy lecturer tried to prove it. But I think that in other ways Wittgenstein was not at all just to Moore. In the first place, Moore did not content himself with assuring us that *he knew*. He attacked the arguments of sceptics, often very effectively. Again, a practical disadvantage of reciting a Mooreian catalogue, Wittgenstein says, is that one gets the impression that knowledge is a magical state of mind which ensures that the world will be in accordance with it (*OC*, 6). Wittgenstein thinks that Moore was led into this error. He says, 'Moore's view really comes down to this: the concept "know" is analogous to the concepts "believe", "surmise", "doubt", "be convinced" in that the statement "I know . . ." can't be a mistake' (*OC*, 21; see *OC*, 178). I have not been able to find a passage in Moore where he suggests such a thing.[2] However, I do find it difficult to believe that Wittgenstein misunderstood Moore, who always went to endless, and sometimes tedious, lengths to make himself clear, and who of course had

[1] The other and more vital part of Wittgenstein's argument, is to understand how, in his view, 'inner processes stand in need of outward criteria' (*PI*, I, 580) and that is another story.

[2] The real offender, I suspect, was Prichard.

conversations with Wittgenstein for many years. It is perhaps interesting to note that Wittgenstein himself was prepared to say that in *some* circumstances 'I know that *p*' was an *Äusserung*, and thus like similar uses of 'I believe that *p*' (*OC*, 510).

Wittgenstein does give, I think, a convincing description of the central use of 'I know', and makes a clear application of his notion of 'language-game' to illustrate his point (*OC*, 564–6). But it does produce such odd results as the following: that the known logical consequences of what is known are not necessarily known. In addition, there will be difficulties about the notion of God's knowledge: thus if God knows something, must there be some account of how He knows it? Moreover, it will not do to say that God 'knows' in some figurative sense, in the way one might say that God sees things. But Wittgenstein never gives the impression that a concept is a tidy thing; there will be, one might say, a theme and variations, 'God's knowledge' being one of these variations.

$$*\quad*\quad*\quad*\quad*$$

Wittgenstein, I think it is fair to say, thought that a consideration of the way in which our concept of knowledge is specialised would throw into relief the features of that quasi-knowledge, as I have called it, which forms the background of our thinking and investigating. That we start off with a mass of inherited belief, has been noted by other philosophers of our time, who are not especially 'under the influence', like Quine and Popper. H. H. Price too shows a lively sense of the pervasiveness of our dependence on testimony, in his book, *Belief*, which is not at all influenced by Wittgenstein. Consequently, I shall not say much about this topic, but I have to mention it as a preliminary to the problem I am next going to discuss, namely, the extent to which we can rationally discuss disagreements with those who radically differ from us in background belief.

But I shall, first of all, remind you of some special features of Wittgenstein's thought in this area.

(1) Background beliefs are not *foundations* of the rest of our beliefs. Wittgenstein's view of it would be better expressed by the picture of a web, or a net in which many elements hang on one another for support (*OC*, 142). He says rather pointedly: 'These foundation-walls are carried by the whole house' (*OC*, 248) and in another place he calls the system of belief 'the element in which arguments live' (*OC*, 105).

(2) People, or perhaps better, communities, have different background beliefs. It is perhaps worth noting that there must be con-

siderable overlap between the background beliefs of different communities. Wittgenstein, so far as I am aware, does not make this point, though we get a hint of it when he says 'In order to make a mistake, a man must already judge in conformity with mankind' (*OC*, 156), and it is implicit in his idea that agreement in judgment is necessary if we are to have a common, or at least universally translatable, language. So I think we must conclude that a large measure of agreement in belief must exist if we are to understand that other people do *not* share all our background beliefs. It is a curious fact of life that human languages are translatable.

(3) Background beliefs don't have to be true; they might be 'part of a kind of mythology' (*OC*, 95). Thus Wittgenstein suggests that a king, in a faraway community, might be taught that the world began with *him*, but obviously does not mean to suggest that this would be true. We must not be misled here by such remarks as: 'The *truth* of certain empirical propositions belongs to our frame of reference' (*OC*, 83, Wittgenstein's italics). I think this only means that we can't be 'mistaken' about some of them, and that we take them as settled when we investigate other matters. 'One cannot make experiments if there are not things that one does not doubt' (*OC*, 337). But not all our background beliefs are like this; some can be tested – he only wishes to say that they 'are not all equally subject to testing' (*OC*, 162). But of course, we do reject much of what we are told, finding it disconfirmed by our own experience (*OC*, 161), or more importantly, I should say, because we are told something else by somebody else. Among our inheritance will be a large number of popular opinions that a critical person will not take seriously. Hence Wittgenstein's remark 'Men have judged that a king can make rain; *we* say this contradicts all experience. Today they judge that aeroplanes and the radio etc. are means for the closer contacts of peoples and the spread of culture' (*OC*, 132).

(4) There are propositions that we know for certain that are *not* part of our inheritance, that, one could say, are certainties of one's special situation: my knowledge of the state of my room, that there has been a table and typewriter in it for a long time, my knowledge of my present whereabouts, of the names of my friends, and so on. About these items, I think Wittgenstein would say that in the circumstances a mistake is impossible. (But n.b., it is interesting to note that at one place he seems to admit another kind of certainty – where one *can* be mistaken: *OC*, 613, where he also says, however, I don't know confidently what I am to answer here'. These are the certainties we *would* resolve to stand by. See also *OC*, 657.)

(5) Wittgenstein makes the interesting observation that some of

this background knowledge is picked up without explicit teaching. Nobody has told us, in all probability that something that was not in the drawer just now when I looked, cannot have materialised there since I closed it (*OC*, 143). Much of our knowledge of what words mean must, I suppose, be of this sort. Wittgenstein also says that we cannot describe our inheritance (*OC*, 102). (Why? Is it that a lot of what we know is hidden from us? Remember that Wittgenstein thought that we often needed reminding in order to see the importance of a concept, about 'extremely general facts of nature' which are 'hardly ever mentioned because of their great generality' (*PI*, fn. p. 56). This is not the sort of knowledge which is at one's fingertips.)

(6) Wittgenstein occasionally uses the words 'what it is natural to think'. One such thing is that the earth never had a beginning. Another, which *he* finds natural to think, is that there are no processes in the brain correlated with thinking. It would be as if there were *no* way of telling from the examination of the minute structure of a seed *what* sort of plant it would grow into; one's sole resource being to remember from which plant the seed had come (*Z*, 608–13). In the *Investigations* he describes the idea that there must be brain processes in such a situation as 'a form of account which is very convincing to us' (*PI*, I, 158) and tries to break this down by suggesting that we ask ourselves 'What do you *know* about these things?' In *Zettel*, he remarks that this 'prejudice' is a consequence of the thought that if things were *not* so, we should have to believe in a gaseous mental entity. These beliefs – what we find natural to think – are part of the background.

*   *   *   *   *

Now for the topic I mentioned earlier: to what extent can we rationally discuss disagreements with those who radically differ from us in background belief? Wittgenstein's view is as follows. A certain amount of rational discussion may be involved. People who are told, for example, that there is, or is not, a God, are taught, or somehow acquire a way of defending their views, of producing 'apparently telling grounds' (*OC*, 107). But after all the arguing, the gap may be unbridgeable, and we are left with persuasion as our only resource; and as an illustration, we are invited to think how missionaries set about converting natives (*OC*, 612). Earlier in *On Certainty* he gives an account of the difficulty in which you might find yourself in these situations. We meet someone who believes that a man has been to the moon. We start with our questions: 'How did he overcome the force of gravity?' 'How could he live without an atmosphere?' and so on, none of which he can answer. But then he says: 'We don't know *how* one gets to the moon, but those who get there know at once that they are there; and even you can't explain everything' (*OC*, 108). We might begin to feel that further conversation was not likely to be profitable. Children, who said this sort of thing, would be told not to talk nonsense, or (very seriously) that it isn't true, or that they'd soon grow out of it.

In thinking about this topic let us make the rather unrealistic assumption that the disputants have unlimited time, goodwill, intelligence, and patience, and perhaps humility. That a failure on these counts could cause a failure in understanding is a point neither new nor interesting.

Let us suppose, then, that we have befriended a person who suffers from what we call delusions of persecution. Let him be as intelligent and sensitive as we please: quick to grasp the points we make to him, even, in many cases, anticipating what we are going to say. He plays chess well, he shows surprising insights into poems that we read to him and writes not a few himself. He is not satisfied with superficial solutions. He is an excellent critic of one's ideas, a good teacher. But he thinks that he is the target of a conspiracy of the most extraordinary devilish subtlety, that the world is full of Moriartys, their hatred directed at him. They are playing cat and mouse with him, he says. An apparent kindness is a Judas kiss. These are the convictions with which he has lived for years. They explain, in a way that he finds satisfactory, all the vicissitudes of his daily life. But being an intelligent man he is easily bored, and loves conversation. If anyone could be rationally 'brought round' from his delusions it is he. But what are we to say if he treats our arguments as part of the plot, as moves to lull him into a false sense of security? Nothing, I think.

Opinions of a single man may be shared by a community. Evans-Pritchard's Azande are, he says, intelligent people, though he says that they are not bothered by 'contradiction' in their beliefs concerning witchcraft, etc. It is obvious from what he writes that they do not show indifference to inconsistencies; rather they regard them like Newman's 'difficulties', of which ten thousand did not add up to a doubt (*Apologia*, beginning Ch. 5). Evans-Pritchard held that it was impossible to convince a Zande of the falsity of his beliefs by pointing to 'difficulties'; beliefs which have been confirmed over and over again, and are part of what he would no doubt call 'common sense'.

Must we say, if we cannot, under the most favourable conditions, rationally win a man over to our side, that our convictions are irrational? Or that there are two sorts of rationality: theirs and ours? Must we conclude that, from a rational point of view, there is *nothing to choose* between such isolated belief-systems? Let us agree one thing: it is all right to say, but quite uninteresting, that 'if we are thinking within our system' (*OC*, 108) what the others say is 'superstition' or something rude like that (*OC*, 611). But what is the point of such talk if it is just propaganda, or reassurance for those who can deceive themselves? What is the point of it if we have to admit that the other people can say just the same about us? However, it is possible to do better than this. We can look at the belief-systems as a whole, and the tradition in which they have grown. There are, in my view, certain rather obvious marks of a good tradition: there must be, as Hobbes noted, a certain peace and stability in the community, and the economic conditions which allow certain people to devote themselves to learning. The curiosity of these people should range beyond the demands of practical concerns. There should be written records of their deliberations, so that ground gained in one generation should not be lost in the next. Above all, there should be a lively awareness of the way human beings, so often fond of their opinions, will readily deceive themselves, reluctant as they are to believe things that are new, or frightening, or injurious to their pride. And in consequence of this they will need to have a certain respect for that clarity of expression which makes their errors open to view; and there needs to be a measure of mutual criticism, if only among the élite. These characteristics pick out a good tradition, whose views are worthy of respect. It will be noted that the witchcraft beliefs of the Azande fail this test in many ways.

(Naturally, primitive farmers or hunters may show certain admirable qualities of mind rare in our wealthy and complex communities. Moreover, I do not wish to deny that there is such a thing as the wisdom of little children. For instance, if one is going in for self-deception, a great deal of academic learning will come in very useful.)

All I want to say at present is that there is *some* way of choosing between belief-systems, even if we cannot settle a point of conflict by rational discussion. There may be other ways: pragmatic considerations are relevant if the beliefs have technological application – thus we might be more impressed by a system of psychiatric doctrine that actually did people good. There are of course ways of choosing that have little relation to truth, which I need not spell out.

However, if there really is nothing to choose between such world-pictures, then there is nothing to choose. And if there really *is* nothing to choose between believing *p* and believing *q* then it is quite irrational to believe either, and this will be important to you if you care that what you think on the matter in question should be true.

This leads me naturally to the remarks I want to make about Wittgenstein's reported views on religious belief. In connection with these reports and lecture notes we should in fairness remember the warning in the *Philosophical Investigations*: 'If my remarks do not bear a stamp which marks them as mine, I do not wish to lay any further claim to them as my property' (Foreword, p. x). Wittgenstein is said by Malcolm to have been 'sympathetic' to religion, and I take this to mean not just that he held it possible for intelligent men to have such beliefs, or even that such men are sometimes interestingly serious in their view of life, but that religious beliefs were themselves worth 'taking seriously'. But I do not think we can conclude that he would have been sympathetic to just *any* religion, or say, to Zande witchcraft beliefs. It is easy to forget the range of actual religious creeds and practices, marking off those varieties of which one approves as 'real' religion, which is of course as pointless an exercise as setting your own boundaries for what you decide to be the 'real' county of Devonshire.

I have argued earlier that Wittgenstein could naturally have had a rough method of distinguishing those belief-systems worth taking seriously from those which he could have just dismissed from his thoughts. Now we should note that among the beliefs that had to be taken seriously were some that were more or less *literal*, rather than figurative in character. This seems to me suggested by the remark (*OC*, 336) 'Very intelligent and well-educated people believe in the story of creation in the Bible, while others hold it as proven false, and the grounds of the latter are well known to the former'. Again, the view on the Last Judgment he chooses to discuss in his lectures involves the extremely literal idea of the particles of one's body rejoining at the general Resurrection. There is, I think, a tendency among philosophers who find something of interest in these lecture notes, to call any more or less literal beliefs in this area 'superstitious', but I doubt whether they have learned this attitude from Wittgenstein. He does indeed say that the unfortunate Fr O'Hara's beliefs were 'superstitious', but this was because they were held by that writer to be rationally defensible, when in fact they obviously were not. No, not quite right: because the weak sort of reasons that could be produced were held to be *relevant* to what he believed, whereas Wittgenstein, like so many, thought that rational foundations for one's convictions in these matters were not called for.

Wittgenstein claimed support for his view that Christianity does not pretend to be reasonable from the writings of St Paul, who, we are told, maintained that the creed was 'folly'. But this is an absurd misreading. St Paul only said that it was folly to the Greeks (and did he mean the *whole* of Christianity or merely the scandal of the Crucifixion?) If I claim that the music of Bach would have been mere noise to the Aztecs, am I saying that *I* think it mere noise? If I say that these remarks of Wittgenstein are most convincing to some philosophers, am *I* saying that I find them most convincing? Now there is a funny sense in which we can say that a belief is 'incredible', when we find it perfectly credible but extraordinary. And in this sense, the Christian story as traditionally conceived by both Protestants and Catholics is indeed most 'incredible', and it was in this way appropriate for St Paul to talk about 'the foolishness of preaching'. But people speak in this way about the findings of astronomers or molecular biologists, without thereby regarding those disciplines as mysteriously irrational. I do not at all wish to tame St Paul's wild words, but only to suggest that they do not necessarily provide a condemnation of Christianity through its own mouth.

Wittgenstein also seems to have held that one could only be said to hold religious beliefs if they somehow profoundly affected one's life. I don't know how this would strike someone learned in comparative religion, but it does not seem true of Christianity. Nominal Christianity is perfectly common, and is perhaps only to be expected by Christians who believe in Original Sin. Admittedly, people cannot hold the nominal belief that if they didn't make themselves scarce they would immediately be dragged into a fire. It is 'part of the substance of this belief' that one is not apathetic. But I think it is a different story when one considers the belief that one *might* be thrown into Hell at some unspecified date in the remote future. One *can* hold such a belief in an apathetic manner, however unwise it may be, just as one can deliberately drink too much at the foreseen peril of one's liver.

Wittgenstein did not think that belief was subject to our wills in the way that we can move our limbs or think thoughts, since belief is not an action. Similarly, understanding is not an action, though one might *make* something of the peculiar command 'Understand this Greek sentence' by learning Greek. It would seem that one could obey the peculiar order to believe something as an order to *bring oneself into* this condition (see Z, 51-2). In this way, our health is subject to our wills, too. And just as we could keep ourselves healthy, so we could keep ourselves believing something, and in all sorts of ways, some more rational than others. And this might be the thing to do if you did not want to be led astray by philosophy and vain deceit. All this is very obvious. Consequently it is curious that Wittgenstein regarded it as something special and unfamiliar that one could be blamed for one's beliefs. The idea of 'culpable ignorance' is at least as old as Aristotle, is familar in the law, and is enshrined in such complaints as 'You ought to have known better'. What is puzzling to *us*, however, is that disbelief in God could be culpable. St Paul thought that God made himself manifest. Aquinas said that anyone who did not believe in God deserved censure for his stupidity. But for us, the thing is no longer a matter of common knowledge, and though it is obviously of importance for our lives to know the truth, if that were possible, a reasonable opinion might not emerge even after twenty years 'hard labour'.

INDEX OF REFERENCES TO WITTGENSTEIN'S WORKS

Zettel (Z)

Remarks on the Foundations of Mathematics (RFM)

INDEX OF NAMES

INDEX OF SUBJECTS

Library of Congress Cataloging in Publication Data
Main entry under title:

Understanding Wittgenstein.

(Cornell paperbacks)
Reprint of the ed. published by St. Martin's Press, New York, which was
issued as v. 7, 1972–1973, of Royal Institute of Philosophy lectures.
Includes bibliographical references and indexes.
1. Wittgenstein, Ludwig, 1889–1951—Addresses, essays, lectures. I. Vesey,
Godfrey Norman Agmondisham. II. Series: Royal Institute of Philosophy.
Lectures; v. 7, 1972–1973.
[B3376.W564U5   1976]   192   76–12818